THE PAGEANT OF JAPANESE HISTORY

THE PAGEANT OF JAPANESE HISTORY

BY

MARION MAY DILTS

*Illustrated by photogravures from Japanese Art
and Drawings by Toyojiro Onishi*

THIRD EDITION

DAVID McKAY COMPANY, INC.

NEW YORK

DILTS

THE PAGEANT OF JAPANESE HISTORY

COPYRIGHT © 1938, 1947, 1961

BY

MARION MAY DILTS

COPYRIGHT RENEWED 1966

BY MARION MAY DILTS

PUBLISHED SIMULTANEOUSLY IN THE DOMINION OF CANADA

FIRST EDITION AUGUST 1938
SECOND EDITION OCTOBER 1947
THIRD EDITION OCTOBER 1961
REPRINTED OCTOBER 1963
AUGUST 1965
JUNE 1967

LIBRARY OF CONGRESS CATALOG CARD NUMBER: 61–15463

Printed in the United States of America

To my Mother and Father
and to Tsunoda *Sensei*
This book is fondly dedicated

FOREWORD

IT IS a matter for rejoicing that a third edition of Marion May Dilts's excellent *The Pageant of Japanese History* is now before us. Appearing first in 1937, it was reissued, with additions, in 1947; now in 1961 it is extensively revised and again brought up to date. The new material includes a rewritten first chapter, which makes use of recent archeological discoveries, scattered material throughout that explains more fully the development of thought and customs strange to Americans, and entirely new chapters on the war, the Occupation, and Japan in the years since the Peace Treaty was signed.

Out of her experiences of living in Japan before the war, a return trip to the country, and a lifetime of interest and study, Miss Dilts had written a book both scholarly and readable. Its scrupulous accuracy, its use of Japanese sources, its range over all phases of Japanese life make it valuable for the mature reader who is approaching the history of the country for the first time. Its direct, simple, colorful style and vivid examples attract the younger reader of high-school or college age. Its objectiveness and sympathy make it especially valuable now when it is so necessary for Americans to understand our former enemy and present ally.

Perhaps never in history has there been such an extraordinary reversal of national feeling. A war fought with unprecedented bitterness has been followed by an alliance based not only on common political interests but on genuine liking between individuals. The growth of this new relationship Miss Dilts has, though necessarily briefly, made credible to readers who have not been in Japan to see it for themselves. Actually, great numbers of Americans have visited Japan since the war and made friends among the Japanese: first the Occupation personnel and then the tourists who have flocked after them. Statistics indicate a great change: 9,111 Americans went to Japan in 1935; 71,585 in 1959.

Our friendship with Japan, so valuable to both countries, requires the firm underpinning of a true knowledge and understanding of the Japanese people, their history, their ways of thought, their culture and their problems. Fortunately we are beginning at last to teach Japanese history in our schools and universities. Travelers planning their trips read about the country before they go. People attracted by Japanese art, Japanese flower arrangement or Zen Buddhism seek to learn more about the civilization out of which they sprang. *The Pageant of Japanese History* fills a real need.

Wallingford, Pennsylvania
July, 1961

Elizabeth Gray Vining

ACKNOWLEDGMENTS

THE years since 1947 when the second edition of *The Pageant of Japanese History* appeared have been so eventful and changeful for Japan that after another visit there, a third edition, carefully revised and brought up to date, seemed very desirable. As the title suggests, the book still aims to present to the reader-observer the Japanese acting and speaking for themselves.

During the past two decades of direct encounter with Japan, Americans in general have shown increasing interest and understanding; American students of Japan have increased tremendously in number and stature and have produced many important writings of which I have availed myself with admiration and gratitude. Dr. Edwin Reischauer of Harvard University, who contributed welcome suggestions for the second edition, has become the first United States scholar-ambassador to Japan, and his writings, I gratefully acknowledge, have continued to influence my thinking. Dr. Hugh Borton also, once a fellow student, has become a recognized figure in the field of Japanese political history. Tsunoda *Sensei* has continued to inspire a rising generation of Columbia University Ph.D.'s and with the special cooperation of two of them, Wm. Theodore de Bary and Donald Keene, has produced a monumental and invaluable volume of translations and interpretations of historical Japanese writings for which I am greatly indebted. Charles Tuttle has made a significant contribution to the current understanding of Japan by his many excellent publications, as have the Japanese periodicals, *Japan Quarterly, Contemporary Japan* and *Bulletin of the International House of*

Japan. Japan Report, issued semimonthly by the Information Office of the Consulate General of Japan in New York, has also provided much information for personal selection and evaluation.

Friendly helpers who have shared their scholarly experience or personal knowledge include K. Lillian Takeshita and Andrew Kuroda of the Library of Congress, Takashi Katsuki of the Freer Gallery in Washington, Kimiko Okamura of Tokyo, and Chiyoko Ichikawa, who with my husband, Paul Kopp, generously assisted with proofreading. Virginia Gilmer typed first drafts and Jean Melnick Buckmaster, who typed the manuscript for the second edition also, gave deeply appreciated assistance with the third.

M. M. D.

CONTENTS

LIST OF ILLUSTRATIONS

PHOTOGRAVURES

TEXT ILLUSTRATIONS

MAPS AND CHARTS

CHAPTER 1

THE EARLY SETTLERS

JAPANESE people themselves until the late 1940's knew very little about the early settlers of their country. As schoolchildren they were taught the myths of the Age of the Gods and of their Empire's founding in 660 B.C. but only a few intellectuals were aware of the findings of scientific studies of their beginnings. Only since World War II have these become generally known.

For thousands of years clans of unnamed primitive folk lived on the thirteen-hundred-mile stretch of unnamed islands off the northeast Asian coast, as tribes of Eskimos and Indians did in North America without knowing how to keep records of their doings. Much of what they considered interesting and important, however, was passed from the memory of one generation to the next and eventually was written down in official histories of both China and Japan. In addition to these sources, scholars have studied ancient remains in the ground, religious customs, and the language of Japan, and from all of them learned something about the early settlers.

The islands of Japan, it seems, were joined with the Asiatic mainland millions of years ago; and also, perhaps, with the Philippine Islands, Java and Sumatra. In the bed of the Inland Sea, fishermen have found the fossils of elephants who certainly could not have island-hopped; and the peoples of this whole area seem to have had much in common.

During the last hundred years archeologists have been digging for traces of the early settlers, and have discovered over a hundred thousand Stone Age dwelling sites scattered from northern Hokkaido to Okinawa.[1] Some Stone Age families seem to have lived on mountainsides, hunting game, fruit, nuts, berries and roots for food; more, however, seem to have lived along the banks of rivers and lakes or the shores of bays, and eaten chiefly fish, seaweed, clams and oysters.

Many of these dwellings resembled South Sea Island homes, with fire holes dug in their earthen floors, and roofs of light thatch supported on corner posts. Around some of them were found stone chopping tools and blades similar to Javan ones.

Near others, in mounds of accumulated shells, were discovered stone axes, knives and arrowheads, bone needles and fishhooks, molded clay bowls and cooking pots. Similar everyday conveniences of Stone Age domesticity were found not only along the coast of Asia from southern China to Siberia, but also in several excavations in our own country.[2] The similar "combed" designs on the ancient pottery, as well as the similar dark skin, straight stiff black hair, thin beards, and high cheekbones which North American Eskimos and Indians have in common with Japanese and Chinese today, lead scholars to think that all four may have had a common ancestry thousands of years ago—migrants from the areas we now call Siberia and Mongolia.[3]

Among Stone Age dwelling sites in the mountains of Japan have been found tools made of the long bones of deer and wild boar, and it is presumed that such animals supplied the early settlers with oil and also with fur for clothing. Skeletons of dogs but not of cats have been found on some of these sites; domestic cats appear to have been brought much later from China.

Coastal dwellers made dugout canoes for six paddlers from fifteen-foot lengths of walnut logs, swords from cedar wood, fishnets, mats and baskets from twisted fibers. Women were fashionable even in this primitive culture, tattooed their skin, filed notches in their teeth and wore costume jewelry made of shells, claws, teeth and red paint. They lived in family groups and moved on to new locations as litter and bad odors accumulated in the old.

In the second century B.C., on the mainland, migrations of primitive people were prevented from moving into the fertile plains of the Yellow River by the Great Wall of China and were channeled into northern Korea. Such a disturbance was created that the Han government set up an armed outpost to maintain order; this gave many primitive tribes their first experience not only of organized government but also of the use of metals. Continuing their migration, these tribes introduced bronze and iron spears and swords to the settlers living in the region now known as northern Kyushu.

Lower standards of living and apparent lack of raw materials in the islands then set up a reverse migration. Emigrants from the islands gained holdings on the Korean peninsula and set up a political center there. Until A.D. 562, they operated as rulers in Korea with the recognition of the Chinese court, but in 660, Korea was unified and allied with T'ang China, and the erstwhile islanders were driven back home.

Dwelling-site excavations reveal a period of transition. Bronze swords, pieces of harness and big bronze bells, mingled with deposits of broken pottery and stone tools, indicate that the early settlers were learning the use of metal.[4] The families with bronze weapons and tools were able to claim more and more land. Old families and newcomers met and mingled. Larger communities developed and organized.

Archeologists have also found remains of subsequent migrations in burial mounds, rather than dwelling sites. There were not very many of these stone-lined burial chambers called dolmens. According to the earliest histories of Japan, the Kojiki (written in A.D. 712) and the Nihongi (written in A.D. 720), they belonged to important rulers and were monuments of great respect. They contained clay figures of people and horses in armor and ornamental trappings, finely made swords of bronze and iron, mirrors of polished bronze, decorated on the back, many shaped vases, gilded bracelets, rings and beads of jade, crystal and other semiprecious stones, such as were used in the Han colony of Lolang on the Korean peninsula (of which more is told in Chapter 2) and were evidence of the rulers' diplomatic relations with kingdoms on the mainland.

Official travelers from China and Korea to the Japanese islands, which they called Wa, made notes of what they saw and heard there, which were later appended to official histories of the Latter Han (A.D. 25–220) and Wei (A.D. 225–265) dynasties,[5] in a section on their barbarian neighbors. According to this Wei account:

> The people of Wa dwell in the middle of the ocean on the mountainous islands southeast of Tai-fang. They formerly comprised more than one hundred communities. During the Han dynasty, [Wa] envoys appeared at the court; today, thirty of their communities maintain intercourse with us through envoys and scribes. . . .
> The land of Wa is warm and mild. In winter as in summer, the people live on raw vegetables and go about barefooted. They have houses; father and mother, elder and younger, sleep separately. They smear their bodies with pink and scarlet, just as the Chinese use powder. They serve food on bamboo and wooden trays, helping themselves with their fingers. When a person dies, they prepare a single coffin, without an outer one. They cover the graves with earth to make a mound. When death occurs, mourning is observed for more than ten days,

FOUR POTTERY GRAVE FIGURES

'CAVATION OF A STONE AGE DWELLING SITE

HORYU TEMPLE

during which period they do not eat meat. The head mourners wail and lament, while friends sing, dance, and drink liquor. When the funeral is over, all members of the family go into the water to cleanse themselves in a bath of purification.

When they go on voyages across the sea to visit China, they always select a man who does not comb his hair, does not rid himself of fleas, lets his clothing get as dirty as it will, does not eat meat, and does not lie with women. This man behaves like a mourner and is known as the "mourning keeper." When the voyage meets with good fortune, they all lavish on him slaves and other valuables. In case there is disease or mishap, they kill him, saying that he was not scrupulous in observing the taboos. . . .

In their meetings and in their deportment, there is no distinction between father and son or between men and women. They are fond of liquor. In their worship, men of importance simply clap their hands instead of kneeling or bowing. The people live long, some to one hundred and others to eighty or ninety years. Ordinarily, men of importance have four or five wives; the lesser ones, two or three. Women are not loose in morals or jealous. There is no theft, and litigation is infrequent. In case of violation of law, the light offender loses his wife and children by confiscation; as for the grave offender, the members of his household and also his kinsmen are exterminated. There are class distinctions among the people, and some men are vassals of others. Taxes are collected. There are granaries as well as markets in each province, where necessaries are exchanged under the supervision of the Wa officials. . . .

When the lowly meet men of importance on the road, they stop and withdraw to the roadside. In conveying messages to them or addressing them, they either squat or kneel, with both hands on the ground. This is the way they show respect. When responding, they say ah, which corresponds to the affirmative yes.

The country formerly had a man as ruler. For some seventy or eighty years after that there were disturbances and warfare. Thereupon the people agreed upon a woman for their ruler. Her name was Pimiko. She occupied herself with magic and sorcery, bewitching the people. Though mature in age, she remained unmarried. She had a younger brother who assisted her in ruling the country. After she became the ruler, there were few who saw her. She had one thousand women as attendants, but only one man. He served her food and drink and acted as a medium of communication. She resided in a palace surrounded by towers and stockades, with armed guards in a state of constant vigilance. . . .

When Pimiko passed away, a great mound was raised, more than a hundred paces in diameter. Over a hundred male and female attendants followed her to the grave. Then a king was placed on the throne, but the people would not obey him. Assassination and murder followed; more than one thousand were slain.

A relative of Pimiko named Iyo, a girl of thirteen, was [then] made queen and order was restored. Cheng [the Chinese ambassador] issued a proclamation to the effect that Iyo was the ruler. Then Iyo sent a delegation of twenty under the grandee Yazaku, General of the Imperial Guard, to accompany Cheng home [to China]. The delegation visited the capital and presented thirty male and female slaves. It also offered to the court five thousand white gems and two pieces of carved jade, as well as twenty pieces of brocade with variegated designs.

Scholars who studied the Japanese language in its earliest recorded forms, and compared it with other languages, found as did archeologists that it seemed to comprise three different influences, the northern and east-central Asiatic being the strongest, but the Polynesian, also present. Though the Japanese adapted Chinese ideographs, which are written symbols standing for ideas instead of for sounds, as our letters do, Japanese is really very different from Chinese. Japanese is polysyllabic with very little inflection, while Chinese is monosyllabic and dependent on tones. For example, the Japanese greeting corresponding to, How do you do? is *Ikaga desu ka,* the Chinese, *Nin hao.* In Chinese, grammatical relationships are shown only by the order of the words in the sentence and verbs function rather indifferently. In Japanese, however, personal pronouns are rare, but the verb plays a most important part. With its various endings indicating aspect, tense and mood, the verb is the key to meaning. These endings, postpositional particles instead of prepositions, suffixes rather than prefixes, make it resemble the Ural Altaic languages of northeastern Asiatic peoples. On the other hand, many of the Japanese names for things closely resemble words used in Malaya and the South Sea Islands; and the symbol for shells is part of the Chinese ideographs for buy, sell, treasure, and coin, as it might well be among coastal peoples, though there is no evidence that shells were used as money in Japan.

Shell   Coin   Sell   Buy

When Japanese scholars studied their native cult, in their search for origins, they found that it contained two kinds of deities, the superiors or gods of their own land, and the deities from elsewhere. Three different influences were apparent in their religion as well as in their language.

Primitive tribesmen of the Siberian plains practiced animal cults and magic for winning good fortune and foretelling the future. They believed that the government of the world was in the hands of a great number of benevolent and malevolent gods or spirits, whom it was necessary to placate by magic rites and spells. They claimed to be able to tell from the way a stag's shoulder blade cracked when it was burned, if, and when, journeys and voyages ought to be started, and paid great attention to the position of the sun and stars when important events were scheduled. They believed that people could go off into trances, and communicate with spirits to find out why calamities occurred—and what should be done to avoid them. An ancient chronicle tells how their Empress Jingu, in the third century, learned in a dream of a "better land than this, a land of treasure dazzling to the eyes where are gold and silver and bright colors aplenty," and went herself in command of an army and a navy to conquer it.[6] Many Japanese still take dreams and fortunetellers seriously.

A very different ingredient of Japanese religion was derived from southern Asia, where people worshiped the heavenly bodies. In Japan, people with South Sea Island characteristics loved the sun for its genial warmth. They sang and danced, clapped their hands and laughed to express their joy and gratitude. They worshiped a sea-god, too, loved bubbling springs and streams of crystal-clear water. They made a ritual of bathing; it was part of their religion to be pure and clean. They thought not of sins but of impurities that had to be washed away. Illness and death occasioned great washing ceremonies, and even desertion of the house of the deceased and the building of a new one for survivors. At the entrance to Shinto shrines in Japan, one still finds large stone or metal basins of water, and worshipers scooping up wooden dipperfuls to wash their hands and mouths before clapping their hands three times to attract the deity's attention to their prayers.

In China, the development of large families for the cultivation of rice fields was of great importance. The forms of worship used there were intended to promote fertility and these forms, too, found their way to Japan. The greatest offenses in the early days of agriculture were the breaking down of irrigation ditches and other acts which hindered the growth of rice. In the spring when the rice was planted and in the autumn when it was gathered, religious ceremonies were held and harvest prayers like this were offered:

> Because the Great Deity has bestowed upon him [the ruler] lands of the four quarters, over which her glance extends . . .

as far as the blue clouds are diffused and the white clouds settle down opposite; by the blue sea plain as far as the prows of ships can go without letting dry their poles and oars; by land as far as the hoofs of horses can go with tightened baggage cords treading their way among rock roots and tree roots where the long road extends . . . therefore will the first fruits for the Great Deity be piled up in her mighty presence like a range of hills, leaving the remainder for him [the ruler] tranquilly to partake of.[7]

Harvest festivals are still celebrated throughout rural Japan and at a shrine in the Imperial Palace grounds in Tokyo. Thanksgiving offerings of rice are made at the shrines, with prayers and ceremonies.

The numerous family groups in various river basins were keenly interested in claiming land as their own and in guarding it against invaders. If tribes wished to occupy new pieces of land they announced that the deity they worshiped wished to dwell there. The idea thus developed of kami, each with his own special region. Beliefs and practices from various homelands were used in support of this idea. Kami were creatures of superior power like the Olympic characters of Homer, extraordinary and awe-inspiring, sometimes spirits sometimes human beings, trees, seas or mountains; foxes became messengers of the kami; bows and arrows helped to extend their domain; magic was used to confirm their plans. Sun, water and fertility practices all enriched both kami and worshipers.

Clan chiefs had to serve their kami on many occasions. When, after settling in a new place, the land was divided among the clan, and the seed rice planted; again, at times of harvest, marriage, or change of leader, kami had to be worshiped. The places where the people met, bringing their offerings of rice [8] and hemp cloth, birds and animals from the hunt, fish and seaweed from the water, became the real centers of community life. There, in addition to religious rites, government and trade were carried on and weapons stored.

When the dolmen era was at its height (around A.D. 400), there were a few kami who, through the efforts of their clans, had come to rule a large section of central Japan, called Yamato, with lesser deities taking orders from them. One such was the sun-goddess, Amaterasu, a kami of both nature and ancestor worshipers, and dispenser of fertility.

Like the early Hebrews, and most early peoples, leaders of Yamato were interested in how they had been created. According to legends later recorded in the Japanese Kojiki (Record of Ancient Matters),[9] in the beginning two deities stood on the Bridge of Heaven and wondered what was beneath. One dipped a sword into the water. Drops falling from the sword when it was pulled out, formed islands, and the pair descended and dwelt on the islands and had a daughter whom they called Amaterasu (Shining in Heaven) and a son, Susanowo (Impetuous Male). Amaterasu was beautiful and gentle, giving light and life to all, while her brother perversely raged between heaven and earth ruining crops and tormenting people generally. In protest to his offensive antics, Amaterasu locked herself in a cave, leaving the world in darkness.

Other deities, assembled in the river bed near her hiding place, made an iron mirror decorated with a string of jewels shaped like a tiger's tooth or claw—as were Korean crown jewels—and laughed hilariously at their scheme for bringing her out.

"Methought that owing to my retirement the world would be dark, how is it that the deities all laugh?" she asked, opening her door.

"We rejoice because there is one more illustrious than thou art," they replied, pushing forward the mirror. Astonished at seeing what she thought was another deity of her own brightness, Amaterasu came forth to gaze, was seized and prevented from returning, and the world again became light.

For his misbehavior, Susanowo was banished to the underworld, but on his way, he stopped at Izumo,[10] on the northern coast of Japan facing the Korean peninsula. In Izumo, he married and had sons and grandsons who ruled that region until they were forced to give it over to Amaterasu's grandson, Ninigi.

Amaterasu bestowed upon Ninigi as emblems of imperial right a marvelous sword and the jewels and mirror by which she had been lured from the cave. "Regard this mirror exactly as if it were our august spirit, and reverence it," the ancient legends quote her as saying. "This land is the region of which my descendants shall be lords . . . May prosperity attend thy dynasty . . . and may it, like heaven and earth, endure forever."

According to tradition it was Ninigi's grandson, Jimmu, who led the way up the Inland Sea to Yamato (Moutain Guarded), where he proclaimed his rule as the first emperor of Japan, on February 11, 660 B.C., but there is no historic evidence that Jimmu was a real person. With the help of Izumo people, who were credited with special knowledge of medicine, silk culture, and the art of fishing, he is reputed to have forced many less-civilized settlers to move farther to the northeast. Some of these were a very different, curly-haired, full-bearded people, known today as Ainu.[11]

According to another Japanese legend, a princess of the divine tribe of Yamato established at Isé a shrine for the treasured mirror, and this with a weaving center developed near by seems to have really impressed the more primitive settlers with the treasures and talents of their conquerors.

In the third century A.D., Isé became the most sacred shrine in all Japan, and has kept this reputation. Every twenty years, beautifully simple structures of ancient design are rebuilt of fresh unpainted wood. Members of the imperial family still worship there on important occasions, and large numbers of Japanese make at least one journey to Isé, with its crystal-clear river and moss-grown rocks among towering cryptomerias. The soldier-priest-poet, Saigyo, in the twelfth century expressed their feelings:

> What sort of thing
> May be within,
> I do not know, but
> From gratefulness,
> Tears rain lightly.

CHAPTER 2

YAMATO LEADERS AND CHINESE TUTORS

(circa A.D. 400–700)

ABOUT the beginning of the Christian Era, when the early settlers of Japan and their Korean neighbors were beginning to know something of the use of metals, the great Han Empire was flourishing in China. The Han Empire had begun in the third century B.C., with the Great Wall, fifteen hundred miles long, already built to protect it against barbarous invaders from the north. It had expanded rapidly by opening trade routes to India, Persia and even to the Roman world. After the Great Wall was completed, large numbers of workmen, who had been employed on this enormous project, and wandering tribes, who found it blocking their forward movement, migrated along it into the northern half of the Korean peninsula. A Han colony of half a million people was established there with Chinese governors and the complete Chinese system of administration. The chief center of this colony was called Lolang.

Many Chinese officials of high rank and families of great wealth transferred their homes to Lolang. They brought with them skillfully made swords and spears; and the saddles, girths and stirrups of their horses were sometimes ornamented with gold. Undisturbed in their splendid tombs have been found lacquer trays and dishes, vessels of pottery and bronze together with coins, mirrors and jewelry of exquisite gold filigree. There is good reason to suppose that such things were used by the living as well as buried with the dead.[1]

Although not one of the noble mansions of Lolang remains standing, and but few traces of them have been brought to light, the foundations of the great government house, when discovered, gave evidence of its former grandeur. This building seems to have been made of bricks and tiles in a great variety of colors and designs, and to have been surrounded by an earthen embankment six hundred feet wide and eight hundred feet long. Here in a continual stream came traders, officials and ambitious travelers from far-distant places. Even the primitive settlers "on the island in the midst of the ocean" knew about the marvels of Lolang, and many of them went back to the mainland whence their ancestors had come to experience first-hand its civilized life, or sent envoys to seek a share of its splendors. Lolang, in its prime, was a most attractive center, radiating its culture for hundreds of miles around.

After four hundred years of power, however, the great Han Empire broke down into three rival kingdoms, and the Lolang colony waned. Then the nearby Korean countries, which before had been weak and backward in comparison with their great neighbor, struggled for possession of the Lolang treasures. Even Yamato leaders and troops went overseas and managed to found a small colony of their own on the Korean peninsula. They won such a reputation as daring, strong and skillful fighters that not seldom envoys from the Korean countries were sent over to the islands with valuable presents for the Yamato rulers, and also with urgent requests for Yamato troops to come help them battle against their rivals. When the Yamato rulers did not respond at once, more envoys came, bringing in addition to the highly prized jade beads, iron swords and bronze mirrors, more precious and novel gifts. At one time they brought an image of Buddha in gold and copper, several flags and umbrellas and a number of volumes of sutras—all accessories of a wonderful religion with which the Yamato rulers as yet were unacquainted. Another time, at the request of the Yamato ruler, they brought "a man learned in divination, a man learned in calendar making, a physician, two herbalists and four musicians."[2]

Conditions on the continent, however, became more and more unsettled, so that whole villages of people from the Han and Korean countries began moving to the islands where they could foresee more security and greater opportunities for themselves. With this wholesale migration the real history of Japan begins.

Men of Yamato returning to their homes brought with them all they could of Chinese coins and medicines, personal finery and household furnishings such as silks, mirrors, lacquered boxes and stands, pottery, silver and glassware and writing materials; and many of the foreigners who came knew how to make such things themselves. They were familiar with ways of fertilizing the soil to raise better crops, with methods of caring for silkworms to get fine strong silk to color and weave into beautifully patterned cloth. But more important even than this, they knew how to read and write and could keep accounts of taxes and trading arrangements.

Since the islanders themselves had never learned these arts, men who were accomplished in writing and reading seemed wonderful to them and were treated generously. They were employed as scribes by the most important clan leaders who, though quite ignorant, realized that they would seem greater themselves if they had remarkable men around them. In return for their services, the Korean and Chinese refugees were given lands where they could build homes for their families, and abundant provisions for living. Often they were excused from the taxes of rice and cloth or the forced labor that ordinary Japanese rendered to the clan heads for the use of the land, and often because of their ability they were granted the best government positions and honored with official rank. Under such favorable conditions they increased in number; they prospered and began to play a very important part in building up the Japanese nation. In the year 540, it is recorded there were seven thousand households of men of T'sin—or about a hundred thousand individuals supposedly of Chinese descent—and in a Japanese Peerage compiled at the end of the seventh century over a fourth of the noble families listed claimed either Chinese or Korean descent.[3]

At first the Yamato leaders simply hired the scribes as they might have hired sculptors to make a statue of a great man, thinking the art of writing to be a special gift, not something which they themselves could learn. But soon they were eager to learn more of the new religion that newcomers had brought along with their material treasures and for which they made glowing claims. "This teaching is among all teachings the most excellent, but it is hard to explain and hard to understand. It can lead to a full appreciation of the highest wisdom. Imagine a man in possession of treasures to his heart's content so that he might satisfy all of his wishes. Thus it is with the treasure of this wonderful teaching. Every prayer is fulfilled. Nothing is wanting. It has come from India to us and there are none who do not receive it with reverence as it is presented to them."[4]

Naturally enough the Yamato men wanted to be able to read for themselves the books of such teachings as these, so they began to study Chinese writings.

The new religion was Buddhism. It had begun with the simple, truth-revealing teaching of a young man in the villages of India, but had seemed so good to those who heard it that they began to spread it and add to it, just as the early Christians five hundred years later did with Jesus' teachings. Just as Christianity gradually spread all over Europe and was adapted to the habits of different peoples, so Buddhism had spread over Asia and, through the years, adopted many other teachings. Buddhist priests had been the bearers of civilization to uncultured masses. They had developed a powerful organization in Asia as Christianity afterward did in Europe, and built beautiful temples filled with sacred paintings and statues of Buddha, their great Enlightened One, surrounded by many of his saints.

It was about a thousand years after the founder of Buddhism lived that his teachings were brought to Japan. At first the Yamato rulers were afraid that by worshiping Buddha they might offend their own land deities, the kami, and very few would take this risk.

Although their native religious beliefs and practices were not organized into any sort of system, and in fact did not even have a name, there were two families prominent in Yamato affairs who for generations had been responsible for the proper performance of ceremonies and rites. In return for the services which they performed these families enjoyed many special privileges. They were, therefore, not at all enthusiastic about the introduction of a new religion. To distinguish their own cult from the new one they dignified it with a name, Shinto (The Way of the Gods) and did everything they could to encourage Shinto practices and to discourage Buddhist ones. When a plague broke out in the country they announced that this was a sign of the kami's jealous wrath. They threw the statue of Buddha into a canal and burned the building where it had been enshrined.

On further acquaintance, however, Buddhism grew to be acceptable. It could hardly be otherwise since the constantly increasing immigrant population which enjoyed such favor was entirely Buddhist. Buddhism stood for progress and the Yamato rulers were not without ambition. Prince Shotoku, a regent who governed for his empress aunt around the year 600, was the first to set an example for the people. He was so deeply interested in the teachings of Buddha, it is recorded, that he became the pupil of a Korean Buddhist scholar so that he might learn to read the scriptures for himself. Many others, like him, learned to read and write because of this new religion.

Prince Shotoku became one of the most loved rulers the Japanese ever had. They still call him The Father of Japanese Culture. With his Korean tutors he is thought to have studied not only Buddhist writings but also the writings of Confucius and other Chinese classics which inspired him to make of Japan an ideal nation. He aimed to do away with rivalry between the big landowners, not by force of arms but by moral teachings and persuasion, and to have one ruler over all the clans who would deal justly with the people and keep harmony throughout his realm. To help carry out his aims he is said to have written what is known in Japanese history as The Seventeen-Article Constitution. In form this was very different from the Constitution of the United States, but like that venerable document it was designed to inspire the confidence and cooperation of the people in a new government experiment. Prince Shotoku's Seventeen-Article Constitution is given here in brief:[5]

Harmony is to be valued, for when there is harmony between the ruler and the ruled and between neighbor and neighbor what can not be accomplished?

Sincerely reverence the three treasures: Buddha, his teachings and the priests.

When you receive imperial commands, fail not to obey them carefully.

Let your behavior be orderly and proper.

Chastise that which is evil; encourage that which is good. Conceal not the good qualities of others, nor fail to correct wrong when you see it.

Flatterers and deceivers lead to the overthrow of the state and the destruction of the people.

Let the court officials attend early and retire late, for the whole day is hardly enough for accomplishing the business of the state.

In everything let there be good faith, for without it everything ends in failure.

Let us not be resentful nor look angry when others differ from us, for each heart has its own leanings. We are not unquestionably sages nor are they unquestionably fools.

Let not the provincial authorities levy taxes on the people; the sovereign is the master of the people of the whole country. They have not two masters.

Let no official sacrifice the public interest to his private feelings.

Let the people be made to do forced labor only when they are not engaged in agriculture or the care of silkworms.

Let all important matters be discussed by many persons.

Needless to say, not all of these ideals of Prince Shotoku were realized, but he sowed seeds which later bore much fruit. It was he, they say, who first encouraged the building of temples. Horyu-ji, one which he had built as a teaching center, though repaired many times in its thirteen hundred years of existence, still bears close resemblance to the original. There on lotus-blossom pedestals two statues still remain in marvelous preservation from Prince Shotoku's day—one of bronze inscribed with a date corresponding to the year 607, and one of wood covered with gold leaf.[6]

In early times the Japanese had counted the years by the reigns of their rulers. Instead of saying that Prince Shotoku was appointed regent in A.D. 593, or according to some such continuous system, they said he was appointed in the first year of Empress Suiko. As a result of this system, or lack of system, there was much uncertainty and confusion about early dates in Japanese history.

During Prince Shotoku's regency, however, a scholar came to his court with books on astrology, calendar making and geography. The Chinese had developed these sciences with great skill. They had two cycles for counting years: a ten-year cycle called after the elements, wood, fire, earth, metal and water; and a twelve-year cycle in which each year was named after an animal, the year of the rat, the ox, the tiger, etc. These names were suggested by the forms of constellations and were similar to our twelve signs of the zodiac.[7] The first year of the ten-year cycle coincided with the cycle of twelve only once every sixty years. Sixty years was therefore used as a unit corresponding to our century. The twelve months were named like the twelve-cycle years, and each month was divided into three parts. The days in each part were named like the ten-cycle years. There were no seven-day weeks, but for convenience the months and days were simply numbered as they sometimes are with us. The days were divided into twelve parts instead of twenty-four so their hours were twice as long as ours.

In the seventh century the Japanese adopted this Chinese system of keeping track of time. Then, figuring back, systematically they gave dates to all their emperors. With naïve ambition, they seem to have exaggerated the lengths of many reigns in order to give themselves a more impressive past. Though modern scholars think it was more likely at about the beginning of the Christian Era when the Yamato clan came to power, officially Jimmu-Tenno, the great-great-grandson of Amaterasu, the sun-goddess, was said to have ascended the throne on February 11, 660 B.C., and this day was celebrated in Japan with parades and patriotic speeches,[8] until official Shinto was banned.

After this new system of dating was introduced Prince Shotoku, together with the leader of a clan named Soga, is said to have compiled the first history of the Japanese emperors, but this work was later destroyed when the Soga's home was burned. Shotoku seems to have been interested in music and dancing too, because according to Chinese books, music softened men's hearts and made them easier to govern. When an immigrant came who knew the Chinese style of music and dancing, the prince regent lodged him in the palace, and had young people come there to learn these arts.

While this progressive regent was governing Japan, the Chinese kingdoms that had been divided since the fall of the Han Empire were united and strengthened again by the Sui Dynasty. Prince Shotoku decided to send an envoy to their new capital, for China, he realized, was the source of all the knowledge and culture of his Korean tutors. The envoy took with him a letter which began, "The emperor of the country where the sun rises sends greetings to the emperor of the country where the sun sets."[9] History says the Sui emperor resented this note of equality from the ruler of a mere island in the ocean, but nevertheless, the following year he sent back with the envoy two representatives from his court and a number of books. The Yamato envoy soon returned to China, this time with a band of eight students, the sons of Korean families who had been welcomed and well established in Japan. They went to study Buddhism and Chinese government; two of them stayed in China studying for thirty years. Before they returned to the country of their adoption, Prince Shotoku passed away.

There was great disorder in Yamato then, for the Soga clan usurped the imperial rights. They had held important positions from very ancient times and had been closely associated with the finances of the ruling clan. When immigrants had begun coming from the continent, the Sogas had employed large numbers of them, thus increasing their own prestige and extending their own power. They were the first clan to worship Buddha and they had supported Prince Shotoku during his regency, but as soon as he was gone they took the reins of government into their own hands, not even hesitating to do away with his sons and grandsons. They brought in half-wild Ainu soldiers from the northeast and ferocious fighters from Kyushu to keep other powerful clans in submission to them. Added to the Sogas' ruthless arrogance, many chieftains had other worries; the immigrant groups by this time, grown large and ambitious, were constantly making greater demands on native clans. The Japanese colony on the Korean peninsula was fast losing importance, for a new dynasty in China was making startling conquests. And Shinto leaders were much disturbed at the success the Buddhists were having in obtaining gifts of land and other favors from prominent people.

In the midst of all these troubles grew up a young man named Kamatari. One of his ancestors was supposed to have accompanied the first members of the Yamato race who came to Japan, and the family from ancient times had been one of those engaged in performing religious rites in honor of the deities of the imperial clan. It also controlled large areas of eastern frontier land, and had often come into conflict with the Sogas on various issues.

At this time there was really no well-organized central government; the country was dominated by a number of clans, each administering certain lands which they had occupied for many generations. Everything these lands produced belonged to the clan and constituted its living and its wealth. The head of the clan directed all its affairs and had full command over all the clan members. Between clans were continual rivalries which drained their strength and enabled the imperial clan to become larger and more powerful. Though the imperial clan had no acknowledged right over any other, many of the other clans became willing to take orders from it. As a system of government for the whole country, however, this could work only when the imperial clan was headed by a ruler who commanded the respect of the other clan leaders, and who could persuade or intimidate them into cooperation. Kamatari saw clearly that such a system was no longer adequate. Times were changing, and the growing numbers of immigrants in the country not only created problems, but also offered opportunities such as the Japanese had never had before.

Kamatari consulted with the students recently returned from China. Just before Prince Shotoku died, the Sui Dynasty in China had been replaced by the T'ang, and the excellently governed T'ang Empire was now the brilliant marvel of all Asia. It was the largest and strongest country in the world, extending from Manchuria to Thai, and from the Caspian to the Pacific.

At its head was an absolute monarch, called Son of Heaven. According to the teachings of Chinese sages the man of greatest virtue in their country was commissioned by the ruler of heaven to be their sovereign—while men of only slightly less virtue and wisdom were to serve him loyally as ministers and advisers. The empire was divided into many provinces, with a governor appointed to each. Then to all grown persons in the country were allotted equal portions of land. The entire government of T'ang was based on agrarian economy. Irrigation canals were dug for the benefit of the farmers, and storehouses were built where the surplus products of good years could be saved for years when the crops were poor. For students were provided schools and a university; a sort of civil-service examination was given for the selection of public officials. Merchants from all over the world flocked to their capital, which is said to have been gorgeous beyond description.

Kamatari, having learned much about the great T'ang Empire from the young men who had lived and studied in China for many years, resolved to make of Japan a small but worthy copy of her continental neighbor. Prince Naka, a son of the nominal empress, was found not only to share Kamatari's hopes, but to have the energy, courage and patience which would be needed to fulfill them. One day as Kamatari was playing football with some young noblemen—not football as we know it but a popular game of that time played by kicking a big soft ball—Prince Naka was playing too, and when he kicked the ball his shoe flew off after it. Kamatari picked up the shoe and returning it to the young prince knelt down and put it on for him. After that they were frequently seen walking and talking together, but since they carried in their hands the yellow scrolls of the Chinese sages and went often to the homes of the students returned from abroad, it was not suspected that they were plotting the downfall of the Soga clan and the building of a new Japan.

The Sogas were so well guarded when they traveled out of doors that it was hard to get at them. It was, therefore, decided to attack the young Soga at court during a celebration of welcome for a Korean envoy. A swordsman was appointed to do the killing, but at the crucial moment he reneged and Prince Naka himself had to carry out the plan. All the other clans who had grievances against the Sogas but had been afraid to do anything now turned to Kamatari and Prince Naka, and within a few days the Soga leaders were all done away with and their palace burned. This was the fire in which Prince Shotoku's history of Japan was destroyed.

Then the First Great Change was begun. It was the keen ambition of Yamato progressives in the middle seventh century to have their country regarded by the T'ang court not as an inferior state, but as a neighbor worthy of respect. Yamato leaders had been treated with deference by the Korean kingdoms and they must continue to maintain their position and influence there. But they must also establish a court of their own as nearly like the T'ang as possible—to which T'ang envoys could be welcomed with proper ceremony, and from which officials of real dignity could be dispatched to China. It was clear that to accomplish this, many clans would have to unite their energies and resources, and there would have to be one man among them with absolute and direct control over all the people.

Though Kamatari and Prince Naka were the guiding spirits of the Great Change, they did not attempt to bring it about in their own names. Realizing that there were other great clan leaders to be considered and conciliated, all their acts were done, all their plans accomplished, on behalf of the imperial clan. They recognized the quality of genius in the family which based its claim to power on the revelations of a divine ancestress. A ruler who bases his right to rule on conquest has constantly to be looking to his fighting forces, for the first man stronger than he is eligible to replace him. But when a family has been commissioned by a heavenly deity to govern a land forever, it has a title as unchallengeable as any can be. Such was the traditional title of the imperial clan; and as official envoys from the continent continued to bring treasures and scholars to this family, its wealth and prestige were further enhanced.

When the Great Change was slowly but surely under way, not Prince Naka himself but his uncle was made emperor.

Kamatari and the prince kept themselves in the background and proceeded carefully. First they adopted the Chinese system of using period names. (When some happy omen or outstanding event occurred the Chinese would start a new era and call it by an appropriate name.) Kamatari and Prince Naka called the era they were beginning Taikwa (Great Change) to prepare the people's minds for something new and interesting. Then they appointed governors for the northeastern border provinces to replace the local chieftains who had only recently won their lands from the Ainu. These governors were to take a census of all the people living in their districts, to collect all the spears and bows and arrows the people had, and to store them in government armories to lessen the danger of revolt. Their next step was to grant to all the people the right of appeal to the emperor. This was to make the people feel that they were being given a special privilege, and also to lessen the power of the clan heads. Before this, if a man had a grievance against his chief he could do nothing about it, the chief's word was final; but now, theoretically at least, a man could ask the emperor to get justice for him. Thus clan rule began to give way to centralized government.

Since no great trouble arose as a result of these changes, as soon as the New Year's celebrations were over in 646, Kamatari and Prince Naka had the emperor issue their Edict of Reform. This contained four new provisions: [10]

Private administration of land was to be abolished. All the property of the country was to be returned to the emperor.

A central government was to be organized with a capital modeled after a Chinese city, and a system of roads, ferries, barriers and post horses to be provided through the provinces. Provincial governors were to be appointed and assisted by clerks familiar with writing and arithmetic.

A census was to be taken of all the people, and the land returned to the emperor was to be given back in equal parts to all the people for them to use.

The old taxes and forced labor required by the clan chiefs were to be replaced by new taxes to be paid to the central government whereby communities which produced special products like silk, flax, cotton, salt, horses, weapons, flags or drums, for example, could substitute these for the regular taxes of rice and labor.

To set an example for the people Prince Naka himself, though a member of the imperial clan and in line for the throne, gave up all claim to the lands and people he had formerly controlled and turned them over to his uncle. Many of the chief landholders followed his lead. Afterward they were appointed as governors or salaried secretaries to oversee the lands and people they had been managing right along. They were paid salaries by the emperor for their service, not in money, for there was still practically no money in Japan, but in the natural products of their district, in fish and timber, salt, silk and such things. These clan chiefs had been so proud of the titles of respect by which they were called, Lord of the Family, or Superior of the Clan, that Kamatari and Prince Naka were afraid they might be dissatisfied at now being called only governor. A Chinese system of ranks was, therefore, revived which, it is said, Prince Shotoku had introduced forty years before.

At elaborate ceremonies the important people of the country were honored with such names as Greater Benevolence, Lesser Benevolence, Greater Righteousness, Lesser Righteousness. Each name stood for a rank or grade of social superiority and political importance. The people of the various grades were distinguished at special court functions by the colors of the robes and caps they wore. Those belonging to the grade of Greater Righteousness wore red, while those belonging to Lesser Benevolence wore blue. The most loyal supporters of the emperor, of course, were given the highest ranks, and only a man of a certain grade could hold a certain official position. The emperor gave special gifts of land corresponding to official rank. Amounts were frequently changed, but at one time they ranged from one hundred and sixty acres for each one of first rank down to sixteen acres each for members of the lower fifth rank, and gifts of produce from the imperial treasury were given to persons of rank below this. So people were eager to please the emperor in the hope of being advanced in rank and of receiving correspondingly increased rewards. No person of rank was required to pay taxes to the imperial treasury.

The Great Change which Kamatari and Prince Naka hoped to see in Japan, however, did not take place at once. Even a hundred years later in many parts of the country it still was not effective. Their efforts to retain some shade of Yamato authority on the Korean peninsula ended in a crushing defeat and expulsion by T'ang reinforcements in 662. And though during their regime four official embassies were sent to the T'ang capital, neither of these great men lived to see in their own country a permanent capital built like a Chinese city. Ten years before he died, Prince Naka, succeeding to the throne as Emperor Tenji, moved his court away from the stronghold of the old clan leaders and landowners in Yamato into a region on the shores of Lake Biwa where there was a large settlement of Korean immigrants who favored his new policies. And it was Tenji-Tenno's envoys who requested the T'ang court in future to call their country Nippon, or Sunrise Land, instead of Yamato. (Yamato proper was only the small central district where the imperial clan had very early established its control.)

Kamatari was well rewarded for his faithful efforts on behalf of the imperial clan. He was granted large estates in a section of the Yamato region, called Fujiwara. From this advantageous position he and his descendants continued to watch over the interests of succeeding emperors. They came to be called Fujiwara as was the land that was granted to them, and Fujiwara came to be the greatest family name in Japanese history.

After Kamatari's death in 669 no official embassies were sent from Nippon to T'ang for over thirty years. The enemies of the

Great Change had a moment of victory and Tenji's son was done away with, but Tenji's younger brother, Temmu, had strengthened his own position by marriage with Tenji's daughter, and succeeded to the throne. Temmu-Tenno established himself at Asuka near a flourishing settlement of Chinese immigrants and with their encouragement, no doubt, his court continued to develop its knowledge and use of Chinese literature and social practices.

Though there were no official exchanges of envoys during this period, there was great law-making activity, regulating in the Chinese way everything from the functions of public officials to the style of ladies' coiffures. No end of time and energy was consumed by Chinese ceremonials of one kind or another, and temples were encouraged with generous gifts and elaborate festivals. Court people began to write Chinese poetry and, more important still, appointed a committee to write an official history of the country as they did in China. The efforts of this committee resulted in the Kojiki and the Nihongi.

In the first year of the eighth century another official embassy was sent to the T'ang court and, soon after, plans were well under way for building Nara, the first capital city of Nippon.

CHAPTER 3

PEOPLE OF NARA, THE FIRST CAPITAL

(EIGHTH CENTURY)

IN APRIL of the year 710 the Yamato court moved into its first real capital. Before that the center of government had been wherever the head of the imperial clan had happened to live. In their own artless dwellings (Tenji-Tenno's is recorded as made of logs with the bark still on) the rulers had conferred with other clan leaders who in turn had given orders from their rustic homes. But the more they learned about the splendors of T'ang cities the more the Japanese nobles wanted to have a real capital of their own. And so Nara was built.

The site chosen was in a valley sheltered on three sides by gentle slopes, a place where as an ancient poem says, "When the bright spring showeth upon the hillsides, the cherry blossoms surpass all the world in beauty and the warblers are ever singing."[1] Several Buddhist temples, already established there on large estates, lent great dignity to the new center. Materials and builders poured in from near and far. Hewn timber, copper, tin and silver, clay products, dyestuffs, silk cloth and hempen cloth, together with skilled laborers, were brought from the various provinces of Japan, while architects, sculptors and painters were brought from the continent, together with works of art and treasures of various kinds. Priests also came, who knew the science of building roads, bridges and wells. It was a great age in which to be alive. The Yamato people had never seen such marvels before.

The city, covering thirty-five square miles, was laid out with broad streets crossing each other at right angles. Instead of the thatched-roof houses of simple construction to which they had been accustomed, now the imperial family and some of the high court officials built palaces of more massive architecture with roofs of colorful tiles.

Since all of these were destroyed a thousand years or more ago, it is not possible to give a clear picture of Nara in its prime, but many of the most treasured palace furnishings and personal belongings, which were used by the imperial family in the eighth century, are still preserved in a storehouse called Shoso-in.[2] Among them are thirty-one rugs of felt with intricate conventionalized floral designs in rich colors, and arm rests of wood in graceful shapes decorated with inlays of ivory, wood, mother-of-pearl and gold. These on special occasions were placed on the floor beside the silken cushions which served as chairs. For serving food there were low lacquered tables and dishes of glazed pottery from China. Many of the treasures appear to have been brought from distant places. A graceful glass ewer has curves strongly reminiscent of Persian design, while the inlaid camels on a mandolin-shaped instrument, and an exquisitely made game board are suggestive of Central Asia. There are cups of rhinoceros horn believed to destroy or disclose poison. There are flutes, foot rules and dice of carved ivory, which probably came from India; ornaments of jade and amber, furniture of red sandalwood, and a log of incense wood, none of which was native to Japan. There are two kinds of harps from Korea—one with twelve strings and one with twenty-three. There are standing screens, decorated with Chinese writing—some of it done by famous Chinese scholars, and some of it colorfully appliquéd in duck feathers. There are scissors and padlocks of gilded copper, and spoons of gilded silver.

Also in this collection of Nara treasures are large needles about a foot long, made of silver, copper and iron, which, it is

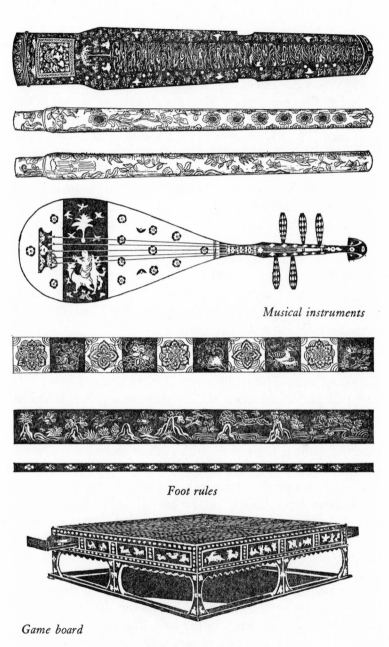

Musical instruments

Foot rules

Game board

Some of the Nara treasures

31

thought, were offered at the Weaving Maiden's Festival by young girls who desired special skill in needlework.[3] In another festival of Chinese origin held on the first day of the rat in the first month of the year, brushwood brooms and lacquer plows were used. There is a broom in the Shoso-in with colored glass beads strung on the brushwood, the handle bound with purple leather and gold thread, with which, it is thought, the empress swept the silk workroom as an act of worship to the deity of sericulture. And there is a lacquer plow decorated with gold and silver with which, it is thought, the emperor plowed on the same day to encourage agriculture. Fragments of two New Year's cards, sent about twelve hundred years ago, are still kept among the Nara treasures. They had cutout designs of gold leaf pasted over thin colored silk, with a message that reads: "Auspicious occasion. Renewal of happiness. Peace ten thousand years. May life last a thousand springs."

Everyday life in the Nara palace was copied as closely as possible after that of the T'ang court. The affairs of the imperial household were directed by a governmental official in accordance with prescribed forms of Chinese ceremony. People had to speak in honorific terms. They had to bow just so, and have a certain number of attendants. Differences of rank were strictly observed. Only persons of the fifth rank or above were allowed to enter the imperial presence.

Court costumes were constantly changing in response to the latest styles from China, but in general ladies wore loosely draped gowns with high necks, and flowing sleeves covering their hands. They had fancy girdles decorated with appliquéd designs, silk cords and glass beads. Courtiers wore voluminous long trousers gathered in at the ankles. They, too, wore ornate belts; an especially fine one was of moleskin with rhinoceros-horn ornaments and a silver buckle. On very festive occasions plum blossoms were worn in the hair. The emperor and empress had headdresses made of lacy gold, set with pearls, rock crystal, coral and colored-glass beads. The emperor had a pair

of scarlet leather shoes with turned-up toes; the backs above
the heels were decorated with gold ribbon and silver flowers
set with pearls and colored beads. The soles were scarlet leather
like the rest, but the inside was lined with white leather and a
pad of white silk. On all formal occasions courtiers wore very
long and elaborate swords. These were not intended for use,
but the length and splendor of the sheath bespoke the rank of
the wearer.

The favorite sports of the Nara nobles were archery, rowing,
horseback riding and hunting with falcons. The ladies rode as
well as the men, either astride or sidesaddle. For less active pas-
times they had various gambling games and a sort of checkers.

Musicians (Nara period)

Often they were entertained by musicians, acrobats, jugglers
and dancers. On one day a year, old, young, highborn and low
gathered together on the streets or in open fields to sing and
dance, to dance and sing, to flirt and fall in love.

But Nara court life had a somber and serious side as well.
Responsible officials were earnest in their desire to make their
country orderly and prosperous; and since the T'ang government was the very best they knew, they studied T'ang practices
carefully with the idea of adopting and adapting them for their
own needs. The Fujiwaras were leaders in this. Kamatari's son,
Fubito, headed a committee of ten for devising a code of laws
to apply to all the people. Many attempts had been made to do
this since Prince Shotoku's time; but the Taiho (Great Treasure) Code was the culmination of them all. This code was based

on the idea that all persons, whatever their rank or from whatever family they came, were indebted to the state and were to be rewarded only as they showed their ability in service. When the Taiho Code was first completed, experts in legal matters were sent with it to provincial governors to explain it and to see that it was put in practice.

The range of things it sought to regulate was very wide: official titles, the duties of officials in various royal households, services to the gods, Buddhist priests, the family, land, taxation, the descent of the crown and dignity of imperial persons, salaries, army and frontier defenses, ceremonies, official costumes, public works, the mode of addressing persons of rank, storage of rice and other grain, stables and fodder, duties of medical officers attached to the court, official vacations, funerals and mourning, markets, arrest of criminals, finding of lost goods, and various other matters.

The most important part of the Taiho Code was probably that which dealt with the administration of the provinces. It was very important that the government be extended to the provinces outside the capital, for it was from the provinces that the court derived its income. According to the new code, provincial governors were supposed to be appointed by the emperor to hold office for from four to six years. Their official duties included supervision of the shrines of local kami, registration of land, the taking of a census, and the selection of able-bodied men to be soldiers or workmen for roads, palaces and timber lands. They were also supposed to settle disputes and mete out justice.

It was the privilege of the provincial governors to recommend officials for the districts into which the provinces were divided. Men whose families had lived on the land for generations and who knew the farmers well were usually appointed. They really did most of the actual work, while the provincial governors remained in Nara to enjoy the exotic novelties of capital life. The chief duty of both provincial and district officials was the collection of taxes. Most of the taxes they were supposed to send to the capital, but they were allowed to keep a certain share of all they collected as salary.

The bulk of the taxes farmers had to pay was in rice which the nobles of the court not only used for food but exchanged instead of money for other things they wanted. There was little money in Japan in those days. Some coins had been brought from the continent and some were minted in Japan after mines were discovered there, but neither kind was circulated widely. The court controlled the issuing of coinage as a special and profitable privilege. Whenever extra funds were needed it issued a new coinage of poorer quality but greater designated value than the previous one, and continued its efforts to put money into general use. The people, however, finding money increasingly to their disadvantage, preferred to use rice as their standard of value in buying and selling. And the court had to be content to collect as taxes not metal coins, but cloth of silk and fiber, purple, red and yellow dyestuffs, hemp, many kinds of fish, garlic, salt, oil (both fish and vegetable), iron spades, paper, willow branches for weaving into baskets, bamboo screens, mattresses, deer horns for medicine, and barrels of sake, the rice wine of which Japanese have always been fond.

The Taiho Code did not become effective for a long, long time; some of its regulations were never practiced. People were not accustomed to anything like it, and where it affected their privileges they often failed to see any advantage in it. Those who had always inherited their fathers' lands, slaves and titles continued to do so; the system of inheritance was deep-rooted in Japan. Though a university was provided for the training of court officials, only noblemen's sons were allowed to enter, and the T'ang civil service system was never introduced. Influence still continued to play its part also (and where does it not?) in the punishment of crimes.

The condition of slaves, however, was somewhat improved by the Taiho Code. From earliest times there had been large numbers of these; some were prisoners of war, some criminals, some debtors, some sold into slavery to save the rest of their family. Able-bodied slaves could be bought for about a hundred bundles of rice; then they and their children continued as the personal property of the purchaser. Like rice, they were also used as a medium of exchange and were one of the units in which wealth was measured. When the clan system began to break down, slaves were especially important for carrying on the cultivation of the land. This is sometimes called the period of slave economy.[4]

In addition to provincial government, literature was a serious concern of the Nara court people. Instead of depending entirely on scribes they were now beginning to be able to read and write themselves. It may be that some of the earlier settlers once had known some form of writing, but scholars have not yet been able to find any proof of this. The early rulers of Yamato had had a Be, that is, a company or guild of reciters called the Katari-be, who kept in their minds the stories and traditions and important happenings of the leading families, reciting them on special occasions. In the fifth and sixth centuries when large numbers of immigrants had begun coming into Japan from Korea and China, those among them skilled in writing and keeping records had been employed as scribes by the Yamato chiefs. But when continental priests came, with rolls of scripture, teaching the way of Buddha, the Yamato people began to study how to read and write themselves.

After one really knows how, it does not seem at all hard to read and write. If one remembers, however, the time and effort spent on learning to write well in a single language which everyone around was using, and then thinks of the Yamato people, grown men and women who had no schools and had never done such things before, having to learn from a few foreign teachers the several thousand characters, more complicated than letters, in which the foreign books were written, the difficulty of their task will be appreciated. Then, having learned to read and write Chinese, they had the added problem of trying to use the foreign characters to write their own language.[5] The process took a very long time.

Two more different languages than Chinese and Japanese are hard to imagine. English and German, or English and Greek, though they have different scripts, in grammar and vocabulary have many things in common; but not so, spoken Japanese and Chinese. When Japanese first tried to write their language with Chinese script, everyone had a different idea as to how it should be done. Three distinct ways developed which may be illustrated very simply like this. Suppose a Japanese wished to write *man*. In his own language the word was *hito*. The Chinese sign for man looked like this 人 . This sign the Chinese pronounced *jen*. One thing the Japanese could do was use this just as the Chinese did and remember that 人 called *jen* means *hito*. Or they could use the sign 人 and call it *hito* instead of *jen*. And there was still another way. They could find a Chinese sign which was called *hi* and another *to* and put them together to express *hito,* regardless of what the signs meant in Chinese. They did all three of these things in their writings in the Nara period. Four literary works from this period have been preserved by editors and copyists down to the present day. These are the two histories called Kojiki and Nihongi, and two collections of poetry called Kaifuso and Manyoshu.

The Kojiki appeared first. It was written in the second of the three ways given above, with Chinese signs in their proper meaning but arranged and pronounced in the Japanese way. The Nihongi and the Kaifuso were done in regular Chinese style, while the Manyoshu was written for the most part with Chinese signs which had the desired sound, regardless of their meaning. The use of these three different methods was very confusing, and it took a vast amount of study afterward to decipher them.

For five or six centuries Chinese court officials had been

keeping records of events in the heavens, like comets and eclipses, together with those of important government affairs. Usually when a change of dynasty occurred these were compiled into an official history—such as the ones from which accounts of Japan were quoted in the first chapter. It was only natural that when the Japanese learned to read and write they should attempt to provide themselves with similar chronicles. Prince Shotoku and Soga are credited with the first venture of this kind. The Kojiki and Nihongi were produced by a historical committee originally appointed by Emperor Temmu. The preface to the Kojiki states that it was based on the facts stored up in the memory of a remarkable member of the reciters' guild, the Katari-be, and that it was written to sift the true from the false before it was too late. At this time, class rivalries had become intense, and preposterous claims were made by ambitious families in the name of their ancestry and relations. To rectify this situation, the court proceeded to guard itself with an authoritative record of genealogies. The Kojiki, completed in 712, was the result.

The Kojiki begins with the creation of Japan by heavenly deities, and the sending of the sun-goddess' grandson to rule over the land, he and his descendants forever. And it goes on with stories of the imperial family, their conquests and relationships with other leading families, glorifying their loyal supporters with superior ancestors like their own. There are no dates in the Kojiki, and the emperors are called by the names of the places where they had their home and court.

Eight years after this was completed, the Nihongi appeared. Neither of these writings were books as we think of them now. They were written with brush and ink on long strips of paper and rolled up on cylinders of ivory or some other semiprecious material instead of being folded flat and cut into pages. They were not printed in thousands. Copies had to be made by hand.

The Nihongi showed much greater literary accomplishment than the Kojiki; it was much better calculated to impress the

T'ang court. The compilers had introduced it with a Chinese theory of creation and embellished it throughout with Chinese literary forms. Emperors in the Nihongi often were given Chinese names, and dates were figured out according to the Chinese system, which put the founding of the Japanese nation by Jimmu-Tenno far back in antiquity.

Though the contents of the Kojiki and Nihongi are similar, the former concludes soon after the death of Prince Shotoku while the Nihongi carries the story on till the end of the seventh century. What evidence there is seems to indicate that some of the same people worked on both and that they added descriptions and anecdotes to their later work which they thought would interest Chinese readers. And, indeed, in the later histories of the T'ang Empire in China the Nihongi was often quoted when Japan was mentioned.

The Kojiki remained obscure for several centuries. But when the Nihongi was completed, it is said, a great court banquet was held in celebration and many poems were written in honor of the occasion. For years and years thereafter courtiers and officials were required to attend special lectures by outstanding scholars on various sections of the Nihongi. This document has served as an official textbook for over a thousand years and was read as part of the New Year's celebrations of the court.

The writing of histories was limited to a very small group of men. In poetry, on the other hand, by the end of the Nara period everyone of any education aimed to participate, from the emperor in the capital to the soldier on the frontier, and from the royal princes to the Buddhist nun. The writing of poetry in Japan has never been professional as it has with us. It became in the days of Nara, as it is now, an accomplishment to be expected of every person of refinement.

The first poem said to have been composed in Japan is credited to Amaterasu's brother, Susanowo, in honor of his Izumo bride, and the only ones recorded in the Kojiki and Nihongi were supposed to have been composed by members of the imperial family. But in the Kaifuso, a collection of one hundred and twenty poems written in Chinese for grand occasions such as enthronements and court ceremonies, sixty-four different courtiers are represented. Over six hundred writers, seventy of them women, are known to have contributed poems in Japanese to the Manyoshu (Collection of a Myriad Leaves).[6]

According to the Kojiki and Nihongi the Japanese were fond of dancing even in the age of the gods. There is the very amusing story of the deity dancing on an overturned tub to lure Amaterasu out of the cave where she had hidden, leaving the world in darkness. The earliest songs of the Yamato race were no doubt made to go with their dancing. They made them as long as they wished and put from four to eight syllables in a line. The ideas they expressed were plain and simple. Most of them were love poems. Others are about experiences we would scarcely think poetic. There is one written by the Emperor Tenji goes like this:

Aki no ta no,	Autumn rice fields,
Kari ho no iho no,	Sort of temporary house,
Toma wo arami	Rush matting may be,
Waga koromo de wa,	My clothes on that account
Tsuyu ni nure tsutsu.	With dew are getting wet.

One man says this means that the emperor was sitting in his palace weeping at the thought of the miserable shelters of the farmers on the land. Another says, "Oh, no, Emperor Tenji himself was working in the field setting an example for the people." [7]

That is the way many Japanese poems were twelve hundred years ago and still are—spontaneous expressions of emotion. If one is familiar with the man and the situation which gives rise to his poem, then it is perfectly understandable. But if one does not know these things, then there seems to be great leeway for personal interpretation. For this reason poems were often accompanied by brief prose prefaces describing the circumstances in which they were composed.

In the early days Yamato people had been accustomed to singing whatever came into their heads without much regard for the propriety of either form or content. Even Kamatari is represented in the Manyoshu with an outburst to this effect: "Wow! I've won her. All men said she was hard to win, but I've won her!" Sentiments direct from the heart are characteristic of the Manyoshu poetry. At this stage the Japanese had learned enough of Chinese script to express in writing what they really wanted to say—but they had not yet developed the smooth facility with which, a century later, court ladies and nobles devoted themselves to poetry for poetry's sake.

Chinese influence, however, was tending to formalize everything in Nippon, and poetry was not an exception. Toward the end of the Nara period the majority of Japanese poems had assumed the standard form called tanka. This form had only five lines. The poetry of the T'ang court in China usually had either five or seven syllables in each line, and the Japanese adopted these line patterns, first a line of five syllables, then one of seven, another of five and then two of seven, making the five lines have thirty-one syllables in all. As you have noticed in Tenji's poem, the tanka has no rhyming pattern. Since Japanese has only five vowel sounds and every syllable ends in a vowel or n, rhymes would be very stupid. Neither has it meter of the compelling sort we are accustomed to in Western verse. The rhythm is given instead by the natural arrangement of the two- and three-syllable elements in the five- and seven-syllable lines.

Nine out of ten poems in the Manyoshu and practically all the poems written in Japanese for over eight hundred years were in the tanka form. They had little of the variety we have in sonnets and quatrains, iambics and dactyls, and in the brief space afforded by the tanka it is obvious one could say but little. One could give only a hint, leaving the rest to the understanding and imagination of the reader. Sometimes a little trick of economy was performed and a lot more meaning was packed into the verses by the quoting of a few suggestive words from some supposedly familiar Chinese poem. It was considered very clever and elegant to do this, but it made severe demands on the reader's knowledge of literature.

The writing of poetry at the Nara court was certainly less of a social pastime than it came to be at the Heian. A number of the poems of this period were written on the occasion of deaths and accessions and were of a ritualistic and ceremonial nature. At farewell banquets, however, poems were sometimes written for the departing guest; lovers often delighted each other with verses of recollection, longing and anticipation. Journeying courtiers also carried writing materials along with them and described in five- and seven-syllable lines, sent to their friends at home, sights and thoughts which occurred to them on their way. A long one in the Manyoshu gives this description, for those left at home, of the events of a voyage:

Like the shining mirror my dear holds in her hand each morn-
ing
Is the shore from which we launched our tall ship manned by
many oars.
We drifted on the tide to open ocean where white waves surged
across the water.
When we sighted Lone Isle, darkness fell on the cloudy margin
of the sea,
As night still deepened we could not see our further course.
And, therefore, tarried in a bay in wave-rocked slumber.
I watched the fisher-girls casting lines from crowded boats in
a row,
And, as the day grew brighter, screaming wild fowl hastening
to the reed marsh.
The sailors shouted making ready, and the fishers launched
their boats across the breakers.
Rowing our tall ship farther we affronted huge ocean billows
that rose and curled and toppled.

In the cloudy distance we passed Home Island which my eyes
    had longed to view,
And onward fared to the hollow Bay of Jewels.
While we tarried there my thoughts returned to homeland and
    tears fell from me.
I thought I would gather pearl shells such as deck the sea-gods'
    arms,
And send them as gifts by runner to my home,
But, finding no runner, left them lying there.

It is an interesting fact that practically all we know of life
away from the capital during the Nara period is contained in
the Manyoshu in the poems of traveling priests and court officials.

It was troublesome to travel in those days, for the roads were
poor and occasionally blocked by robbers. The frequent streams
had but few ferries or bridges across them and persons of rank
either rode their horses through the shallows or were carried
over on the backs of laboring people. Since there were no inns,
all provisions for the journey had to be carried along.

Ordinary farmers in the country lived in the crudest sort of
shelters with bare earth floors strewn with wisps of straw on
which the family huddled together at night to sleep. If they
labored from sunrise to sunset and had good fortune they could
raise enough rice to live on and make enough cloth to cover
themselves, but a poem in the Manyoshu says, "Then would
come the village headman with his rod in hand calling for
taxes or service in loud and angry tones." If their crops were
poor on account of heavy rains or droughts or insects, then,
"No smoke rose from their hearths but spiders wove their webs
about the iron cooking pots, forgetting rice was ever cooked in
them." If some member of the household was called away to
do forced labor building a governor's mansion or fighting on
the frontier, the rest of the family had not only to do his share
of the work at home, but in addition to their regular taxes provide his livelihood and equipment wherever he might be for

as long as he was away. A courtier sent out from Nara as counselor to the governor of a distant province was passing along a
mountain trail when he saw a shrunken corpse lying by the
wayside and wrote in a poem his thoughts:

> White clothes made by a dear one
> From dried hemp grown in the garden.
> A girdle bound three times
> Around the wasted frame—
> Returning home from having done forced labor
> Hurrying on in pain,
> Eager to see wife and parents
> Here the gentle soul departed.
> The hair is disheveled, the body looks chilly—
> His family? His native place?
> No answer.

From poems in the Manyoshu we also learn how Nara people felt about overseas voyages. They were indeed experiences
to strike terror in the heart. When parties were about to embark on the "Dread Way Perilous of the Great God of the
Sea" they gathered with their families and friends at the Sumiyoshi Shrine (near the modern city of Osaka on the Inland
Sea, which even in those days was a great port). Praying here
for the voyagers' safe return, they made offerings of jars filled
with rice wine and of cloth of mulberry bark.

It is no wonder that any Japanese who went to China to
study was thought of very highly and honored by his countrymen. There was one man named Kibi no Mabi who left
Japan in the early days of Nara when he was twenty-two years
old, and remained in China studying for seventeen years. Later
he went again as an official envoy to the T'ang court. Japanese
official history says that the Chinese were favorably impressed
by his dignity and sincerity and were inclined to think well of
the country he represented.[8]

When Kibi no Mabi returned to Japan the first time, he

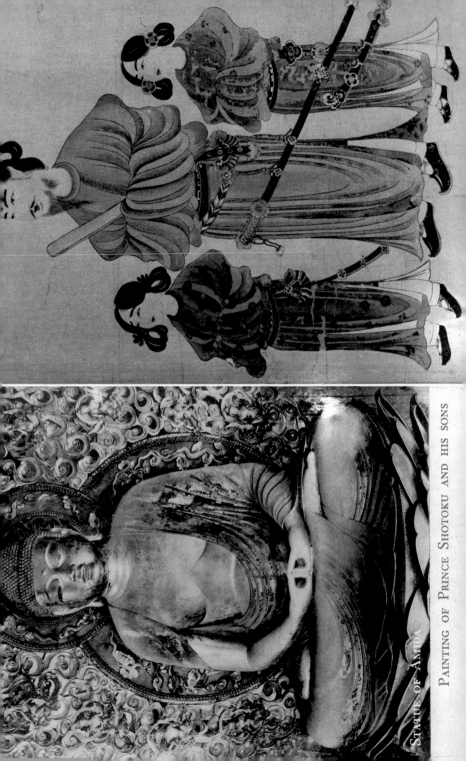

STATUE OF AMIDA

PAINTING OF PRINCE SHOTOKU AND HIS SONS

brought with him a great store of knowledge and books on many subjects. He gave many lectures to the Nara court on the forms of etiquette and ceremony considered proper in China, and on the classics of Chinese literature. He was made head of the university established at Nara for training officials and before he died had become an important minister of state. Kibi no Mabi is also said to have been the inventor of a simplified set of phonetic symbols called katakana, which the Japanese use for writing as we use our alphabet. Though the katakana more likely were developed later, the fact that Kibi is credited with their invention shows how great and clever a man people thought he was, and how much they respected him.[9]

Even toward the end of the Nara period, after considerable experience with navigation, a voyage was a terrifying undertaking. One mission returning from China set out from the Yangtze River with four ships, each carrying over a hundred people. These included the chief envoys, their subordinate officials, secretaries, interpreters, doctors and diviners, carpenters, seamen and crew. Soon after setting out they ran into a storm. One envoy and forty of his followers were washed overboard and drowned. After a day or so at sea a mast snapped and a ship broke into pieces. Those who could clung to the pieces which floated and were finally washed ashore. One ship reached Japan safely after only nine days of battering at sea, while another took forty days to make the trip. The last ship of the four was wrecked on an island and the passengers were made captives. This was perhaps a more unlucky mission than most, but such disasters were not uncommon. Even with fair skies and smooth sailing the discomforts of a hundred or more people crowded together for many days on one of those small ships may well be left to the imagination.

But discomforts and dangers notwithstanding, official embassies continued to go from the Nara court to the T'ang at approximately fifteen-year intervals. What they especially desired to bring home with them were books—books on govern-

ment, on writing and phonetics, on calendar making and astrology, and the official historical works of the Chinese court. Not
only did court officials by their courageous voyaging prove the
intensity and sincerity of their interest in T'ang culture, but
Buddhist priests also, continually coming and going between
the continent and the islands, gave convincing proof of their
faith in the possibilities of Nippon. Famous priests from China
and even from India came out to the islands to teach and ordain
new followers; while less famous, perhaps, but no less zealous
priests from Nippon made the perilous trips to China to study
and bring back treasures for their temples. Indeed it seems
more than likely that the Buddhist priests played a very important part in inspiring, directing and sustaining the interest
of the Japanese people in things Chinese.

CHAPTER 4

BUDDHIST PRIESTS AND THEIR
NARA TEMPLES

(EIGHTH CENTURY)

FROM the good start Prince Shotoku gave them the Buddhists
had continued to go forward improving their economic condition, extending their public works and making their influence
felt in ever widening areas. Before the Nara capital was built,
an imperial edict was issued ordering every family to have a
Buddhist altar and read the scriptures daily in the home. Since
very few people knew how to read, this edict probably was not
generally effective, but it is recorded that there were already
thirty-four temples and fifteen nunneries built throughout the
country, and that several Ainu even had been prepared for the
priesthood and sent out as missionaries to the northeastern
frontier.

Buddhist temples were large institutions. They spread over
several acres of ground in the midst of beautiful scenery, and
were enclosed by walls too tall for a passer-by to look over.
In the south side of the wall was an ornamental gateway
covered with a gently sloping roof. The whole enclosure represented a realm of enlightenment. In the center was the Golden
Hall where the statue of Buddha was enshrined. Surrounding
this were the pagoda, in which his earthly life was represented,
the bell tower, the drum tower and various other buildings
connected by covered passageways and porches. There were
buildings where the priests slept, ate and studied, and others
where they cared for orphans and aged people, where they

taught lay students the holy scriptures, where they dispensed medicinal herbs to people who were sick, or prayed and performed rites for invalids.[1]

The Golden Hall was not a very large building but it was

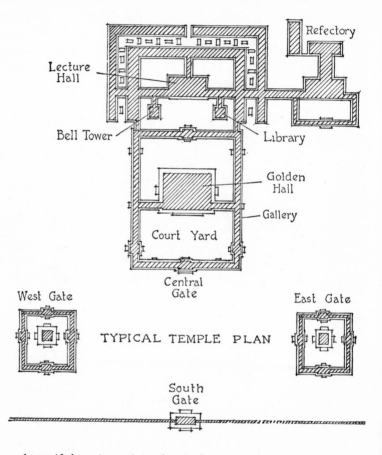

TYPICAL TEMPLE PLAN

as beautiful as its priests knew how to make it—and this is saying a great deal, for Buddhist priests had had long and rich experience in all forms of art. A gilded statue of Buddha occupied the central place, surrounded by wall paintings, ceremonial banners of richly colored silk brocades, and other accessories of worship made of precious materials by devoted hands. Here on regular occasions the scriptures were solemnly intoned and priests in slow and rhythmic procession performed the sacred rites accompanied by the beat of hand drums and the music of wooden flutes. Attendants, either standing or sitting in worshipful pose on the floor, could not help but be impressed by the mysterious and exotic beauty of the sacred ceremonies.

It was not only a great honor but also a very profitable thing to be a priest in those days. The temples had the best of everything in the country. In addition to gifts of land they received the very best the people had to offer in rice, wine and sea food, in silk and hempen cloth. They owned most of the books and the works of art imported from the continent. The temples were the homes of all the best scholars and artists. As such they provided more luxury, more culture and more security than any nobleman's palace. Their number, however, was limited and it was a much-sought-after privilege to be a priest.

Prominent priests and abbots of the temples were all able men of wide experience. Most of them had either been brought up and trained on the continent, having taken refuge in Japan from wars and political disturbances in their native lands, or had gone to China to study with Chinese masters and teachers; one had even come from India. All of them had traveled. They knew the ways of the world. There was a loved and learned priest who tried five different times to come to Japan from China but each time was shipwrecked and nearly died. On the sixth attempt, a very old man and completely blind, he arrived safely on the same boat with the famous political scholar Kibi no Mabi, mentioned in the previous chapter. Another priest named Gyogi was a great personality. Gyogi traveled all over Japan and wherever he went drew such crowds to listen to him that he was jailed for a while as a disturber of the peace. He taught the people how to build roads and bridges, how to dig wells, and how to make harbors safe for ships. He planted small trees and gardens of herbs which were good for medicine, and brought the people relief from famine, pests and plagues. He also solicited offerings for the building of an enormous statue of Buddha at Nara which he did not live quite long enough to see completed.

There are two kinds of Buddhism—one emphasizing the teachings of the historic Buddha himself, the other, teachings which later grew up about him. It was the later form, called Mahayana, which was brought to Japan. The entire collection of these teachings is called the Tripitaka. The Tripitaka is to the Buddhist what the Bible is to the Christian, and as the Bible is made up of many separate books written at different times and places by different people, so is the Tripitaka. It includes not only the narrative scriptures called sutras but also essays and commentaries. Certain of these which became great favorites were chosen as a basis for the distinctive rituals and tenets of different sects. The Lotus Sutra [2] and the Sutra of the Benevolent King were the most popular ones at Nara. These sutras had been written originally in Sanskrit, then translated into Chinese as the religion was carried eastward. They were still copied in Chinese when they reached Japan.

One of the first requirements for a priest, therefore, was that he be able to read Chinese script. For this reason most of those who aspired to the priesthood in early days were members of Chinese or Korean families who had migrated to Japan and had brought some knowledge of reading and writing with them. But there were many native Japanese, too, who by diligent effort were able to qualify for the advanced studies of a temple. The advantages of the priesthood were a great stimulus to learning.

The copying of sutras was not confined to temples—a special government bureau was organized for this purpose. Only men who had learned to write very beautifully were allowed to copy the texts and only the most excellent of all was allowed to write the titles. There were proofreaders who reread each copy twice and imposed penalties on the copyist if they found more than five errors on a sheet. Then there were dressers who joined the separate sheets of paper into a long strip, dyed it with a brownish stuff distasteful to insects, mounted it on a roll and fastened it with a silk cord. There were specialists to make writing brushes from rabbit, deer and badger fur, and paper polishers who rubbed the paper with a boar tusk to smooth it. Paper was made at two different places in Nara from mulberry bark, hemp, straw and rags. Painters were employed also to decorate the ends of the rolls and a space at the beginning of the scroll. The full staff included more than two hundred people and could complete about six thousand copies a month.[3] This Sutra Copying Bureau was one of the most important factors in the development of Japanese art; from it later came the families of official artists for the service of the court.

Besides reading, writing and religion, medicine and civil engineering, the Japanese learned from the Buddhist priests the science of blending metals and the art of casting and engraving them. In the course of years they became especially skilled in this.

Buddhist priests also encouraged the raising of silkworms, silk weaving and dyeing. In the early days of Nara, textile experts were sent to twenty-one provinces to teach the advanced art of weaving brocades and twills. These experts had recipes for the exact amounts of various kinds of plants which would give exactly the desired shade to a fixed length of silk when it was boiled with exactly so much vinegar and wood ash over exactly so much fuel. There are fragments of silk still remaining from the Nara age, some of which though dyed with madder root twelve hundred years ago are even now a fresh rich red. Blue and green were derived from a kind of marsh grass and a shrub called the wild orange. Fragrant jasmine blossoms supplied the yellow. The designs used often included birds, flowers, trees and insects.[4] While much of the silk used by princes and priests was imported from the continent, the best of the native textiles also were sent to the court and temples as tribute.

The Buddhist priests were certainly an inspiration for Yamato. "Look forward," they taught, "not backward; build temples, not tombs; cremate your dead and make your monumental offerings works of art which may bring enlightenment to children yet unborn." Though they kept the favor of the powerful and wealthy, they did not scorn the poor. The most beautiful pagoda, they demonstrated, may be built from the roughest timber.

The Yamato people admired these priests greatly and trusted them—for advice in dealing with their continental neighbors, for the healing of their ills and the satisfying of their desires. And for these things the Yamato people paid well.

The Buddhist priests had advanced so far and so fast that they did not think it enough to be merely the rulers of temples. They began to see Japan as a Buddhist kingdom entirely under their control. To that end they appointed officials of the Buddhist order similar to the officials of the state. Some of the shrewdest members of the court, seeing danger ahead, tried to put brakes on the Buddhist progress and develop within their own ranks leaders of equal merit. The strongest of these were the Fujiwaras, the descendants of Kamatari. It was they who promoted the codes of law for governing the country. One of Kamatari's sons named Fubito became prime minister soon after Nara was founded, and his four capable sons all held important offices. One of his daughters was the mother of the heir to the throne, and another daughter by another wife was a likely person for the heir to marry. With the Fujiwaras in such a good position to defend the imperial interests the day when a Buddhist priest would take the place of the emperor seemed very far away. The Fujiwaras themselves, to be sure, were not beyond Buddhist influence, but they had their own talents and their own ambitions.

Fubito's younger daughter did marry the emperor and,

though not immediately, was proclaimed Empress of Japan a few years later. This was the first time in the history of the country that such an honor had been bestowed upon a girl not born of the imperial family. Fubito, however, had not lived to enjoy it. Not long afterward some poor fishermen from Korea landed in Japan with smallpox which spread through the population like wildfire. Among those who lost their lives were Fubito's four promising sons.

As the plague raged on, priests advised the court to turn to Buddha. In Buddha, they said, lay the only hope for the nation. Emperor Shomu allowed two and three thousand persons at a time to become priests and nuns and attach themselves to the more than two thousand temples then existing in the country. Lavish offerings were made for prayers at the Nara temples. And still the plague raged on. Then it was decided to build a bronze statue of Buddha over fifty feet high and a special sanctuary to contain it. To help this project along, Emperor Shomu ordered that, in every province, a temple be built with a seven-story pagoda and a nunnery. "Let the sound of the tools that are raising the image of Buddha reverberate in heaven!" urged Fubito's daughter, Shomu's Empress Komyo. "Let it rend the earth asunder for the sake of the fathers, for the sake of the mothers, for the sake of all mankind!" [5] Thus she encouraged the people in their giving and toil.

Metals, timber and fuel were brought from all over the country. A million pounds of bronze were to be melted and molded. Such an enormous metal statue had never been cast before nor has one of such size been cast since. Six attempts at casting ended in failure, and then the son of a Korean immigrant who had come to Japan in Tenji-Tenno's time finally succeeded. He turned out a perfect figure of Buddha sitting on a pedestal shaped like a lotus blossom, backed by an enormous halo studded with minor statues of Buddhist saints all united in adoration. For his remarkable achievement he was honored with the fourth rank of the court.

At this point, the priests did some clever propagandizing. They had it announced far and wide that gold was discovered for the first time in Japan and this was a sign that the deities were well pleased. They had some of the precious metal transported to Nara with great ceremony and gilded the great bronze Buddha. Emperor Shomu abdicated his throne and gave it over to his daughter so that he might be relieved of government duties and devote himself wholly to worship—or so it was reported. Such a thing had never before been heard of in Japan. Though his daughter was no longer young, she was still unmarried and had no heir to succeed her. The chances for the Buddhist kingdom looked very bright indeed.

On the two-hundredth anniversary of the date when Buddhism is officially supposed to have been brought to Yamato, the dedication ceremony for the great bronze Buddha was held. A grand procession moved solemnly along the broad avenue from the palace toward the Todai temple, led by the new Empress Koken followed by her father and mother, the retired Emperor Shomu and his wife the Empress Komyo. Hundreds of lesser court people followed, robed in voluminous gowns of colored silk. At the entrance to the new sanctuary the procession was greeted with music and feasting.

Ten thousand priests and musicians in brocade robes were there performing with rhythmic motion. On two stages outside the temple, groups of figures wearing large, grotesque masks performed rhythmic dances. Inside the temple was candlelight, incense and perfume. A crimson cloth covered the floor. Before the great Buddha offerings were laid; gilded copper flowers on six silver stands, crystal balls, white tortoise-shell cups.[6]

At the climax of the ceremony former Emperor Shomu and his empress proclaimed themselves "servants of Buddha and the three treasures." [7] Then, wearing a crown, Shomu mounted a platform forty feet above the crowd while the priests and musicians chanted. A very large brush was there with endless yards of light-blue-silk cord suspended from it. Shomu clasped the brush in his hands. The spectators below clasped the cord that they too might have a part in the rite of painting black pupils on the great gold eyes and making the Nara Daibutsu an image filled with the spirit of light. This image was not thought of as the real deity any more than the statues or crosses in Christian churches are thought to be really Christ. It was a symbol which made the deity seem near, real and understandable.

These were great days for the Buddhists in Japan. It was their golden age. Their ambitions seemed scarcely to exceed their grasp; their highest hopes seemed all but fulfilled. A priest named Dokyo was their head. By gift, purchase and reclamation they had come into possession of as much land as was controlled by the imperial household itself. And temple land was free from taxes. Dokyo was given rank higher even than the prime minister, and his annual income was very large. Empress Koken jilted the Fujiwara whom previously she had extravagantly favored with affection, lands and titles, and took Dokyo for her lover. Only one more step to the throne!

But this step never was taken. The landlords rebelled against Buddhist domination and the best soldiers in the country refused to fight for it. "Since the establishment of the state," it was proclaimed, "the distinction between sovereign and subject has been observed. The successor to the throne must be of the imperial family. The usurper is to be rejected." [8]

The country was in a turmoil. Before long the Empress Koken passed away and Dokyo was made an ordinary priest again. Conditions in Nara made it expedient for the court to establish itself elsewhere, and so the first capital was abandoned and a new one started in another valley thirty miles to the north.

The temples, however, remained at Nara, and on the grounds of one, Todai-ji, was the Shoso-in, the temple storehouse mentioned in Chapter 3 which was built of roughhewn logs and which, alone of all the buildings that stood in the heyday of Nara, was to survive intact the ravages of storm, fire, war and time. In the Shoso-in were stored all the treasured possessions of Emperor Shomu which his widowed empress, Komyo, had dedicated to the Todai temple after his death in 756. The document of dedication reads:

> His Majesty the late Emperor was illustrious and his virtue filled the universe . . . He suppressed wickedness and exalted the doctrine of Buddha . . . Priests of the purest virtue and deepest learning came to his empire from afar . . .
>
> . . . Alas, of his term on earth there could be no prolongation and his spirit has departed . . . Nine and forty days have now elapsed, but each day my grief grows deeper and sadness weighs ever heavier on my heart . . . I have therefore resolved by the performance of good deeds to give succour to his august spirit. To this end, and in obedience to the will of his late Majesty, these his relics, that in truth are national treasures, I donate to the Todai-ji by way of offering to Buddha for the repose of the Emperor's soul. May these gifts, I humbly pray, help its progress to the Temple in the Lotus World. May he there always enjoy heavenly music, and may he finally be admitted to the Sacred Hall of the Buddha of Light! [9]

A list with detailed descriptions of over six hundred and fifty items followed this devout dedication, and a number of these are still carefully preserved. More offerings were made a little later and many of the temple treasures used in the great Eye Opening and other ceremonies were also stored in the Shoso-in, together with a hundred suits of armor, eighty swords, a hundred and three bows, ninety-six quivers full of arrows and twenty-one chests of medicines.

In the course of centuries, some of these objects were withdrawn by members of the imperial family and twice thieves broke in through the floor, but nearly five hundred dated objects from the eighth century were preserved in the collection. The expansion and contraction of the logs with the weather, it is explained, has guarded the precious contents well against both dampness and dryness. They were further protected by an imperial seal which kept the building locked except during a few weeks of good weather in the autumn.

For the annual opening, a messenger sent from His Imperial Majesty in Tokyo, with officials of the Imperial Household Museum, proceeded up the freshly raked sand path to the threshold. Here all slipped out of their footgear and with fresh water from a wooden dipper washed their hands ceremonially, drying them on soft white paper. Great formality attended the unsealing and unlocking of massive wooden doors before they swung open on their wooden pivots. Then the treasures were officially inspected and cared for, and by very special permission visitors with electric flashlights might view the remains of the glory that was Nara: palace furnishings and personal adornments, mirrors and musical instruments, swords, saddles, bows and arrows, scepters, masks, and rosaries, brocade banners, bronze censers and flower baskets.

An interesting though unspectacular part of the collection were the medicines in their little earthenware jars. These, too, were given to Todai-ji in adoration of Buddha, and theoretically any person suffering from illness and in need of them could apply to the head priests of the temple. The clergy had a practical monopoly of medicines and their application. One priest was sent to China especially to study medicine. Its chief use in those days was to promote long life and to keep men virile; the curing of disease was secondary.

The parts and organs of the body, in accordance with Chinese philosophy, were designated Yin or Yang, i.e., passive or active in essence, and also by the five elements—wood (liver), fire (heart), earth (spleen), metal (lung) and water (kidney); and medicines were similarly designated according to their origin and properties. Sickness, like all other evils, they thought was caused by a lack of harmony between the active and passive elements, and medicines were chosen to restore a harmonious relationship between them in the body.

A kind of pepper was used to warm the stomach, cure rumblings in the intestines, pain in the shoulder, headache, toothache or nasal catarrh. Croton seeds from India were used to open the passages of the body, kill worms and cure snake bites. Magnolia wood from Cochin-China was pulverized and made into pills or given with ginger juice for typhus, diarrhea or nervousness. Petrified dragon bones "with a simple sweet taste" were supposed to protect one from devils and to quiet the mind; powdered and heated they were a dose for malaria. Rhubarb was used as a tonic and laxative, mica powder for carbuncles, nutgall to prevent perspiration and for dyeing the hair, a form of arsenopyrites for rat poison, hedgehog skin from northwest Asia and Africa for hemorrhoids, and sheep fat from Korea to cure colds and gout and to expel wind. These remedies and many others were to be found in the Shoso-in.[10]

All in all this collection of treasures in the Nara temple storehouse is unique. Nowhere else in the world has an age been represented by such a variety of objects so carefully preserved throughout more than a thousand years.

CHAPTER 5

THE IMPERIAL COURT, KYOTO

(NINTH AND TENTH CENTURIES)

AFTER the affair of Empress Koken and Priest Dokyo the whole country was in confusion, and naturally enough. Only two hundred years before, the Yamato people had known little of what we call civilization. They had been entirely illiterate, and practically ignorant of both organized religion and organized government. In the two centuries from 600 to 800, they had tried three great experiments. They had learned to read Chinese script and tried to adapt it for writing their own language. They had tried to attain the fulfillment of their desires by following the teachings of Buddha and his priests. And they had made an effort to establish a centralized government such as there was in China.

Quite naturally confusion followed change. It was not surprising that each of the several Japanese books written in Chinese script used the foreign symbols in a different way, or that the Buddhist priests to whom the Yamato leaders had looked for guidance had attempted to seize the supreme power themselves. Nor was it surprising that government by public officials could not be made effective throughout the country at once, for both the geography of the land and the psychology of the people were very different from those of China.

Instead of broad, fertile plains and a few wide torpid rivers separating vast areas, here were rocky slopes, stony valleys and innumerable little torrents cutting the country to bits.

Instead of worldly-wise philosophers were men and women of action with material ambitions.

Japan was still a young country with frontiers beyond the reach of court officials where small farmers could escape from burdensome tax collectors and where energetic leaders could develop their own domains. On the large island to the south and west were independent clans of bold seafarers; in the north and east beyond Mount Fuji were the Ainu and a vigorous breed of settlers.[1] The Nara priests had enshrined the sea-god in one of their temples, hoping thus to win the cooperation of seafaring clans in importing treasures from China, but these worshipers of Hachiman had refused to fight for Dokyo. The settlers on the northeastern frontier rose up in revolt when the government tried to expand and take toll of their forests, fields and mines. Even among the clans close to the capital there was keen rivalry. But now a new generation of Fujiwaras had grown up since the great epidemic, as determined as their ancestor Kamatari had been to establish the supremacy of the imperial family.

Fujiwara Momokawa was determined that the emperor should be an able man. He stayed forty days in the palace refusing to move, until at sword's point it was agreed that the prince of his choice was to succeed to the throne.

Though this prince was a great-grandson of Emperor Tenji, his mother was a girl of Korean descent, not of the Yamato nobility, and his position, therefore, had not been very high. He had belonged to the junior grade of the fifth rank and had earned his living as head of the imperial university at Nara. Fujiwara Momokawa saw in this, however, an excellent recommendation for his protégé, for in the university little respect was paid to Buddhism. There they were concerned with the study of Chinese history, Chinese institutions, and the teachings of the Chinese sages, which had to do with the responsibilities of rulers, with loyal and proper conduct toward people of higher and lower rank, and were closely associated with good government. Furthermore, through his mother's relations this prince had the support of a large colony of continental immigrants who had settled in the province of Omi near Lake Biwa and who had grown very rich and important because of their great skill in weaving silk and their monopoly of sake brewing. Both of these industries had flourished when the Nara temples flourished, but when the clergy fell from favor, they had to look for other patrons. Thus, in addition to being a Chinese scholar, and more independent of the Buddhist priests than were many courtiers of his day, this prince united the interests of the wealthy and progressive immigrant group with the interests of the Yamato leaders, chief among whom were the Fujiwaras.

When he became emperor, Kwammu began planning at once for the removal of the capital from Nara. The priests of the Nara temples were loath to have the court carried away from their control since it meant the loss of the many gifts and favors which they had enjoyed under Shomu and the empresses. There were also old clan leaders whose interests were closely affiliated with Nara, who opposed the move in every possible way and for ten years struggled to prevent it. The Fujiwara minister in charge of the plans for the new capital was assassinated. Even after the new capital was built, a rebellion was instigated within the imperial family and an attempt made to move back to Nara. But plans for the new capital were carefully laid.

The site chosen, thirty miles north of the old, enjoyed three chief advantages. It was away from the center of the scheming Buddhist priests; it was convenient to a settlement of Chinese and Korean immigrants, willing to support the new regime; and it was on the direct route from the Inland Sea via Lake Biwa to the northern frontier where uprisings were growing more serious. Emperor Kwammu's capital was called Heian-kyo (Capital of Peace) and the new era which it instituted was called the Heian Era. People often referred to Heian-kyo simply as Miyako (The Capital). Later, it came to be better known as Kyoto, and since that is the name most familiar today, Kyoto it will be called in this book.

The great cities of the world all seem to be on rivers. The T'ang Chinese had a superstitious saying which they applied when they chose the site for their capital: "For a capital, three hills and two rivers." [2] And it is said the Japanese court thought of this also when they chose the location for their new center of government and planned to model it after the magnificent T'ang capital. Kyoto was supposed to be a very fortunate choice, for it lay in a valley protected on three sides by mountains which opened toward the south, and through this valley ran two beautifully clear streams.

To separate the city from the surrounding fields a wall was built enclosing a section of land about three miles square. A moat was dug just beyond the wall and through it flowed fresh water. In the northern part of this enclosure was the imperial palace. Its grounds stretching for about a mile in each direction were also surrounded by walls with three gateways on each side. The Kyoto of Kwammu's day was not such a splendid city as is often imagined. The imperial palace and the government buildings around it were built in part with materials transported across the valley from the demolished Nara palace.

The most spectacular edifice was the Great Hall of State. It stood on a spacious stone platform, surrounded by red-lacquered balustrades; its roof of blue-green tiles was upheld by fifty-two pillars painted a rich red. The imperial throne stood on a dais in this hall with a canopy and golden phoenix over it, bespeaking the schoolmaster emperor's fondness for things Chinese. [3] Near by was the hall where nobles and court ladies gathered to attend official entertainments, and the Hall of Martial Virtues with its field for archery, riding and equestrian games. Further secluded were the hall in which state ministers and nobles of high rank conferred with the emperor, and the living apartments of the emperor and his consorts, called the Cool Refreshing Hall. Just outside the wall on the southern side was a large estate, comprised of several buildings, which Kwammu gave for the university. Here also, many of the nobles had residences.[4]

Broad avenues traversed that part of the city not occupied by the official enclosure, dividing it into equal districts called first ward, second ward and so on to the ninth. The avenues, wide

Typical palace and garden

enough for ten bullock carts abreast, were traversed by narrower thoroughfares lined with one-story unpainted houses roofed with shingles or thatch, where the townsfolk lived. Shrines to the old deities of the land were located here and there, as well as temples to Buddha and the Chinese sage, Confucius. The booming of the temple bells let people know how time was passing.

Merchants were not scattered everywhere in the city as they

are today. They were established in a large market where, on scheduled days, people would display the products and wares which they wished to sell. These were brought from many provinces. Business was still carried on chiefly in terms of rice: thirty bundles of rice, say, for a roll of silk; three bundles of rice for a hoe, etc.

Modes of transportation in Kyoto varied with the rank of the traveler. High officials sometimes sat in curtained palan-

Market scene

quins which were carried around on poles in the hands of a group of servants. Sometimes they rode in two-wheeled carts drawn by oxen and attended by many servants walking. Those of lesser rank and importance rode on horseback. But the undistinguished, by far the greatest in number, went everywhere on foot.

The Japanese capital was small compared with the Chinese one it copied, but none the less attractive for that. People flocked to it as if charmed, and as time went on built nearly forty thousand homes there.

Emperor Kwammu did everything he could to make Kyoto the real center of the country with government authority extending from it as far as possible in all directions. He built new roads, repaired bridges and improved old ferries to facilitate travel between the provinces and the capital.

Government through the ages, as everyone well knows, has been a great system for collecting taxes, and this was the chief concern of the Heian regime. The Nara government had failed because it had paid little attention to the collection of taxes. Large areas of the land, whose yield was its greatest source of revenue, had got away from it and into the hands of priests and officials who were immune from taxes. That is why, when Emperor Kwammu came to the throne, he issued an edict forbidding the gift or sale of land to religious organizations, and limiting the building of temples and the number of men and women who might become priests and nuns. Many officials, too, had added to their own lands at the expense of the government which they were supposed to serve. They not only accepted lands from farmers who could not pay their taxes, but also reclaimed land from mountain slopes and river beds by using forced labor, and held it as their own instead of turning it over to the emperor. By these methods district governors who handed their office down from father to son were able to build up very large estates for their families. There was also the possibility that a dishonest tax collector might simply keep the taxes for himself and report that he had been unable to deliver them to the capital because a bridge was down, the roads were bad, or the storehouse where the tax rice was kept had been struck by lightning.

All these malpractices Kwammu-Tenno sought to remedy. He tried to put into effect the Chinese system of office based on merit instead of inheritance, and made a great effort to do away with officials who sought special privileges for themselves. When lightning struck too often in the same district the governor was investigated. Inspectors were appointed to audit the tax records in all the provinces, and the emperor himself often performed official tasks until he found a man whom he thought honest and efficient to relieve him. The farmers who had left their lands and migrated toward the frontier, he ordered to return to their native places, and for their protection he had granaries built and stored up rice for times of need. He also tried to get people in the provinces to pay their taxes in money if they had any, for money was more convenient than rice to use in the capital market, and was of less use than rice in the country. There had never been much money, however, and now more and more of it, instead of fulfilling its intended function, was being melted and made into huge bells and Buddhist statues.[5]

The Ainu up in the northeast, supplemented by rebellious farmers, were another one of Kwammu's great problems. While his father was ruling, they had won a victory over the provincial defenders, and again not long afterward had defeated them on sea as well as on land, causing the death of over a thousand of the emperor's soldiers. Whenever a court official was sent there to try to collect taxes they were stirred to fresh revolt and finally began pressing southwestward. "They gathered together like ants and dispersed like birds."

Then Kwammu, whose name means Prosperous in War, organized imperial troops from among the sons and younger brothers of provincial officials. Two thousand suits of leather armor he provided for them, and three thousand suits of iron armor. He appointed a man named Tamuramaro, of extraordinary height and hawklike eyes, as permanent Sei-i Tai Shogun, Great Barbarian-subduing General. Tamuramaro drove the rebels farther and farther back and killed some of their chiefs. At last many of the ringleaders who survived fled to the northernmost island, Hokkaido. Those who remained agreed to obey the shoguns who were sent to rule them. An occasional burst of resentment occurred later and there were a few rebellious sons of courtiers on the frontier, but aside from these minor disturbances the country enjoyed peace for three hundred years. Tamuramaro was the first warrior honored with the title of shogun, and the last shogun of any importance during the Heian Era. At the end of the twelfth century, however, the whole of Japan came to be ruled by a shogun and continued to be until 1868.

But to return to the early ninth century and Emperor Kwammu; he had broken with the Nara Buddhists, it is true, but he did not fail to appreciate the good their priests had done in developing civilization in Yamato. Though his own interests centered more largely in the wisdom of Chinese sages, his courtiers and court ladies were enthusiastic attendants at the beautiful temple ceremonies and willing believers in the power of Buddhist prayers to save them from disaster, disease and death. Kwammu did not attempt to suppress Buddhism entirely; he merely tried to free the government from Buddhist domination.

As it happened there were two brilliant young priests who saw things much as he did and were willing to work with him. One was Saicho; the other, Kukai.[6]

Saicho belonged to a family of Chinese immigrants who had settled near Lake Biwa. He was ordained at Nara when he was eighteen years old, but growing dissatisfied with the conduct of the Nara priests, went off into the mountains near his native place to think and pray alone. When Kwammu founded Kyoto, a little monastery built by Saicho already stood on Mount Hiei, north of the site, to defend it from the evil spirits which Japanese seemed to think lurked in that direction. Before long there were many places of worship and learning on the slopes of Mount Hiei, but the priests devoted themselves to religious services and did not meddle in politics during Kwammu-Tenno's lifetime.

Kukai was a descendant of a warrior clan which had for generations served as imperial guards at Isé, but which had been implicated in a plot to prevent the removal of the capital from Nara and were, therefore, in disfavor with Emperor Kwammu. Young Kukai, however, managed to go to China with Saicho, as some modern scholars think, to restore the fortunes of his family. There he remained three years, studying with both Indian and Chinese masters, traveling and collecting many books and works of art. Upon his return he had no more than begun to make a good impression on the Heian court when another relative was indicted for plotting against it. Though this made Kukai's position difficult, it could not prevent his rise. He personally contrived to be on good terms with everyone of influence, made friends of Shinto priests and courtiers as well as rival Buddhists. His name is written with the Chinese symbols for sky and ocean which signify broadminded, and this he surely was.

Before Kukai died he succeeded in establishing a teaching center similar to Saicho's, though not so near the capital, on Mount Koya, winning the support of Kwammu's emperor sons and the loyalty of many of Saicho's disciples. His monastery later became "the largest and perhaps the most flourishing in Japan. His memory lives all over the country, his name is a household word in the remotest places, not only as a saint, but as a preacher, a scholar, a poet, a sculptor, a painter, an inventor, an explorer, and—sure passport to fame—a great calligrapher. Many miraculous legends cluster about his name. A great light shone when he was born, a bright star entered his mouth, by his prayers he could cause wells of pure water to spring up from foul places, could make rain fall in times of drought and conjure away the pains of an ailing emperor." [7] His tomb is still visited every year by hundreds of pilgrims. Approached through a mile-long cemetery with mossy monuments to thousands of faithful followers, it rests in the dim shade of tall cryptomerias and fragrant incense smoke. In the quiet beauty of its surroundings worshipers find exaltation and peace.

For a time Mount Hiei and Mount Koya were at odds, but gradually Saicho's group grew interested in Kukai's teaching. "Everything in the world," he wrote in his *Juju Shin, Ron* (*Ten Steps in the Development of Religious Consciousness*) "has something of the God spirit in it, and there is no real difference between man and nature or body and soul, but all are essentially one." According to the doctrines of Kukai's sect, every human desire could be fulfilled by the performance of prescribed rituals, the details of which were kept secret among the priests. Certain rites assured health and long life—others wealth, fine weather or promotion in official rank. No teaching was so full of hope and promise as this. It made the people feel as though anything were possible. This was most encouraging for a young nation which was trying to appear as dignified as ancient China.

Court people flocked to the temples and made generous offerings to the priests for performing mysterious services. Their gifts were sometimes so extravagant that the court found it necessary to issue an edict limiting the amount that might be given by persons of different ranks. Princes of the imperial family might give five thousand yards of cloth—members of the sixth rank not more than three hundred. This new Buddhist movement, however, as already noted, had its centers on mountaintops rather than in the capital and offered no political threat to the government.

In an energetic attempt to make practical use of his Chinese studies by building up a body of able government officials competent in bringing about order and peace in his domain, Kwammu-Tenno gave the Yamato people a sense of self-confidence greater than any they had known since, three centuries before, they had lost their standing on the Korean peninsula and their country was flooded with immigrants far more gifted than themselves. The feeling of inferiority and helplessness which made the Nara court look so eagerly to the foreign priests was disappearing, and native leaders of Yamato were ready to direct affairs themselves in their impressive new capital. Fortunately for them, the T'ang Empire which had seemed all-powerful was now beginning to be weakened by Tatar invasions.

The first code of laws in Japan had been issued by Kwammu's great-grandfather, Tenji, from his palace in Omi in 662.
Japanese officials after that time seem to have been very much
interested in legislation. Tenji's code underwent a revision from
672 to 686, and in its revised form was distributed throughout
the government offices in 689 or a few years later. Then in 701
the Taiho Code was compiled and it also was revised seventeen
years later. These revisions represent the process of adaptation
of the Chinese models on which the Japanese codes were based.

Many differing opinions developed concerning these laws,
and as a result Kwammu appointed one of his ministers to
prepare a version of them with a commentary which should
be considered authoritative and official. The resulting document, called Ryo no Gige (Commentary on the Code), is still
in existence. It deals with the functions of the departments of
state and the duties of officials. While the Nara court had
provided statutes on paper, the Heian court put into practice a
classical system of government. At the head were the emperor
and the department of religion and under them eight ministries
of state, with officials and employees totaling well over six
thousand people. These were associated with the central government alone, and did not include provincial officials. A list
of the eight ministries and their various bureaus, with a brief
description of their functions as given in the Ryo no Gige, af-
fords a good idea of what an elaborate, complex and costly
business the Heian court was as early as the ninth century.[8]
The functions of the emperor and the department of religion
are described in detail following this list.

The Ministry of Central Affairs had as its chief officer
usually an imperial-family prince, in constant attendance upon
the sovereign to advise on matters of ceremonial and precedent,
drafting of imperial edicts, compilation of official chronicles,
and the keeping of records of the services, promotions and
ranks of court ladies and palace women, of registers of population, provincial land and labor taxes, monks and nuns. A secre-

tary was to inquire into the conduct of court officials so as to decide on promotions; eight chamberlains were to maintain discipline at court; ninety attendants were to wear swords, keep guard within the palace and act as escort before and behind the imperial carriage. Inspectors were to oversee the palace storehouses the keys of which were kept by a palace woman official. Masters of the Bells dispatched official communications to the provinces by giving bells as token of the messenger's right to use post horses and seals to make the message authentic. Bureaus and offices under this ministry: managed the affairs of the empress' household; acted as escorts; took charge of books, documents, maps and drawings and of the copying, binding and repair of sacred writings used for court ceremonies. Others including bootmakers, saddlers and needleworkers kept personal properties in good repair and made wearing apparel. The Bureau of Divination was in charge of astrology, calendar making, watching the water clocks and striking the hours on gongs and drums.

The Ministry of Ceremonial, in addition to keeping registers of officials, both central and provincial, administered the universities, examined the approximately four hundred students, celebrated festivals in honor of Confucius, lectured upon the Chinese classics, taught arithmetic and the reading, writing and pronouncing of Chinese.

The Ministry of Civil Administration was responsible for genealogies, marriages, funeral rites and receptions for foreign envoys: this included a Bureau of Music with professors of singing, dancing, Chinese and Korean music, flute and drum playing; eight flute makers and about three hundred and fifty singers and students.

The Ministry of Popular Affairs included a Bureau of Statistics and the Tax Bureau for administering labor taxes, family obligations, rewards for meritorious conduct, servants and slaves, bridges and roads, harbors, fences, bays, lakes, mountains, rivers, woods, swamps and rice lands in all provinces and also the receipt, custody, hulling, milling and issue of grain delivered as tax.

The Ministry of War maintained registers of military officers, their services and rewards, and of the allocation of troops, arms and equipment for war service and ceremonial fortifications. It included: the Remount Office in charge of feeding and training horses and oxen for military use and post stations; the Arsenal Office; the Military Music Office; the Ship Control Office; and the Falconry Office which supplied and trained hawks and dogs.

The Ministry of Justice investigated and judged offenses, imprisonment and claims for debt and administered prisons.

The Ministry of the Treasury was in charge of receipt and issue of tax goods from the provinces: coins, gold, silver, jewels, copper, iron, bones, horns and leather, fur and feathers, lacquered hangings and curtains, weights and measures, price fixing, and miscellaneous tribute goods. It was also in charge of the supply and maintenance of palace furnishings and the cleaning and arrangement of palace apartments.

The Ministry of the Imperial Household administered crown lands producing food and taxes for the palace, provided meals and banquets, carriages and palanquins, sunshades and fans, firewood and charcoal. It supervised the cleaning and lighting of apartments and gardens; it had a Bureau of Medicine, with professors and students of medicine, acupuncture, massage and exorcism; herb gardeners and a guild for providing cows' milk; other offices were responsible for the imperial table and wine, water supply and ice chambers, oils and fats for lighting and cooking, public slaves, palace women, ponds and gardens, making copper and iron articles, bricks and tiles, wood and pottery receptacles for food and drink and dyeing.

To supply this great body of court officials and court servants called for by the Ryo no Gige there were, according to a genealogical record of the time, eleven hundred and eighty-two families of rank. These were divided into three important classes and a few miscellaneous ones. Those of imperial lineage, descended from Amaterasu herself, numbered three hundred and thirty-five; four hundred and four families were descended from the companions of Amaterasu's grandson Ninigi and his scion, the first emperor, Jimmu; and three hundred and twenty-six families of nobles were of Chinese or Korean origin. These must have been a most impressive group. From their numbers also were appointed provincial officials and the Kebiishi (Transgression Inspection Agency). The function of the Kebiishi was to apprehend lawbreakers. Operating at first only in the capital, it later extended its activities into the provinces and helped to increase the government's prestige.

Young sons of these noble families were educated for office at the imperial university or in the private schools of their own clan, where studies were based entirely on Chinese writings. The Heian court held in highest esteem not only the wisdom of the ancient Chinese classics, but also the minutest details of the manners and customs of the contemporary T'ang court and endeavored with earnest enthusiasm to deport themselves according to T'ang standards.

Throughout the greater part of the ninth century, groups of students and scholars traveled to and from the T'ang court at frequent intervals in their effort to establish a perfect reproduction of it in Japan. Toward the close of the ninth century, however, Japanese returning from the mainland began to report that the T'ang Empire was no longer what it had been; orderly government no longer existed; trade and the arts no longer flourished. A favorite adviser [9] of the emperor's then offered his opinion that Japan no longer had anything to gain by sending official envoys overseas; he recommended that the Heian court, instead of persisting in imitation, make an effort to digest what had already been learned and develop new ways for putting the knowledge to use.

This advice was followed and brought about noteworthy changes not only in government, but in literature and art as well. The resulting forms of the latter, which today are held to be classical and representative of the Golden Age of Japanese court life, will be described more fully in the next chapter.

In the realm of government, the new tendency led to the passing of more and more of the actual administration into the hands of an able few. The Fujiwara family came to be The Court. They exercised the real power and controlled the country, while many official titles were borne by men who performed no serviceable duties. The imperial family, to whose prestige the official recognition of Chinese rulers had contributed largely, now came to be of less and less importance in affairs of state. The emperor's function became increasingly that of a high priest. The performance of religious ceremonies made such demands on his time and energy that he had little left for politics and statesmanship.

Even during the century of Buddhist domination the old cult, Shinto, had persisted. Though Japanese worshipers had given a large share of their attention and offerings to the Buddha of Light, still they had not forgotten Amaterasu, their own Shining-in-Heaven goddess. The majority of the people, not only farmers on the soil but great property owners and provincial leaders, had never turned wholly away from their native deities of heaven and the land. The government took most respectful cognizance of this and encouraged the populace in the worship of their local divinities, as well as in the worship of the divine ancestors of the rulers.

In the Ryo no Gige, the department of religion, with the emperor as its high priest and object of worship, was given precedence and greater authority than the ministries of state. This department was made responsible for oracles and divination by which government officials were supposed to be guided, as well as for the traditional ceremonies connected with the accession and enthronement of the sovereign. It also had to perform a number of prescribed observances throughout the year: rites held in early spring for freedom from calamity, and bountiful harvests, prayers for freedom from sickness offered at the end of the third month; and in the fourth, festivals in honor of food and wind deities together with offerings of summer garments at the Isé shrine. On the last day of the sixth month, rites had to be celebrated at the crossroads outside the capital to induce the gods of the crossroads to prevent evil spirits and pestilences from entering Kyoto. The prayer recited on this occasion had no doubt been in use for generations. It beseeches the deity of the crossroads:

> Whenever from the Root-country, the Bottom-country, there may come savage and unfriendly beings, consort not and parley not with them, but if they go below, keep watch below; if they go above, keep watch above, protecting us against pollution with a night guarding and a day guarding.

And it goes on:

> The offerings furnished in your honor are bright cloth, shining cloth, soft cloth and rough cloth. The tops of the sake jars are raised up, and they are filled, and the bellies of the jars are ranged in order. Of things that dwell in the mountains and on the moors, the soft of hair and the coarse of hair are offered. Of things that dwell in the blue sea plain, the broad of fin and the narrow of fin, even to the weeds of the offing, and the weeds of the shore. Peacefully partaking of these plenteous offerings laid before you in full measure like a range of hills, hold guard on the highways, preserving from pollution the sovereign grandchild firmly and enduringly, and make his reign prosperous.
>
> Also be pleased peacefully to preserve from pollution the imperial princes, the ministers of state and all the functionaries, including moreover the people of the Under-Heaven.
>
> An official of the department of religion humbly fulfills your praises by this celestial, this great pronouncement.[10]

Following the celebration at the crossroads was one required for preventing the destruction of the imperial palace by fire.

This included a somewhat similar prayer in worship of a fire kindled by the official in charge rubbing together two pieces of wood.

In the eleventh month there was a very important thanksgiving ceremony in which the emperor, together with the gods, partook of wine and food made from rice of the new crop. There were many other rites and services also, less important perhaps than these, which had to be performed.

Before each ceremony those participating were required to observe a period of abstinence and purification varying in accord with the importance of the occasion from one day to one month. There were partial and complete abstinence and regular and great purifications. During periods of abstinence, officials were not permitted to pay visits of condolence upon a death, call upon the sick or eat meat; death sentences could not be pronounced nor criminal cases judged; no music could be played and no unclean or inauspicious tasks performed. Complete abstinence meant that all work was suspended and only duties related to ceremonial observances were performed. At the accession of an emperor, the court observed partial abstinence for a month, complete abstinence for three days. Regular purifications were held at the end of the sixth and of the twelfth month; great purifications, on such occasions as the appearance of a comet, the outbreak of an epidemic, the finding of a dead body in the palace, or the officiating in a festival of a Shinto priest recently involved with Buddhist services. Purification rites included bodily ablution, presentation of offerings, and the emperor's declaration to his ministers and people, by virtue of his relationship with Amaterasu, that he was "graciously pleased to purify them and cleanse away all their offenses."

Once a year there was prescribed a ceremony of Luck Wishing for the Great Palace, when a procession of officials from the department of religion and virgin priestesses entered the palace carrying two eight-legged tables on which were boxes of precious stones, cut paper, mulberry bark, rice and bottles of sake. The officials read the ritual while the priestesses went throughout the palace, even to the emperor's bathroom, sprinkling rice and mulberry bark and sake, and hanging strings of precious stones at the four corners of each room.

A not insignificant part in Heian religious observances was played by the sacred mirror, one of the Three Imperial Regalia.[11] Every new moon, offerings of rice cakes, paper, cloth, eggplant, fish and shellfish were presented by ladies of the palace at the Place of Reverence where the mirror was kept; and many other special rites were performed at Isé.

At many Shinto festivals gaiety prevailed; sake cups were passed around, and the voices of official singers joined with the flutes and harps. Ceremonial dances were performed by priests and priestesses, sometimes even by the Vice-minister of Religion himself. Not seldom those taking part later proceeded to the race course, and the festival, which began with ritual very early in the morning, was concluded in the evening with galloping matches.

In and around the capital there were over seven hundred shrines, and in the provinces over two thousand others, kept up at the expense of the imperial treasury. The offerings presented by the emperor on ceremonial occasions were divided by the department of religion and given to representatives from these various shrines who were supposed to offer them to the gods in their own localities. This network of shrines and elaborate program of rites and festivals served to perpetuate the power of the imperial court in a peculiarly Japanese manner.

CHAPTER 6

THE POWER AND GLORY OF THE
FUJIWARAS

(TENTH AND ELEVENTH CENTURIES)

FROM 669, when Kamatari won for the family its name, until 1016, when Michinaga became regent and brought the Fujiwaras to the zenith of their power and glory, was over three centuries. After this, Fujiwaras were still to rule Japan for another hundred and fifty years. No other family in history has continued to dominate a nation for an equal length of time.[1] The secret of their success lay in adherence to three principles, two of which may be stated briefly in familiar phrases: knowledge is power and in unity is strength. The third principle is distinctively Sino-Japanese, ancestor worship and blood relationship as the foundation of the state.

Kamatari's greatness had lain not so much in breaking the power of the Soga clan as in setting for his own family an example of intelligent eagerness to learn. He had devoted himself for years to studying the teachings of scholars returned from China, and though the voyage was filled with perils had sent his eldest son to the continent in search of firsthand knowledge.

In the latter part of the seventh and in the eighth century, when they became keenly aware of their own limited knowledge, young Fujiwaras, with determination, turned their minds to learning everything they could from the cultured priests and other talented immigrants in their midst. Quick to absorb

experience from others, they became the leaders in all the legislative activities of the court, and headed the committees for
compiling the official histories throughout two centuries. In
spite of the loss of four promising sons in the smallpox epidemic
and the efforts of the clever Nara clergy to thwart their best-
laid plans, the Fujiwaras, by diligent self-improvement, were
able to create new opportunities for extending their influence.
Under their leadership, the government overcame its trusting
acceptance of Buddhist authority and moved away to establish
an independent center of its own.

Had only a few members of the family been fired with
ambition they could not have gone so far, but the Fujiwaras
worked together with remarkably little friction. Daughters
as well as sons cooperated in furthering the fortunes of the
family as a whole. While sons became priests and abbots of
temples, daughters married into the imperial household to
consolidate their political power. Fujiwaras very early realized
the advantages of uniting their interests with those of the
imperial family, administering for the emperor and in his
name, rather than taking possession of the throne themselves.
In this way they not only strengthened themselves politically
against possible rivals, but also greatly improved their economic
position. From the taxes he received the emperor had to pay
the expenses of government, a large part of which were the
salaries of Fujiwara officials. In addition, he had continually
to reward special services, usually with the gift of a manor, so
that his acreage of taxable land was continually decreasing. The
Fujiwaras, on the other hand, were the most frequent recipients
of these grants of land, on which they were not required to pay
taxes, but from which they were free to collect as much as they
could. Their income was thus constantly increasing.

By installing their daughters in the imperial household, the
Fujiwaras were able to keep well-informed of what went on
there and to make their influence felt at all times. Further than
this, they emphasized the importance of the divine ancestry

of the imperial family, as shown by the high-priest function of emperors in the previous chapter, and encouraged filial piety in general; disrespectful acts or attitudes toward parents were considered the height of immorality. Little princes, well-trained in these precepts, were willing to trust their grandfathers in everything. With the sanction of this Chinese principle of ancestor worship, Fujiwaras were often able to keep boy rulers on the throne and act as regents for them. Before one grew old enough to take matters into his own hands he was retired and replaced by one still younger. Emperors of superior piety showed their grandfathers greatest honor by retaining them as regents even after coming of age. Such emperors were usually kept so involved in choosing the colors of the robes to be worn by officials of various ranks, deciding the proper length of jeweled swords, learning Chinese etiquette, and performing Shinto rites that they had little mind for more pressing problems of government.

Occasionally able scholars of attractive personality appeared who won favor with an emperor, though they were not of the Fujiwara clan. But when any of these threatened to oppose the Fujiwara will, they found themselves in trouble. On one such occasion the whole city of Kyoto was thrown into a panic by a herd of wild horses, which the Fujiwaras let loose to demonstrate the need for their firm governmental control to keep the country from anarchy. Scholars of political bias different from theirs were dismissed from the court and usually sent to some place of obscurity.

Soon after the cessation of official relations with the declining T'ang court in 895, there was a period during which the line of great Fujiwara statesmen seemed to have run out. One emperor was able to take the actual power into his own hands and rule the country without dictation from his Fujiwara ministers for almost a quarter of a century. For two or three generations, though they continued to fill official positions, no great men were produced in the distinguished family, and it was further weakened by jealous rivalries between its various members over which should provide the mother of the next emperor. But the Fujiwaras by this time had vast resources at their disposal, and the greatness of their reputation carried them on. Then came Michinaga!

Michinaga had the good judgment and good fortune to enlist in his service a rising military clan named Minamoto. The Minamotos were strong-armed men, experienced in rural administration, the collection of taxes and the enforcement of law and order. They gave Michinaga the power he needed to reunite the Fujiwara family, and forwarded to him regularly in the capital revenues from estates much more extensive in area and much more rich in yield than those belonging to the emperor himself.

Five of Michinaga's daughters were married to successive sovereigns and he became the grandfather of five crown princes. He was the supreme power in government for many years. "This life of mine," Michinaga wrote in a poem, "is akin to the full moon, nothing seems to me wanting." And over his cups he muttered, "It is no disgrace to make one's daughter a princess. The empress is not so badly off in having a father like me. Her mother must be very glad to have such a husband." [2]

For his family Michinaga had a marvelous palace built. Provincial officials vied with each other in bringing treasures for it, aiming to surpass their rivals for the great man's favor. According to the description of a court lady of the time this palace was as beautiful as a polished jewel and surrounded by exquisite landscaped gardens with pools that shone like spotless mirrors. On the clear surface of the waters, whence pure white and pale pink lotus blossoms raised their lovely heads, were reflections of the palace, its towers and storehouses, which looked like a painting of Buddha's paradise.

Close by was the Fujiwara family temple. When it was being built treasures were taken even from the imperial palace, and a provincial governor was ordered, "Though you neglect your official duties, do not neglect to furnish materials and labor for Hojo Temple." Here, amid its other glories, in a venerable row stood a Buddhist figure thirty-two feet high and a hundred other gilded Buddhist statues.

In the early eleventh century, when Michinaga was in his prime, life in both temple and palace was very gay. Priests talked of a paradise where court life continued on a more colorful and more luxurious scale, and where all the sins of the flesh were forgiven at the mere mention of a sacred name. They fostered a belief in their special powers to keep away ill fortune, disease and death, and encouraged the building of temples and monasteries in connection with palaces, where spectacular ceremonies could be performed for the enjoyment of courtiers and court ladies.

There was such a demand for Buddhist statues at this time that distinguished families of artists and schools of sculptors began to appear. Priest sculptors had always been able to supply the demand hitherto, but when Michinaga began to build Hojo-ji he hired a sculptor named Jocho and his school of assistants. Jocho and his school did not simply copy Chinese statues as ardor for things Chinese had somewhat subsided. Rather, they gave their deities the distinctly Japanese forms of beautiful human models such as they saw in the palaces and temples of Kyoto with lovely bodies, round faces and slender eyes and brows.

These statues were all carved from wood, but not necessarily from a single tree trunk as statues had been in earlier times. Now methods of joinery were developed and the head, arms and hands were carved separately and fastened to the torso. Figures of Amida Buddha had their faces and bodies covered with gold foil, but lesser deities and saints were given a heavy coat of ivory-white flesh paint. Their robes, lying in smooth, graceful folds, were painted to represent the richest of silk brocades with a variety of gorgeous colors and intricate patterns of gold foil. Often they wore crowns, necklaces and armbands of most elegantly carved gold. Figures attending the deity often resembled court ladies in beautiful flowing draperies, riding or dancing on clouds or playing musical instruments. For background they had gilded wooden canopies of most marvelously lacelike perforated carvings in designs of flames, flowers, vines, clouds and saints. The interior of the temple, the pillars, walls and ceilings, were elaborately decorated with paintings, mother-of-pearl inlays and open carving.

But the sculptors of the days of Fujiwara splendor did not surpass the painters. One splendid temple painting, almost seven feet high and fourteen feet across, still preserved from that era, shows Amida Buddha on a cloud in the midst of a happy host of celestial beings who look very much like priests and court ladies. They are playing on various kinds of drums, flutes and stringed instruments, and one is singing, with a broad smile on her face. All are adorned with elaborate jewelry. The figures are drawn in fine lines of lively red and filled in with vividly contrasting olive green, rich blues and yellow reds, lavishly overspread with gold.[3]

Other paintings of which Fujiwara court folk were very fond showed the beautiful and merciful Amida Buddha coming over the green hills of their own beloved Kyoto landscape to welcome the faithful believers. This deity, Amida, is represented in such lovely form that it is sometimes referred to as the Goddess of Mercy. Among Buddhist deities, however, sex is transcended: there are not males and females, but only perfect, all-sufficient beings.

When noble ladies fell ill, priests rather than doctors attended them. Handsome young priests, according to one court lady's diary, in elegant brown robes and mantles of thin, lustrous silk murmured incantations and fanned themselves the while with clove-dyed fans.[4] Everything was done esthetically.

For this the court had the smooth-running Fujiwara government to thank. It is easy to skip over the orderly processes of

administration, the steady working of a well-regulated organization, and pass quickly on to more spectacular activities, but the
important functions which the Fujiwaras performed in maintaining law and order should not be overlooked. Their strong,
able government, which gave the country peace for over three
hundred years, played a larger part than their brilliant court
life in making their regime the Golden Age of Japanese history.

The characteristic orderliness of the Fujiwaras penetrated
even the social sphere. Most of the activities of the court were
prescribed ones, regulated in accordance with the annual calendar of court functions. Two-thirds of this calendar was devoted
to religious ceremonies, both Shinto and Buddhist: the New
Year's service to the sun-goddess, followed by services throughout the year to important deities of nature and state, and homage to the imperial forefathers; many and various Buddhist
rites, visits to temples of different denominations, and an elaborate practice of prayers. Time was also prescribed for a drinking
bout on January 2, poem contests on several occasions, contests
of archery and polo, picnics in spring to view cherry blossoms,
outings in autumn to see the red maples and golden grasses and
to listen to the chirping of insects. Dates were set for horse
races and parades of decorated oxcarts, fetes for wisteria and
chrysanthemum, for new-moon and full-moon festivals, wrestling matches, exhibitions of shells and pictures, and initiations
of dancing girls.[5] The court at certain periods had as many as
two hundred and fifty men musicians and fifty dancing girls
to enliven its ceremonies.

When little princes became twelve years old they were feted
with initiation rituals. Their long childish locks were cut off
and, dressed for the first time in man's attire, they performed
The Dance of Homage before the assembled court. The hero
on such occasions was given presents, such as fine horses from
the royal stables and trained hawks from the royal falconry.
His friends and followers in uniform robes of violet, pink,
white or yellow, according to their rank, were showered with

baskets of fruit and delicacies, and boxes of cakes. Sometimes on this day the young prince was betrothed. Then the Moon Lords and Cloud Gallants, as the courtiers were called, assembled to drink a love cup and the initiate took his place among them. Other court entertainments are vividly described in *The Tale of Genji,* a lengthy narrative of the adventures, mostly amorous, of the shining Prince Genji and the Fujiwara court circle.[6]

Here like figures in a picture of fairyland they spent the day gliding away across the lake to the pleasant strains of the tune called the "Royal Deer." Suddenly the boats halted, and the ladies were invited to go ashore at the fishing pavilion which was finished in a manner combining elegance with extreme simplicity.

As the parties spread along the empty galleries and across the wide deserted floors, there was such an interweaving of gay colors as would have been hard to outdo. The musicians were again called upon and soon were joined by a troupe of dancers. It seemed a pity that darkness should be allowed to interfere with these pleasures.

When night came on, a move was made to the courtyard in front of the palace. Here flares were lit, and on the mossy lawn at the foot of the great steps not only professional musicians, but also various visiters from court, and friends of the family, performed on wind and string, while picked teachers of the flute gave a display in the mode beginning on alto A which symbolizes spring. Then all the zithers and lutes belonging to different members of the household were brought out onto the steps and carefully tuned to the same pitch. A grand concert followed, the piece "Was Ever Such a Day?" being performed with admirable effect.

Even the grooms and laborers who were loitering amid the serried ranks of coaches drawn up outside the great gates, little as they usually cared for such things, on this occasion pricked up their ears, and were soon listening with lips parted in wonder and delight. The concert continued till dawn—already the morning birds were clamoring in a lusty chorus.

Part of the race course was not far away from this side of the palace and a good view could be obtained from the porticos and outer galleries which soon were thronged. Persons of quality were hidden behind green shutters or curtains, dyed in the new-fashioned way, with color running down into the fringe. Among the dresses of the visiters were many elaborate Chinese costumes specially designed for the day's festivity, the color of the young dianthus leaf tending to prevail. Some were in their summer gowns, green without and peach-blossom color within. There was a great deal of rivalry and harmless self-display, which was rewarded from time to time by a glance from one of the young courtiers who were assembled on the course.

Genji arrived on the scene at the hour of the sheep (1:00 P.M.). It was interesting to see the competitors, so differently arrayed, each with his following of smartly dressed squires and assistants. The sports continued till evening. The ladies, though understanding very imperfectly what was going on, were at least capable of deriving a great deal of pleasure from the sight of so many young men in elegant riding jackets hurling themselves with desperate recklessness into the fray.

The races were followed by a game of polo played to the tune of "Hitting the Ball." Then came a competition of rival pairs in a Korean dance. All this was accompanied by a great din of bells and drums, sounded to announce the gaining of points on one side and another. When it began to grow dark there was indoor entertainment with a distribution of prizes among the successful riders and a great banquet. It was very late indeed when the guests began to withdraw.

With a continuous round of prescribed ceremonies and entertainments such as these to keep them busily amused, and most of the luxuries of the nation concentrated in Kyoto, it is small wonder that the Fujiwara court people had little interest in life beyond their own circle. They went on short trips to mountain temples and to country places near the capital, but they never traveled into other provinces if they could possibly avoid it. Even courtiers who were appointed to provincial posts sold their offices to others and remained in the capital whenever they could so manage. It is interesting to read of their reactions to things outside their customary environment.

Lady Sei, for example, jotted down the following notes about a spontaneous little excursion to hear the cuckoos singing at a place just outside the city:

Presently we came to the house of Akinobu and someone suggested we should have a look at it. The house itself was a poor affair and very cramped, but quite pretty in its way. Everything was very simple and countrified—pictures of horses on the panels, screens of wattled bamboo, curtains of plaited grass—all in a style that seemed to be intentionally behind the times. Sending for some stuff which I suppose was husked rice our host made some girls—very clean and respectable—along with others who seemed to come from neighboring farms, show us how the rice was threshed. Then the grain was put into a sort of machine that went round, two girls turning it and, at the same time, singing so strange a song that we could not help laughing. Then refreshments were brought on a queer old tray stand such as one sees in Chinese pictures. As no one seemed much interested in its contents, our host said:

"This is rough, country fare. If you don't like it, bother your host or his servants till you get something you can eat. We don't expect you people from the capital to be shy."

"You don't want us to arrange ourselves around the tray stand like a lot of maid servants sitting down to their supper," I protested.

He ordered the things to be passed around, but while this was going on rain threatened and we hurried back to our carriage.

And again she writes:

When one thinks of it, to be in a boat at all is a terrible thing! It is bad enough, even in reasonably shallow water, to trust oneself to such a conveyance; but where the water may be any depth—perhaps a thousand fathoms—to embark upon a thing loaded up with goods and baggage of all kinds, with only an inch or two of wood between oneself and the water! However, the low-class people who manage the boat do not seem to be in the least frightened, but run up and down unconcernedly in places where a single false step would lose them their lives.

Even the loading of a ship, when they bang down into the hold huge pine trees two or three feet in circumference, some times half a dozen at a time, is an amazing thing. Rich people, of course, go in ships with cabins, and those who are lucky enough to be in the middle of the ship do not get on so badly. But those who are near the sides get very dizzy.[7]

The writing of notes such as these and of diaries was a favorite pastime of Fujiwara court ladies. A charming literary style was thus developed which became one of the chief glories of the Fujiwara age.

As the Japanese had grown familiar with Chinese script, different groups had begun to invent abbreviated forms for the symbols, a sort of shorthand which they could use among themselves. There were several styles of Chinese writings for them to copy. One was an angular, disconnected style, which had been used before the days of brush and ink, when the Chinese wrote with chisels on stone or with lacquer on strips of bamboo; another was an informal running style much more convenient to use when one wanted to write quickly. The first style was called in Chinese "writing in the house," and the informal style "writing in the field." In the Nara period about four thousand different Chinese symbols came into use in Japan.

Scholars liked to use as many different symbols as they could, just to show how learned they were. If they wished to write a Japanese sentence, for instance, in which the sound "wa" occurred six times, they might use six different symbols all of which the Chinese pronounced wa, even though they had no connection whatever with the meaning of the sentence. The result was something like a rebus puzzle, only much more difficult to read.

As the Japanese readers gained familiarity not only with Chinese but also with Sanskrit, the language in which Buddhist scriptures originally were written, they discovered that the sounds of their own language could be classified; there were just forty-seven pure ones. Then different groups chose

a ア あ	sa サ さ	na ナ な	ma マ ま	ra ラ ら
i イ い	shi シ し	ni ニ に	mi ミ み	ri リ り
u ウ う	su ス す	nu ヌ ぬ	mu ム む	ru ル ろ
e エ え	se セ せ	ne ネ ね	me メ め	re レ れ
o オ お	so ソ そ	no ノ の	mo モ も	ro ロ ろ
ka カ か	ta タ た	ha ハ は	ya ヤ や	wa ワ わ
ki キ き	chi チ ち	hi ヒ ひ		
ku ク く	tsu ツ つ	fu フ ふ	yu ユ ゆ	
ke ケ け	te テ て	he ヘ へ		
ko コ こ	to ト と	ho ホ ほ	yo ヨ よ	wo ヲ を

JAPANESE PHONETIC SYMBOLS[8]   ン ン ん

forty-seven Chinese symbols, one for each sound, abbreviated them a little, and used them phonetically as we do our alphabet. One temple would have a set of symbols abbreviated in a certain way, another temple would have an entirely different set, abbreviated in an entirely different way. Officials had sets peculiar to themselves, and sometimes lovers made up sets for their own private use. Two such sets came to be used much more than others. One based on the writing in the house was called katakana (part sign) and one based on the writing in the field was called hiragana (handy sign).

It is sometimes claimed that Kibi no Mabi, the great scholar-minister of the Nara period, who went to China twice and was exiled as governor of the Kyushu Dazaifu, invented the katakana, but so few of these abbreviated symbols have been found in the writings of his time and even later that this is hardly likely. It seems more probable that the katakana now in use developed in the ninth century from studies of the sutras, mainly under the guidance of two abbots from Mount Hiei, and that this particular set came to be better known than many others because of the great influence of this center of religion and learning. The hiragana, though said to have been invented by Abbot Kukai, the founder of Mount Koya, were also the result of a lengthy process of selection and change and a sort of survival of the fittest. There was not an official standard set of either kind of kana until after the Restoration in 1868.[8]

After the annals, Kojiki and Nihongi, and the anthology, Manyoshu, had appeared, several other official chronicles and collections of poetry had been compiled; there were legal and religious writings too, but the earliest Japanese fiction we know of was written in the Fujiwara age. It was a humorous sort of fairy tale and legend called "The Old Bamboo Hewer's Story," [9] which pretended to explain why smoke always rose from the summit of Mount Fuji. This story was soon followed by several others which made very popular entertainment for courtiers and court ladies.

Courtiers and officials seemed to think it much more dignified to write in the Chinese language, just as lawyers and college officials in America even today seem to think it more dignified to use phrases of Latin or Greek. They spent no end of time and effort trying to write things which could be mistaken for the work of Chinese scholars and poets.

But the ladies wrote in Japanese, in their own natural way of talking. The novels, notes and diaries which flowed profusely from their brushes now are known as the classical litera-

EXCERPT FROM CARICATURE SCROLL

SCREEN SHOWING COURT LADIES DRESSING PRINCESS

TWO EXCERPTS FROM THE HEIKE SCROLL

BYODO-IN

ture of Japan. The prose works of several of these Fujiwara court ladies have been translated into English as have the verses of a great number more.[10]

Along with this natural style of writing a new style of painting also developed, called Yamato-e. Yamato-e were pictures of Japanese people in Japanese settings, drawn and colored in a typically Japanese manner. Two outstanding characteristics are the amusing way in which artists drew an eye or a nose with a single stroke of the brush, and left off the ceiling instead of a side wall to show the inside of a room.

Many Yamato-e were graceful illustrations for *The Tale of Genji;* others with none of the elegance of these were caricaturish drawings of street crowds or of miraculous happenings at some shrine or temple. They usually told a story, either in a series of different views or in a continuous scroll picture.[11] Like Japanese books, which are made to begin where Western ones end, these Yamato-e narratives start at the right and proceed toward the left of the scroll.

The age of Fujiwara supremacy was a golden age for women in Japan. A beautiful and clever girl had unlimited possibilities for social advancement; her chances were much better than a man's. The empresses were all Fujiwara girls in their early teens who needed counsel and coaching in etiquette, the arts, and the ways of life. Their parents were ready to go to any length to secure the most talented companions for them. Many of these more experienced ladies also found favor with the emperors themselves. Fujiwara princes were able to bestow on amiable and entertaining beauties gifts of rank and riches to satisfy the most ambitious. With every detail of everyday life as carefully prescribed as it was in the late days of Heian, no courtier presumed to be spontaneous or original; court ladies offered his only chance of adventure. Since they also played principal roles in political intrigues, they were very important indeed and acted accordingly with very great freedom.

For example, Lady Murasaki, author of *The Tale of Genji,* in her early twenties had been left a widow with a baby daughter, but being keenly admired by the great Michinaga she was appointed as companion to one of his empress daughters, and had every opportunity of knowing intimately the ways of the court life she described so well.

Fujiwara power and glory was brought to its climax by Michinaga, and Japanese classical culture reached its greatest height during his regime. His life was a perfect pattern of the classical tradition even to the end. When his faculties began to weaken, according to time-honored custom, Michinaga took the tonsure and became an ordained layman. This provided a pleasant relief from the performance of court formalities and was supposed to insure salvation in the future. His ordination ceremony was held at Nara and, if one may believe the poetic description of it given in *Eiga Monogatari (Tale of Splendor)* [12] was as spectacular as the Great Eye Opening of the Nara Daibutsu. In the year 1028, at the age of sixty-two, Michinaga passed away.

CHAPTER 7

COURTIER GIVES PLACE TO PROVINCIAL SOLDIER

(TWELFTH CENTURY)

THE JAPANESE have a very old hymn that says:

> The sound of the temple bell
> Echoes the impermanence of all things.
> The flowers of the teak tree declare
> That they who flourish must be brought low.
> The proud ones are but for a moment,
> Like an evening dream in springtime.
> The mighty are destroyed at the last;
> They are but as dust before wind.[1]

Even the Fujiwaras' moment at last drew to a close. Unproductive themselves, they had depended on the tillers of the soil and the tax collectors to provide them with luxuries, but the limited agricultural resources of the country were no longer sufficient to satisfy the desires of the ever-increasing court circle. More and more absorbed in the fastidious life of Kyoto, courtiers had gradually passed on their provincial duties to the less favored ones of their number. But these, as the wheel of fortune turned, became the real power of the nation.

The working people of the country were called by court officials The Great Treasure and a very great treasure they were indeed. Patiently the farmers leveled and cultivated their little pieces of ground, piled firm banks of earth around them and covered them with water. They sowed the seed rice and transplanted the tiny, grasslike shoots when they began to grow. The whole summer long they guarded the delicate plants ceaselessly against insects, storms and droughts until the time for harvest. When they handed over to the tax collectors a large part of the fruits of their labors, there was scarcely enough left to feed the family through the winter.

Japan was not suited as many Asian countries were for rice cultivation: the land consisted chiefly of volcanic mountain slopes rather than broad flat river valleys; the warm season was relatively short, and interrupted by heavy rains and typhoons. Where three crops a year could be harvested, rice was capable of sustaining an enormous population, but in Japan it was different. The Yamato court ate rice because the Chinese court did; Yamato farmers raised it because they were required to, but for their own food they grew hardier grains such as millet, oats and barley.

The peasants' wives and daughters made cloth of bark, hemp and cotton. Some of them raised silkworms and wove silk. This, too, required an enormous amount of labor. Trays had to be carefully prepared for the cocoons to be spread out on; then endless bushels of fresh green mulberry leaves had to be picked for the ravenously hungry little worms when they hatched. When the new cocoons were finished they had to be dipped in boiling water and the fine silk filaments of which they were made had to be unwound with very steady hands and even tempers before they were ready to spin into threads for weaving into cloth. It was a long, painstaking process, and when it was over a generous share of the precious fabric was sent as taxes to the capital.

Taxes were based on units of land. It was found by experience that a square patch of ground two paces, or six feet, long on each side would yield about as much rice as an average man would eat in a day. Their years being made up of twelve months of thirty days each, a year's supply for one man would require three hundred and sixty such units, or a plot of ground about one hundred and fourteen feet square. Ten such plots were called one cho. One cho, or about three acres of rice fields, may be thought of as the holding of an average peasant's family; in addition, they sometimes had some ground planted in other cereals, and in mulberry and lacquer trees.

By the twelfth century, the rice tax had mounted to almost one third of the total yield; thirty per cent was claimed for the court in Kyoto and two and a half per cent for the support of the provincial governor. For each cho of land it held, a family was also supposed to pay in taxes: one piece of silk fabric ten feet long and two and a half feet wide, three pieces of pongee and four pieces of cotton goods of the same size, and a proportion of the other things produced in the district. It was said that in the latter days of the Fujiwaras the court took seventy per cent of the produce of the land and left to the people only thirty per cent. In addition to taxes, every man from twenty-one to sixty-six years of age was likely to have to give one month of labor a year, cutting and hauling timber, mining iron ore and sulphur, making repairs on roads, official residences and public buildings.

Japanese farmers have always been marvelously hard-working and loyal to their masters, but under such conditions they could not pay their taxes and live. Very often they turned their land over to some provincial landlord who was less exacting than the Kyoto officials.

The court at the time of the First Great Change had claimed that all the land of the country belonged to the emperor and that theoretically he had both the right to collect taxes from it all and the responsibility for officials' salaries and other expenses of the court. The best arrangement it seemed rather than having all the taxes brought to the capital and then divided was for the emperor to allot a certain section of land to each official and require each to collect his own share of taxes. Since the Fujiwaras held most of the highest-ranking positions in the court, they also were allotted most of the land. Other officials, however, had received grants from time to time, and provincial manors were also given by emperors with large families to their younger or less-favored sons whom they could not afford to support in the expensive style of Kyoto.

These sons were expected to go out and secure their own living, and many of them did so successfully. They were looked up to by the country people because of their ancestry and admired for their skill in horsemanship, hunting with hawks, and writing. Because they did not have to keep up with the extravagances of life in the capital these former courtiers could get along very nicely by taxing the farmers much less than the Fujiwaras or the emperor did. Farmers, therefore, much preferred to work their lands for them rather than for the central government; and these men were glad to increase the number of fields and farmers from which they might draw income for themselves. When agents from Kyoto came around, such provincial landlords sometimes used force to defend their gains; they began to enlist in their service men experienced in handling spears and bows.

Two of these families of provincial landlords prospered and flourished remarkably. One was named Taira or Heike; the other Minamoto or Genji. Taira and Minamoto are the Japanese pronunciations of the Chinese symbols Hei and Gen; ke and ji mean family or clan.

Clever Fujiwara regents saw that the way to treat these growing warrior clans was not to oppose them but to get their cooperation. They used them for collecting taxes from Fujiwara estates and for settling disputes with rivals. The system worked very well indeed at first; warrior clans, gratified to receive the recognition of this great court family, vied with each other for favor by adding lands to the Fujiwara domain. They reclaimed large tracts of land from mountainsides, river beds and marshes, and sent very generous gifts up to the court. It was the cooperation of the Minamoto warriors that made it possible for Michinaga, the most spectacular of the Fujiwaras, to achieve the supreme power and glory of his family. But any government that delegates to others its right to collect taxes is in imminent danger.

The Heike and Genji were more vigorous and energetic than the Fujiwaras. They had lived on the land and they loved it; they sympathized with the hard-working farmers. Gradually they began to lose their respect for the Fujiwaras and to gain some notion of their own importance and possibilities. They realized that they were the real power of the country on whom the government depended, and from this consciousness grew a military caste.

While the Taira and Minamoto were the most powerful families of this military caste, they were by no means the whole of it. There were several other families only slightly less strong, with bands of loyal followers recruited from among the farmers. These families, seeing that the government was no longer able to enforce its laws, made rules and regulations of their own. They paid little attention to orders from the court, but they saw to it that their own family regulations were strictly enforced. This created a situation very much like the one which existed in the very early days of Japan, when there were many clans, before Prince Shotoku tried to organize a central government.

Japanese soldiers had always worshiped a special deity, and now this deity came to play an especially important role. In the chapter on the early settlers there was a story from the two oldest annals of Japan about an empress who commanded an army and navy overseas expedition. For divine aid, guidance and protection in this undertaking, she had appealed to a sea-god called Yawata (Bubbling Tremendous Waves) who was enshrined on the coast of the island Kyushu. When she returned victorious and gave birth to a son, he was held in high esteem as a symbol of victory. In the course of centuries the memory of this son seems to have become merged with that of the deity, and the old sea-god, still called Yawata, continued to be worshiped in Kyushu as the god of wars and victories.[2]

During the Nara period, when the Buddhist priests were trying to build the Daibutsu, they found it to be desirable to enlist the support and friendship of the whole country, so they summoned these rugged Yawata worshipers to bring their deity to the capital and enshrine him among the temples. There the highest ranks were conferred upon him and he was given a new name in Chinese script, pronounced Hachiman (Eight Banners). The priests said that these stood for the eight right ways of Buddha. They thought Hachiman would thus be induced to cooperate with them in importing religious articles from China and Korea. Not long afterward a messenger was sent to his shrine at Usa to ask his approval for letting the priest, Dokyo, become emperor. The answer brought back to Nara was: "Since the establishment of the state the distinction between sovereign and subject has been observed. There is no instance of a subject becoming sovereign. The successor must be of the imperial family, the usurper must be rejected."[3]

This patriotic stand had made Hachiman very popular with the Fujiwaras while they were still trying to consolidate their position with respect to the throne, but once they were in power they neglected Hachiman. In the days of peace and splendor people worshiped chiefly the Fujiwara ancestral deity, Kasuga, and the merciful Buddha Amida. No matter what they did, they were forgiven by simply believing in Amida. This must have been a great comfort to dissipated courtiers.

With the rise of the military caste, however, Hachiman again came into his own. New shrines were built in his honor and old ones repaired. His spirit inspired, unified and strengthened the warrior class.

After the middle of the eleventh century there were emperors who took advantage of Fujiwara laxity and tried to take control again themselves. They could not succeed, however, without revenue, and taxes were not only collected but also kept by the military clans.

Originally these provincial soldiers had been engaged to defend court interests in distant places. But as court incomes were reduced and court gifts and favors necessarily curtailed, many temples accustomed to enjoying the generosity of princes and nobles felt the pinch of circumstance, blamed Fujiwara extravagance and sent armed monks to Kyoto. Three thousand of them from Nara and Mount Hiei battled in the streets of the city and threatened Michinaga's son. Provincial soldiers had to be called into the capital. They kept coming in increasing numbers at the invitation of ambitious officials. In the middle of the twelfth century the Tairas and Minamotos took opposite sides in an imperial succession dispute. From the war that developed between them, the Tairas emerged victorious with the court in their hands.

Previous to this Taira victory all offices of the fifth rank and higher had to be filled by the nobility. No military man could hold them. Tamuramaro, the honored shogun, who had finally subdued the Ainu was the only exception in history. He had been raised to the third rank and made a councilor. Now upon Taira Kiyomori likewise was this honor conferred.

Son of a brave member of the imperial guards appointed governor of a province on the Inland Sea to rid its shores and waters of pirates, Kiyomori grew up familiar with the ways of the sea and ships. He came to feel very strongly that the future of the nation lay, not in agriculture, but in export and import trade.

While a provincial governor himself Kiyomori had had convenient channels in the Inland Sea deepened and widened for the passage of merchant vessels, and had reinforced the shore of an inlet to make a safe anchorage. On this work, it is recorded, fifty thousand laborers were employed for twelve years, all men from his own estates. The harbor which they made was the beginning of the port of Kobe which today is one of the busiest in the world.

Kiyomori also had a lighthouse erected so that ships might

sail in safety at night; and when he became head of his clan he adopted as a sort of guardian deity for his family Beautiful Island Princess, one of the three guardian deities of the sea, enshrined at Itsukushima. In honor of this deity he built a very beautiful shrine on an island in the Inland Sea, the red-lacquer gateway of which is often seen in tourist pictures of Miyajima today.

Victorious over the Minamotos at the age of forty-two, the farseeing head of the Heike was a great influence in Kyoto. His clan came to have thirty of the sixty-six provinces of Japan under its control; and soon Kiyomori succeeded in replacing many Fujiwara officials by members of his own family. His daughter was married to an emperor. He whose father had been laughed at for his awkward dancing and rustic squint when first he came to court was now the arbiter of fashion, and "Not to be a Taira was not to be a man!"

Kiyomori's palace, according to later courtly raconteurs, consisted of a hundred and seventy buildings in a park which covered more than ten square miles. Other buildings occupied by his family and retainers numbered over twenty-five hundred.

> In their many gorgeous costumes, his sons and daughters were resplendent as the flowers of the field. Nobles and illustrious people crowded before their gates like throngs in a market place. Gold, jewels, damask, brocade, no rarity or treasure did they lack. And for poetry and music, fishing and riding, even the emperor's palaces were not more renowned.[4]

Granted special permission by the retired emperor to ride as a head of state in an ox-drawn wagon or palanquin Kiyomori did not forget his maritime ambitions.

The country had developed into a nation by the interplay of three groups, the rugged, hard-working farmers in the northeast, the adventurous seafarers of the southwest and the cultured court group in the center. Impressive at first on account of their treasured swords and mirrors, and then on account of their entourage of artists and scholars, the court group with the official recognition of China had always maintained a certain prestige. But they had never been independent. Threatened by the Nara clergy they had called upon the followers of Hachiman in Kyushu, threatened by revolting Ainu they had called upon troops from the northern districts, and always they had relied for their safety upon a certain balance between the northeastern and southwestern elements.

Two hundred and fifty years before Kiyomori's day official relations with China had ceased and during all that time Japan had had practically nothing to do with her neighbors on the mainland. Only seldom during that interval had trading boats come to Japan, and more infrequently still had student priests gone to China. What little intercourse there had been was carried on through the southwestern part of the country.

Now Kiyomori allied himself with that southwestern interest. He could see only plodding poverty in the limited land resources on which northeastern farmers based their ideas of economy, and this did not suit his temper. Kiyomori was an original thinker, unbound by the conventions of his day—a man of will, and a man of action. He succeeded in getting Chinese and Korean traders to bring their ships and cargo to his port, and advocated expanding this trade as a means to national prosperity. And yet, withal, Kiyomori was naïve. He took great pride in the success and high position he had achieved through his own efforts and outdid the Fujiwaras in showy, luxurious living. When at last he was able to make his grandson emperor, with little regard for the strong undercurrent of ill-feeling and resentment that was rising up against him, he pushed the interests of the southwestern element still further.

The better to establish Japan on a maritime basis he required the whole court to leave their sheltered capital founded by Emperor Kwammu and glorified by the Fujiwaras, and to establish a new capital on the coast of the Inland Sea. Very much against their will did officials, nobles, court ladies, artisans and tradesmen expose themselves to the fogs, salt winds and discomforts of a city in process of construction. They could not even imagine anything good existing outside Kyoto. The older ones among them, large landowners especially, kept raising bitter opposition to the seacoast capital. The priests in the great temples, too, more than indignant at having their patrons transported from their midst, joined forces with the court and called in Minamoto soldiers from the northeast. Six months after it was moved the court returned to its sheltered valley and three months later Kiyomori died. Since his sons were not men of the caliber to carry on his plans, the first attempt at Japanese trade expansion came to an untimely end.

The court moved back to Kyoto in December, 1180, but it was never the same again. Despoiled by the removal, frequently beset by the fires of malcontents, shaken by typhoons, it was a wretched place. The whole country was in upheaval.

"Misfortunes succeeded each other," wrote an eyewitness. A great fire reduced to ashes the southern gate of the palace, the Hall of Audience, the University buildings, the Home Office and the houses of sixteen nobles, and took the lives of an immense number of people and cattle. A great whirlwind blew all the houses of three or four city wards flat on the ground and crippled countless people. All this in addition to the miserable moving, and after that: [5]

> Either there was drought in spring or summer or there were storms and floods in autumn and winter, so that no grain came to maturity. In all the provinces people left their lands and sought other parts, or, forgetting their homes, went to live among the hills. All kinds of prayers were begun and religious practices revived, but to no purpose whatever. The capital, dependent as it is on the country for everything, could not remain unconcerned when nothing was produced. The inhabitants in their distress offered to sacrifice their valuables of all kinds, but nobody cared to look at them. Buyers made little account of gold, and much of grain. Beggars swarmed by the

roadsides, and even respectable-looking people, wearing hats and with their feet covered, might be seen going from door to door. Sometimes they fell down before your eyes. Countless persons died on the roadsides and their bodies were not removed. It was worse on the riverbanks where there was not even room for horses and vehicles to pass. Porters and wood-cutters became so feeble that firewood got scarcer and scarcer and people pulled down their houses. It was strange to see pieces of firewood adorned with vermilion and gold and silver leaf.

Such conditions did not arise in a moment. They had existed in varying degree ever since the splendor of the Fujiwaras had begun to bankrupt the country in the tenth century and social upheaval had begun to take place.

In the course of this confusion, the Tairas went down and the Minamotos rose once more. Those who had once been serfs and peasant farmers became equals of the best. Court people were allowed to continue as well as they could in the capital, but all the business of government (as described in the next chapter) was carried on in camp headquarters at Kama-kura, a sort of fishing village three hundred miles northeast of Kyoto near the modern port of Yokohama. Young Yoritomo, of the Minamoto clan, was the new leader of the nation.

Courtiers who once had spent all their days in idle song and dance and poetry now had to earn their own living. Many of them turned their talents to account by composing flattering narratives about the new military heroes which they recited or sang to the accompaniment of a zither. The new rulers, and the country people, who had had but slight acquaintance with the talents of the court before, were enthusiastic about this form of entertainment. Some of the stories which were sung in this way were later written down and also frequently repre-sented in painting.[6]

In the era which these chanted tales describe, the court was giving way to military dictatorship; the center of the stage was shifting from the capital to rural districts and social leaders spent their time not in ceremonies and festivals, but in battles and preparations for battles. In this era personal valor came to count for more than rank or family; affability and stylized conduct gave place to reckless egotism and defiance of established authority. Lacquer armor replaced the colorful brocade robes of court officials with silk trains several feet long. Religion, which had been taken so lightly, now began to receive serious consideration.[7]

The Tale of Heike, the most elaborate of the heroic narratives describing the conquest of the Tairas by the Minamotos, was composed by destitute courtiers and, perhaps, a bit overembroidered by their elegant hands. Several descriptions and episodes from it give such a vivid picture, however, of life in this age of transition that they seem well worth quoting.[8]

> The commander in chief of the Taira forces was at this time twenty-three years old and his costume and bearing were beautiful beyond the power of brush to depict. His general's armor, an ancestral treasure, laced with Chinese leather, was carried in an armor box before him, and on the road he wore a robe of red brocade under light-green body armor. He rode a dappled gray horse and his saddle was mounted in gold. The second in command wore a robe of blue brocade under armor with black lacings and rode a large and powerful black horse. His saddle was ornamented with powdered gold lacquer. With their horse trappings, armor and helmets and even their swords and bows flashing and glittering as they rode they were a splendid spectacle.

> When the commander in chief summoned his guide to the eastern provinces and asked, "Are there many samurai in the eight eastern provinces who are as mighty archers and as bold as you are?" the guide replied with a scornful smile, "Do you consider me a mighty archer? Why I only draw an arrow of thirteen handbreadths and in the eastern provinces there are any number of soldiers who can do that. A really famous archer

never draws a shaft of less than fifteen and his bow is so strong that it needs four or five ordinary men to bend it. They are bold riders too, and their horses never stumble even on the roughest ground. When they fight they do not heed even if their own parents or children are killed, but ride on over their bodies and continue the battle. Men of the western provinces are different. If their parents are killed they retire and perform Buddhist rites for the repose of their souls—if their children are slain they are overcome with grief and can fight no more. They dislike the summer because it is hot and grumble at the cold of winter."

The hour of the hare (6:00 A.M.) was the time fixed for the beginning of the battle between the Heike and the Genji, and so on the preceding evening the outposts of the Heike went forth to observe the disposition of the enemy. The farmers and inhabitants of the neighborhood, in terror at the movements of the armies, had fled away, some to the moors, some to the hills and some in boats on the sea and river and had kindled their cooking fires everywhere. The Heike, seeing them on all sides, exclaimed, "Ah, see! The campfires of the Genji are without number. The mountains, sea, river and plains all are full of warriors. What is to be done?"

About the middle of the same night the waterfowl of the marshes of Mount Fuji were startled by something or other and rose suddenly with a whirring of wings like the sound of a mighty wind. The Heike soldiers hearing it, shouted, "It is the Genji army coming to attack us from the rear—we must fall back to the river or we shall be cut off."

Panic-stricken, they abandoned their positions and fled without even taking their belongings with them. Some snatched up their bows without arrows or arrows without a bow, springing onto each other's horses and even mounting tethered animals and whipping them so that they galloped round and round the tie post. Some had procured singing girls and dancers and were making merry with them when the alarm took place. These women were hustled, thrown down and trampled in the confusion, and their cries added to the uproar.

Then at the hour of the hare the Genji advanced to the river and shouted their war cry three times. The heavens echoed and the earth shook, but from the Heike side there was only silence. When the vanguard approached their camp there was not a man to be seen, not so much as a fly stirring, so they gathered up the armor left behind and bore away in triumph the curtains of the headquarters that had been left standing.

Then Yoritomo alighted from his horse and taking off his helmet, washed his hands and rinsed his mouth. Turning toward the imperial palace he reverently made obeisance and said, "This victory is owing to the favor of Hachiman."

Now since the priests of Nara had made clear their feelings for Kiyomori and had shown many signs of rebelling against him, Kiyomori sent troops to attack them. Though it is said nothing drastic was intended, one of the soldiers set fire to a few houses; the wind veered around in all directions so that flames spread hither and thither and most of the temple buildings were soon in a blaze. Even the great Buddha of gold and copper whose eyes the Emperor Shomu had painted was fused with the heat so that its full-moon features fell to the pavement below. Never before had there been such a destruction of sacred treasures.

The Genji forces continued to gain in power and before long one of their number named Yoshinaka had made common cause with the monks of Mount Hiei and was pressing on the capital. The Heike abandoned all hope of saving the city and planned to take the emperor with the sacred jewel, sword and mirror away to places of safety. As they fled from Kyoto to the Inland Sea they set fire to all their mansions and the houses of their followers. Though in former days the Heike had flourished like the flowers of spring, now they were falling like the autumn leaves. Looking for some safe refuge they were driven from one place to another by threats of the Genji or Genji allies.

A faithful friend gave them one hundred large boats to replace the little ones in which they had been keeping themselves. Then they sailed to a large island and on its shore built a palace of rough timbers, but it was so common they shrank from permitting his eight-year-old majesty [Kiyomori's grand-son] to live there, and the real palace was a ship. Courtiers spent their days in the thatched huts of fishermen and their nights on shipboard.

Plunged in sorrow deep as the tide, their lives were frail as frosted grasses. At dawn the clamor of the sea birds increased their anguish and at night the grating of the ships on the beach tormented them. When they saw the flocks of herons in the distant pines their hearts sank, wondering if they were the white flags of the Genji, and when the cries of the wild geese were wafted from the offing they trembled lest it might be the oar beats of the foe by night. The keen breeze lashed their blackened eyebrows and painted faces, and the salt spray pene-trated their delicate eyes which homesick longing often filled with tears. For their green-curtained chambers of scarlet they had exchanged the earthen walls of the reed-hung cottage, and instead of the scented smoke of their braziers rose the briny fumes of the fisherman's driftwood. The features of the court ladies bereft of cosmetics and swollen with continual weeping were changed almost beyond recognition.

While the Taira still held possession of a few provinces in the west, Yoritomo ruled supreme in the north and east; and Yoshinaka lorded it over the capital. His soldiers wearing on their backs quivers of twenty-four arrows tipped with falcon feathers swarmed everywhere in Kyoto. They entered any place at their will to plunder, broke into people's storehouses and even waylaid citizens on the street and robbed them. Yoshinaka was ordered to stop this violence, but he just laughed and said his men had to be taken care of. His swaggering was more unendurable than that of the Heike. Even Yoritomo thought he was going too far and sent his younger brother, Yoshitsune, to put Yoshinaka in his place.

After one desperate battle Yoshinaka fled from the city with a small band of followers. He was arrayed in a robe of red brocade under a suit of armor laced with Chinese silk. By his side hung a magnificent sword mounted in silver and gold and his helmet was surmounted by long golden horns. Of his twenty-four eagle-feathered arrows most had been shot away in the previous fighting; only a few were left drawn out high from the quiver and he grasped his rattan-bound bow by the middle as he sat on his famous gray charger, fierce as a devil, on a saddle mounted in gold. Rising high in his stirrups as he met a band of his enemies, he cried with a loud voice, "Yoshi-naka you have often heard of—now you see him before your eyes! Come, take my head and show it to Yoritomo!"

Then he and his three hundred fell upon their six thousand opponents—cutting, slashing and swinging their blades in every direction until at last, only five of them still surviving, they broke through the enemy ranks. Among these five was a girl named Tomoe who had taken the field many times with Yoshinaka and handled her sword and bow so well that she had won matchless renown in encounters with the bravest cap-tains. Now in this last desperate struggle Yoshinaka called Tomoe to him and said: "As you are a woman it were better that you now make your escape. I have made up my mind to die either by the hand of the enemy or my own; and I would be shamed to die with a woman." But Tomoe was still in fine mettle and would not forsake her lover. "Ah, for some bold warrior to match with," she exclaimed, "that you might see how fine a death I can die." A band of thirty valiant men rode up at that moment. Plunging into them she seized their captain, dragged him from his horse and calmly cut off his head. Then stripping off her armor she fled away to the east.

Then Yoshitsune, determined to wipe out the Heike and re-store to the capital the three imperial regalia (the jewel, the sword and the mirror) which the Heike had carried off with them, set out with a band of followers. The Heike at this time had made their way back toward Kyoto and were encamped at a place on the seashore, protected on all sides by steep cliffs. "Is it possible for a stag to pass there?" Yoshitsune enquired of an old hunter who knew the country well. "Where a stag may pass, there can a horse go also." And Yoshitsune rode over the cliff at the head of his thirty retainers. The whole force of three thousand followed after them. For more than a hundred yards the slope was sandy with small pebbles so that they slid down and landed on a level place. Thence downward it was all great mossy boulders, steep as a well and some fifty yards to the bottom. It seemed impossible to go any further and the soldiers were recoiling in horror thinking they were in a trap, when one sprang forward shouting, "In my part of the country we ride down places like this any day to catch a bird. We would make a race course of this!" Down he went, followed by all the rest, and the Heike in a panic fled out of their stronghold and onto the sea once more.

One of the Heike leaders then, seeing that all was over, turned toward the west to repeat the death prayer. "O Amida Nyorai who sheddest the light of Thy Presence through the ten quarters of the world, gather into Thy Radiant Heaven all who call upon Thy Name!" Just as his prayer was finished a Genji soldier from behind swept off his head. Not doubting that he had taken the head of a noble foe, but quite unaware whose it might be, the Genji soldier, searching the armor, came across a piece of paper fastened to the quiver on which was written the verse:

> Tonight my lodging,
> The shelter of a pine tree
> And my host, a flower.

Another Genji captain seeing a single horseman attempting to escape to one of the ships in the offing beckoned with his war fan crying out, "Shameful to show an enemy your back! Return! Return!" Then the Heike warrior turned his horse and rode back to the beach. Springing upon him and tearing off his helmet, the Genji captain beheld the face of a youth of sixteen or seventeen, delicately powdered, with blackened teeth and features of great beauty. "How pitiful to put this youth to death," the Genji captain thought, mindful of his own son, and was about to set the Heike warrior free when a troop of Genji horsemen rode up. "Though I would spare your life," the captain explained, "the whole countryside swarms with our men. You cannot escape them. If you must die, let it be by my hand, and I will see that prayers are said for your rebirth in bliss." His eyes swam with tears and his hand trembled so that he could scarcely wield his blade. "Alas," he cried, "what life is so hard as that of a soldier? Only because I was born of a warrior family must I do such cruel deeds." And he pressed his face to the sleeve of his armor and wept bitterly. Stripping off the young man's armor he discovered a flute in a brocade bag that he was carrying in his girdle. "Ah," he exclaimed, "it was this youth and his friends who were amusing themselves with music within the walls this morning. Among all our men of the eastern provinces I doubt if any has brought a flute with him. What esthetes are these courtiers of Heike!" The flute was named Saeda (Little Branch) and had been given as a present by an emperor.

One evening as the sun was sinking and both forces on the shore were preparing to rest for the night a small Heike boat appeared some seventy or eighty feet from the water's edge and swung round broadside. A girl hung a red fan on a pole fastened to the gunwale of the boat.

"Summon the best archer we have," ordered Yoshitsune, "and show the enemy how we can shoot."

Yoichi was called, a lad barely twenty years old. He was wearing a robe of greenish blue with the collar and edges of the sleeves ornamented with brocade on a red ground. His armor was laced with light green and the mounts of his sword were silver. With bow under his arm and helmet slung to his breast-plates, he came into the presence of Yoshitsune and bowed respectfully.

"I cannot say that I can hit the fan for certain," Yoichi said, "and if I should miss, it would be a lasting reproach to the skill of our side. Would it not be better to entrust it to someone who could be quite sure?" This angered Yoshitsune. So Yoichi said, "If my lord commands, I will try." Then he mounted a fine black horse with saddle ornamented with gold and, taking a fresh hold on his bow, gripped the reins and rode into the sea till he came within bowshot of the boat. The wind was blowing strong; the waves were running high. The ships were rising and falling on the swell and the fan was fluttering in the breeze. The Heike had ranged their ships in a long row to see better, while on land the Genji lined the shore in expectation.

Yoichi prayed to Hachiman and the deities of his homeland. "I pray you grant that I may strike the center of that fan, for if I fail I will break my bow and put an end to my life." Then he opened his eyes again, drew his bow with all his strength and let fly. The shore echoed to the whirr of the arrow as it flew straight to its mark. The Heike in the offing beat applaudingly on the gunwales of their ships while the Genji on the shore rattled their quivers till they rang.

The forces of the Genji increased while those of the Heike grew less with the continual desertion of their followers. On the twenty-fourth day of the third month of the second year of Genryaku, at the hour of the hare (6:00 A.M.), the final battle between the Taira and Minamoto began at Dan-no-ura.

The two hosts of the Genji and Heike faced each other scarcely thirty cho distant on the water, and as the tide was running strong the Heike ships were carried by the current against their will while the Genji were naturally able to advance on them with the tide.

One of the Heike leaders shouted: "These eastern fellows may have a great name for horsemanship but they know nothing about sea fights. Let their Commander Yoshitsune be the special object of your attack. He is a little fellow with a fair complexion and his front teeth stick out a bit so you will know him by that. He changes his clothes and armor often—so take care he doesn't escape you!"

The fleet of the Genji was more numerous, but as their men shot from various places here and there their force did not show to advantage. Yoshitsune himself, who was fighting in the forefront of the battle, was greatly embarrassed by the arrows of the foe that fell like rain on his shield and armor. Elated by their victory on the first attack, the Heike pressed on and the roar of their shouting mingled with the booming of their war drums.

Both sides set their faces against each other and fought grimly without a thought for their lives, neither giving way an inch. As the Heike had on their side an emperor endowed with the ten virtues and the three sacred treasures of the realm, things went hard with the Genji. Their hearts were beginning to fail them when suddenly something like a cloud or a white banner floating in the breeze came drifting over the two fleets from the upper air and finally settled on the stern of one of the Genji ships.

When he saw this Yoshitsune, regarding it as a sign from Hachiman, removed his helmet and, after washing his hands, did obeisance, his men all following his example.

Later on, the men of Shikoku and Kyushu all left the Heike in a body and went over to the Genji, so the struggle was decided in their favor.

Then the widow of Kiyomori in an outer dress of dark-gray mourning color, with her glossy silk skirts tucked up, put the sacred jewel under her arm and the sacred sword in her girdle and, taking the emperor (her grandson) in her arms, spoke thus: "Though I am but a woman, I will not fall into the hands of the foe, but will accompany our sovereign. Let those of you who will, follow me."

The emperor was eight years old that year and his appearance was very lovely with his long black hair hanging loosely down his back. With a look of surprise and anxiety on his face he enquired, "Where is it that you are going to take me?"

Turning to her youthful sovereign with tears streaming down her cheeks she answered: "Face the east and bid farewell to the deity of the great shrine of Isé, and then the west and say the prayer that Amida may come to welcome you in paradise. There is a pure land of happiness beneath the waves, another capital where is no sorrow. Thither am I taking our sovereign." Thus she comforted him and bound up his long hair in his dove-colored robe. The child sovereign put his beautiful little hands together and did as she had told him. Then holding him tightly in her arms she said, "In the depths of the ocean we have a capital," and sank with him at last beneath the waves.

Now the whole sea was red with the Heike banners and the insignia which Genji had torn off and cut away; it looked like a river in autumn flecked with the maple leaves the wind brings down. The deserted, empty ships rocked mournfully on the waves.

CHAPTER 8

CAMP ADMINISTRATION AT KAMAKURA

(THIRTEENTH CENTURY)

MINAMOTO YORITOMO, who emerged from the struggle described in the previous chapter to become Japan's first military dictator, had a romantic career. As a boy of eleven he lived at the palace of the emperor's second wife who was the fashion leader of the time. Since his father was a chief of the imperial guard, it seemed likely he would grow up in the fastidious society of leisurely and self-indulgent courtiers. When Yoritomo was twelve, however, his father was defeated in a skirmish with the Taira and had to escape from the capital in the dark of night. The boy, not wishing to remain in the hands of enemies, ran after his father's party, but somehow or other missed them and had to hide with peasants. His father was caught and killed. By natural succession Yoritomo became head of the Minamoto clan, and as such was in imminent danger from the Taira. But his mother was a charming lady, and when she appealed to Kiyomori to spare the life of her sons, the heart of the great man melted.

Instead of being beheaded, Yoritomo was sent to live in the custody of a Fujiwara family in the Mount Fuji region. Not at all broken in spirit by this experience, the boy at once set about making friends in his new surroundings. Though the leading families of the region were of Taira descent, instead of turning with Kiyomori toward the sea and the court, they had, like the Minamotos, kept up their interest in the land. They were not kindly disposed toward their relatives in Kyoto.

Chief among these eastern landlords and highly respected by them was a man named Hojo Tokimasa, the father of Masa, a most remarkable daughter. Hojo Tokimasa was favorably impressed with Yoritomo, and willing to cast his lot with this heir of the Minamotos rather than with some of his own blood relatives. His daughter, Masa, seemed to share his sentiments. On the night set for her marriage to a Taira governor deputized by the court she eloped with Yoritomo.

This raised rather than ruined Yoritomo in the estimation of the eastern landlords and, with the backing of his father-in-law, he became a sort of champion for them. Minamoto ancestors were fully as illustrious as the Taira's and the interests of Heike in the provinces were more closely allied with those of the Minamotos than with those of their Kyoto cousins. When Yoritomo led troops to the capital to free it of Kiyomori's domination, about as many Tairas as Minamotos followed him. When he returned victorious to the east the owners of large estates were willing to make him their chief.

Yoritomo established himself as Lord High Constable in the fishing village of Kamakura, and from there he directed the affairs of the surrounding country. After Kiyomori's death, the government in Kyoto was totally ineffectual. It could neither keep order nor collect taxes, and several of the able men in its employ were glad to enter the service of the new government at Kamakura, called the Bakufu, or Camp Administration. On the advice of these men of experience Yoritomo appointed three committees: one for carrying on general affairs, one for hearing and judging lawsuits, and one in charge of soldiers. He also obtained permission from Kyoto to appoint military governors and land stewards to supplement and supplant the governors and officials appointed by the court. In this way he was able to reward those who had fought for him, and to extend his own influence. But, more important still, he was able to levy and collect taxes from privately owned lands in return for the military protection which his government offered.

By leaving the court undisturbed, and restoring many of the old nobility to the offices and estates which they had held before the rise of Kiyomori, he won favor with them. By rebuilding many temples which the Tairas had destroyed, repairing the great Buddha at Nara and having another large one cast in Kamakura, he made friends instead of enemies of the Buddhist priests. Shinto priests and the followers of Hachiman were likewise gratified when they found the lord high constable lavishing gifts upon the shrine to the god of victories which had been erected near Kamakura by the Minamotos two centuries before.

In ten years Yoritomo, by negotiation and conquest, had under his control the entire eastern half of the country. Then he revisited Kyoto. Great preparations were made for his coming. Dwellings were furnished for him and his companions on the site where the Tairas' magnificent palace once had stood. The court was thrilled with curious anticipation for the coming of this wonder-working strong man from the east. Even the cloistered emperor went out secretly to watch Yoritomo and his followers pass.

Though he stayed five weeks in the capital, bestowing costly gifts on the court, the temples and shrines, Yoritomo's hope of being appointed shogun, with the right to move troops as he pleased, was not readily fulfilled. It was not until two years later that he won the coveted commission, Commander in Chief of the troops of the nation—a commission which he could hand down to his sons and grandsons.

And as fate would have it, neither Yoritomo himself nor his sons were long to enjoy this privilege. Returning from a bridge-opening ceremony in 1199 Japan's first military dictator was thrown from his horse and fatally injured at the age of fifty-three. His sons who fell heir to the family possessions and the title of shogun were soon put out of the way. His widow, Hojo Masa, however, rallied Yoritomo's followers and managed to maintain the stability of the Bakufu.

When some of the Kamakura generals, with their strong leader gone, were inclined to desert the camp government and try to make a name for themselves with the Kyoto court, she called them together and, with trembling voice, pleaded from behind a bamboo screen as befitted a respectable lady:

> Nobles and retainers of Kamakura, if ye recollect the past direct administration of the emperors, your fathers had to do military service at court for three years, besides bearing many burdens. It often happened that many, when discharged, had to return home barefooted because of poverty. But my late husband, touched by such conditions, reduced the term of court service to six months and abated many burdens. Now the court is trying to overthrow me. Is it possible that a government which has achieved so much should be punished? The loss of my beloved husband and two sons was already sufficient sorrow, yet I had to see my dear father pass away only recently. Now comes a moment of life or death for my government. Those of you who remember what my husband and father did for you, give me your hands in allegiance . . . But if some would prefer to render service to the court, speak out at this moment.[1]

Everyone present was touched by the earnestness of her appeal and the dignity of the soldiers' life as compared with the ways of the court. All swore to share the fate of the Kamakura government, and thereafter fought as one man for the victory of the Hojo regime.

The kind of life these military men had led on the frontier was the best possible training for ruling the nation at that time. Though originally they had been the less-favored members of the nobility, or erring ones banished far from courtly ease and pleasures to atone for their misdemeanors, they were now the aristocracy of power. While courtiers had been dissipating their energies in idle amusements, these men had been working hard. In the great Musashi plain they had found more extensive fertile fields than anywhere else in Japan; the climate there was less fickle than farther south and west—but it was also sterner.

Untiring industry and long perseverance had been required to develop the district, and united action had been required to defend it. These men, therefore, loved the land to which they had given so much. And they knew full well the value of working together, sacrificing together, if need be, for the good of all.

For twenty-five years after Yoritomo passed away, Hojo Masa carried on the government he had planned. Ama Shogun, the widow or nun general, she was called. Though neither of her sons who succeeded their father had been allowed by rival generals to live long enough to amount to anything as rulers, Masa organized a Council of State which, under the leadership of her brother and his descendants, gave Japan a century of government as just, efficient, strong and economical as any the country has ever known.

The thirteen members of her Council of State swore a solemn oath that they would give no regard to ties of relationship, but would speak out unafraid of powerful houses. Every opinion the council expressed or order it issued was to be upheld by every member. There was to be no dissension or criticism of one member by another, for this would destroy their solidarity and give men a chance to laugh at them.

Lawsuits were settled promptly with good judgment. Even when an envoy from Korea came complaining of the ravages of Japanese pirates on the coast of his country, the matter was given prompt consideration, the pirate leaders were punished and their booty was restored to its owners. A real effort was also made to reduce the cost of government and lessen the taxes on the people as shown by the following anecdotes about various Hojo rulers.

Once, when the fence surrounding the Hojo regent's home was in need of repair, some government officials wished to replace it with an embankment, but the regent refused, saying the suggested change would take too much labor, and would not protect him nearly so well as the bravery of his comrades.

On another occasion when a young Hojo regent was coming

to visit his mother she set about patching some torn places in the sliding paper walls. Her brother said, "Let me give it to so-and-so to do; he understands such things." But she replied, "His work will not be any better than mine," and went on pasting square after square. "It would be easier to repaper the whole thing," her brother suggested, "and, besides, the patches look ugly." Then the regent's mother explained, "I am doing it like this on purpose, to teach young people to mend evils while they are small." [2]

There are also stories about Hojo regents who disguised themselves as pilgrims and traveled through the deep snow to find out how poor people were living. One of them wore only old clothing and ate only two simple meals a day as an example for his officials. Both he and they worked from dawn till dusk, devising and supervising effective measures of relief.

A Hojo regent's widow obtained permission from the government to establish a temple of divorce where helpless wives could stay for two or three years and be protected from cruel husbands.

The officers appointed to the provinces by the Hojo government were visited at regular and irregular intervals by inspectors from Kamakura, and people were encouraged to report any maladministration and dissatisfaction with officials. Every autumn inspectors were sent out through the country to estimate the crops and thus keep a check on tax returns of rice and produce. Storehouses were kept filled with rice, to be dispersed to the people in time of bad crops and famine. There were no longer any estates completely immune from taxes. All landholders were to receive justice and protection, and all were, therefore, required to pay taxes.

The emperor, resenting the thoroughgoing way in which the Hojo regents were taking over the functions of government, raised a revolt against them, but his efforts were worse than futile.[3] He himself was deposed, three former emperors were sent into exile, and the Hojos put on the throne a boy they

knew they could manage. As a result of this unsuccessful coup
the Hojo regents were enabled not only to clear many princes
and courtiers out of the capital, but also to take possession of
many lands valuable as rewards for faithful followers. Two
officials were appointed to represent the Kamakura government
in the capital and keep watch over the imperial family, to
prevent further conspiracy. These officials used the buildings
prepared on the Taira estates for Yoritomo's visit as their mansions and offices. The fire-swept imperial palaces and court
office buildings were entirely neglected. The spacious grounds
were frequented only by hunting parties. The university was
no more. Emperors lived here and there in the homes of im-
poverished nobles.[4]

While country people in general were better treated by the
new regime, even with Hojo economy, misery prevailed: national bankruptcy was aggravated by earthquakes, plagues and
famines.

Buddhist priests of necessity changed their programs. They
now catered to persons of wealth and leisure by building temple
hostels in beautiful scenic places, and encouraging the practice
of making pilgrimages. They also encouraged courtiers and
officials, who found themselves in difficulties with their rivals,
and their plans gone far awry, to withdraw from active life
and retire to some temple.

Instead of the gay confidence and optimism that character-
ized the religion of Fujiwara days, now there was pessimism.
Instead of saying, "Eat, drink and be merry and make generous
gifts to us for obtaining your salvation," now they said, "The
times are so bad there is no use trying to do anything about
life here. Shun it as much as possible and simply believe in
Amida's all-embracing mercy and willingness to save you."
Just repeating the deity's name, with faith, was sufficient for
some denominations. They did away with learned discourses on
the scriptures, with complicated theology and creeds, for the
masses were ignorant and unable to read. They said, "You

must look in your own heart for the truth, and work out your own salvation."

A fisherman's son named Nichiren turned preacher and went through the streets of Kamakura accompanied by followers, beating sticks and drums. "We have seen many signs in heaven and in earth! A famine, a plague, the whole country is filled with misery! Horses and cows are dying on the roadsides and so are men; and there is no one to bury them. One half the population is stricken, and there is no house that has entirely escaped, hence many minds are turning to religion." Thus Nichiren addressed the people. "Others again in accordance with the secret doctrines of Shingon use copious sprinklings of holy water from the five vases. Some write the names of the seven gods of luck on pieces of paper and affix them by the hundreds to the door posts of their houses, while others do the same with the pictures of various gods of heaven and earth. But let men do what they will, the famine and the plague still rage, there are beggars on every hand, and the unburied corpses line the roads. The truth is missed and distorted by squinting eyes . . . Repent and be converted to the true faith before the hour of utmost disaster arrives." [5]

Nichiren felt sure that Japan was to be a fountain of blessing to the whole world in coming ages, but at present needed chastisement. The Japanese nation was living in winter, but spring was sure to follow.

"It will not be long before the great Mongols will send their myriad warships and attack this country," he prophesied. "Then the whole people will surely abandon all the sanctuaries they used to revere and join in crying, 'O Master Nichiren, save us!' " [6]

He was right about the Mongol warships. From early times boats from China had come to Japan with treasures of various kinds for the imperial storehouses, for which sulphur, arrows, pearls, herbs, straw mats and timber were traded in exchange. When the imperial treasury could no longer stand the strain

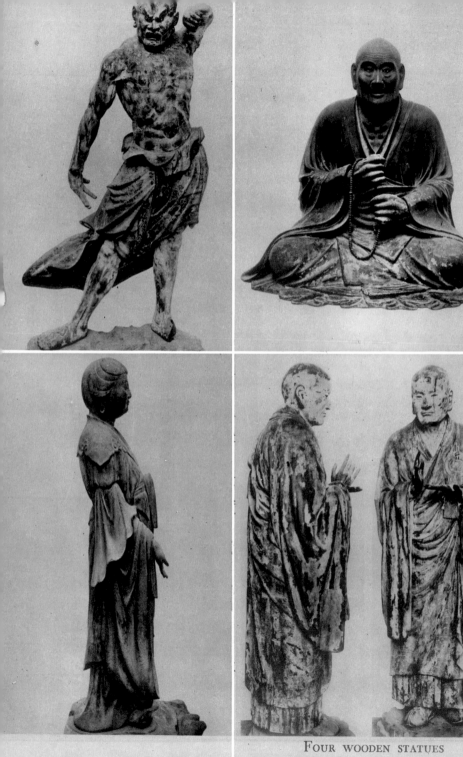

FOUR WOODEN STATUES

of such trade, the Fujiwara took it over, and when their resources were dissipated it was Taira Kiyomori's turn. The lavish way in which he traded in Chinese goods wiped out the fortune of his family in one generation. The Kamakura shogunate, made up of thrifty northern farmers, refused to trade. They had seen the folly of overspending. Homemade things were good enough for them. So Chinese boats stopped coming.

Some people, however, were not satisfied. Though they had little of value to trade with China, there were many things in China which they wanted, and buccaneering began. The coasts of Korea and China were continually pirated by little boats from Japan. When the Mongols came to power they wished to put an end to this illicit trade and establish more orderly relations.

It was about this time that the great Venetian traveler, Marco Polo, reported: "There is a very large island called Zepangu [which was the way he caught the name Nippon] fifteen hundred miles from the coast of China, where gold is so abundant that the riches of the King are incalculable and even the roof of his palace is covered with gold. The inhabitants, though living quite separate from other nations, are fair, handsome and of agreeable manner." [7] Marco Polo did not visit the island, but when this description, fantastic as it was, reached Europe, men became very eager to trade with the Orient. This was one of the factors leading to the discovery of America.

To arrive at some agreement with the rulers of Japan the Mongols sent several groups of envoys. One of them arrived in Kyoto when the courtiers were preparing for an emperor's fiftieth birthday party. The message they brought from the great Mongol, Kublai Khan, concluded something like this: "We beg that hereafter you, O King, will establish friendly relations with us. Is it reasonable to refuse intercourse with each other? It will lead to war, and who is there who likes such a state of things? Think on this, O King." [8]

The courtiers suspended their birthday party preparations

and drafted what they thought was a suitable reply. The Kamakura officials, however, refused to give it to the envoys and sent
them back empty handed.

Not long after this a fleet of several hundred ships attacked
two small islands off the mainland of Japan, capturing or killing the people and plundering whatever they could find of
value. Then they sailed on to Kyushu. The news was rushed to
Kamakura by riders on swift horses. A thrilling appeal was
made to all armed men to put aside petty differences and rally
in defense of the nation. Every man who could use bow and
arrow and sword, and get a horse to take him there was urged
to hasten to Kyushu. The Mongols, however, did not wait;
local leaders had to meet them alone, with only courage and
terrible swords to confront poisoned arrows and heavy stones
hurled from machines. Though face to face with an adversary
there was none who could withstand their spirited blades, at a
distance Nipponese soldiers were helpless. When dusk came,
the Mongols returned to their ships, intending no doubt to
land again and continue fighting next day. But during the
night a storm arose. And with the dawn, the Kyushu people
discovered that the attacking fleet was far out to sea and headed
for Korea.

The Kamakura government thought that Kublai Khan would
not be so easily thwarted, and they thought right. Soon more
envoys arrived bidding the Nipponese ruler to come and pay
homage at the Mongol ruler's new court in Peking. This message infuriated the Hojo regents. They cut off the envoys'
heads and undertook great preparations for both offense and
defense. They instructed officials in the coastal provinces of
western Nippon to get together helmsmen and sailors for a
fleet, and they ordered the Kyushu landlords to build stone
ramparts on their shores. For over five years they kept on preparing. Then another envoy came from the great Mongol. The
government cut off his head and continued strengthening
defenses.

Finally the second great fleet appeared, part of it made up of Koreans, and part of it of Chinese just recently conquered by the Mongols. Over four thousand ships, they say, there were altogether, some of them carrying a hundred men or more, and horses in addition. But this time the Japanese did not allow them to land so easily. They took out little boats to harass the fleet by surrounding single vessels and setting fire to them and

Ships filled with samurai

attacking crews which tried to get ashore. For seven weeks the fighting continued along the shores of Kyushu. For seven weeks the resolute soldiers of Nippon, behind miles and miles of earthen embankments, checked the advances of the Mongol marines. But losses were heavy on both sides.

Princes and courtiers in Kyoto spent all their time fasting and praying and having priests perform religious rites to bring about victory. The emperor sent his autographed prayer to the shrine of Hachiman in Kyushu. It read: "The enemy of the country must be vanquished."

"Throughout the length and breadth of the land could be heard the tapping and roll of temple drums, the tinkling of sacred bells, the rustle of the sleeves of vestal dancers and the litanies of priests. In thousands of temples wood fires were kept burning and the smoke of incense ascended perpetually." [9]

The fighting continued fiercely for seven weeks and three days. The reports which reached the capital spread panic. All work and business was suspended. Even courtiers suffered from a dearth of supplies. Then suddenly the sky grew dark, and again there arose a mighty wind of tornado proportions; the Mongol squadrons were jammed together at the mouth of the harbor where they were lying. Vessels shattered to pieces. Men plunged into the water. The wreckage piled so high and solid that it formed a bridge from one shore to the other. The soldiers who went ashore were captured and put to death. Only a fraction of the ships and men escaped to the continent again.

Then what rejoicing there was all over the country! Then what a clamor the priests put up! The victory was theirs, in answer to their prayers. And they demanded suitable rewards. Both court and Bakufu were very generous with them, but still they clamored for more. And the fighting men, who had left their farms in the northeast and gone down to the defense of Kyushu, they also asked the Bakufu for recompense.

Nothing had been gained by the war, however; there were no spoils to divide. And there was still danger that the Mongols might return, because of repeated scares troops were kept in Kyushu for almost thirty years. Even if they had wished to, the Hojo regents would have found it very difficult to satisfy all of the claims presented to them. With the passing of the years, however, their standards had relaxed, their sense of responsibility had grown dull. Instead of being reared in the robust thrift and simplicity of his forebears, the eighth Hojo regent was brought up like an imperial prince. This caused great discontent among the thousands of fighting men who, though they had gone into debt in defense of the country, found no recompense or justice forthcoming from the Hojos. Their only hope, it seemed, lay in a civil war. Then if they were among the winners, there would be the estates of the losing side to take over and redistribute among themselves. It was not long before many of these malcontents, and monks too, had turned their backs on the decadent dictators and rallied to the support of the Emperor Go-Daigo, of whom more will be told in the next chapter.

These were the days of the sword. From earliest times, a sword had been one of the three sacred symbols of the emperor: for generations in ancient times the use of metal swords had remained as the exclusive right of the ruling family. When not in use these early swords were kept in Shinto shrines to impress worshipers with the power of the imperial clan. In the Nara and Heian periods, nobles and officials came to share the privilege of wearing swords, but the swords they wore were nothing but bejeweled wooden things which served as decorations of rank. Swords which could stand the test of use were given only on special occasions such as the dispatching of expeditions to the north against revolting Ainu or the sending of delegations to the Chinese court, and then they were bestowed with ceremony and only to the highest in command.

As the Fujiwaras left more and more responsibility in the hands of provincial officers, these latter were allowed to carry swords. And when Tairas and Minamotos came to guard the capital they provided themselves with swords on their own initiative. Even then, however, there was only one sword to a family, and the member to whom it was entrusted was regarded with highest respect. Combat was not on a large, impersonal scale. It was the hand-to-hand encounters of provincial swordsmen well aware of each other's reputation that made possible the rule of the shoguns or military dictators.

With the establishment of the Bakufu at Kamakura, swordmaking became a prosperous industry and remained so for seven centuries.[10] Because of their superb quality, Japanese swords were in great demand in China and came to be the chief item in export trade. The best Japanese swords of the thirteenth century are the finest of any in the world. A good one, they say, will cut a hair floating in the air, or a pile of copper coins without being nicked.

To make a "noble blade," the swordsmith first of all had to lead a pure and moral life. His craft was like a religion to him. For each sword he started to make the smith went through a period of prayer and fasting and used charms of various kinds in his home and workroom to keep away evil influences.

The first step was the forging. Several tiny strips of steel were welded together to make a bar about six inches by two inches, by half an inch. This was cut almost in half and folded back on itself, then forged to its original size again. Several bars like this were forged, and cut and folded, and reforged twelve or eighteen times. Then all were welded together and cut and folded and reforged half a dozen times more before they were beaten out into a blade.

The second step was the tempering. In this process the whole blade except the edge was covered with a clayish mixture and heated in a bright charcoal fire until the back reached red heat and the edge white. Then it was plunged into water of a certain temperature. This made a very hard, sharp edge and a resilient back.

The polishing and sharpening was the most difficult and complicated process. It took weeks and weeks of most perfectly controlled and painstaking labor. When it was completed and the maker's name was incised on the tang, the sword was ready for mounting. The hilt, fastened on with a simple little bamboo plug, was easily removed when occasion arose to show the smith's signature, but when the sword was being used it held absolutely firm. Marvelous little pieces of carved metal were bound to the hilt with shark skin and silk cords to give a good grip and serve as ornamentation. The guards also were ornamented with gold and silver alloys in exquisite inlay designs. A master swordsmith's masterpiece was of enormous value; even lesser craftsmen's good swords sold for a small fortune.

Since in addition to the exacting and costly process of making a sword, learning how to use one required years and years of devoted training, effort and discipline, it is small wonder that skilled swordsmen formed a distinct and distinguished class of society. Groups of them attached themselves to important landowners and were given regular salaries in property and rice in return for their readiness to use swords when needed. These swordsmen in the service of landlords came to be called samurai.

Centuries later it came to be the custom for each samurai, and for samurai only, to wear not one but two swords in lacquer sheaths thrust through his belt. There were long swords for encounters, and short ones for cutting off the head of a defeated opponent, or for cutting open one's own stomach. A true samurai never hesitated to give his life in order to prove his sincerity or to defend his honor. Like the ancient Greeks, it is explained, the Japanese thought that the soul of man dwelt in his stomach. And ripping open the stomach was equivalent to saying, "I will show you my soul. See for yourself whether it is polluted or clean." [11]

Good swords themselves were supposed to have some hidden power or spirit akin to a soul in them. The gift of a good sword carried with it a sacred trust and inspiration, for the quality of the blade was thought of as reflecting the character of the owner, and owners sought to live up to the reputation of the sword handed down to them. Some swords had the reputation of preserving peace by their inner power without dealing death. It was a serious matter to unsheath a sword, for once it was unsheathed it had to be used effectively. Otherwise the sword was dishonored, and the samurai, too, for showing such haste in drawing and hesitation in using it.

From the thirteenth century on, as samurai came to play an increasingly important part in political, social and economic affairs, they became increasingly more class conscious. There grew up among them a certain code of conduct, not written down as rules and regulations, but impressed deep in their minds and hearts. It was their way of life. They called it Bushido (the Way of the Warriors). Bushido had much in common with European chivalry, but a great deal more which was peculiar to itself. Bushido was often spoken of as the Soul of Japan. It became the basis of the most popular Japanese literature, and most Japanese movies had samurai as heroes. Heroic ballads and stories of famous samurai, of how they lived and died, are still favorite features on Japanese radio and TV today. The following story of Akechi Mitsuharu, given here without its usual embellishments, is one which continues to delight Japanese listeners.

Besieged by a rival general, Mitsuharu set fire to his castle on Azuchi hill, and with less than two dozen men, all that remained of his six hundred samurai, attempted to escape to his other castle on the opposite shore of Lake Biwa. Confronted by the enemy en route, every one of his men fell, bravely fighting. Mitsuharu himself was able to charge through the enemy on his horse and plunge into the lake. The sight of this single horseman, his coat of white silk twill painted with a dragon and clouds by a great artist of the day, the red and blue saddle and trappings of his mount moving close to the water, was so beautiful to behold that the enemy on the banks forgot themselves and cheered.

Landing on the further shore, Mitsuharu rode his horse to a shrine and there dismounted. Taking out a sheet of paper and a writing brush from the kit he carried in his girdle, the hero wrote, "The horse which swam across the lake with Mitsuharu on him," and tied the piece of paper to the horse's mane. He had no further need of his horse, but wishing to save its life, left it with its bridle fastened to the shrine and walked alone to his castle.

At dawn the next morning he appeared at the window of his watchtower shouting, "I have a word to say to the general of the advancing army, I, Akechi Mitsuharu. Will he come closer?"

When the enemy came forward Mitsuharu went on: "My master fell in an ill-fated battle, and his wife and children are about to end their lives here. I shall set this castle on fire and die also, but rare treasures that once belonged to Lord Nobunaga are kept in this castle. We ourselves may perish as the fortunes of war decree, but these treasures in truth belong to the world at large and ought to be preserved for thousands of years to come. I will hand them over to you with a list. Pray take them to your master for safe keeping."

Having said this, by means of sashes he slowly lowered the treasures, wrapped in silk brocade bedding, into the hands of the enemy general.[12]

Though it was often said that Bushido made Japan what it was at best, it was also true that Japan as it was in the thirteenth century was what made Bushido. It was not something new which appeared suddenly, but the natural outcome of the deep and widespread influences of Buddhism, Shinto and Chinese ethical teachings, and the economic and social conditions of the time. The newer sects of Buddhism were creating in people's minds a calm acceptance of whatever life had in store, and a not unfriendly feeling toward death. The Jodo sect taught that death is rebirth in paradise. And the Zen sect that life is a continual dying.[13]

Shinto taught pious reverence and gratitude toward one's own ancestors and especially for those of one's superiors. It is interesting to note in this connection that when worshipers went to ancestral shrines to pay their devotions, they were almost always confronted by a round mirror of polished metal. The mirror seemed to say, "To serve truly and reverence others, first of all you must know yourself. Look and see what ugliness and beauty, what evil and what good there is in you. Know yourself."

The ancient Chinese ethics emphasized loyalty in all relationships and propriety in behavior. Now the condition of Japan was such that men in power needed the support of many strong-armed men, and men who had only their strong arms to defend them needed to band together under the protection of an influential landlord. Life was not easy for anyone; the spirit of daring and bearing was often put to the test.

As a result of all these influences, Bushido developed among provincial troops in the Kamakura period. In the centuries that followed it took a stronger and stronger hold on the hearts of the people; it was their ideal and has not entirely disappeared even from contemporary Japan.

Samurai had no patience with vague moral theories and but little respect for knowledge unless it was of the kind men reveal in character. They were men of action and, without any explanation, executed what they thought was justice. If their lord needed something belonging to someone else, they would see how highly the owner really valued it by the defense he offered. "Let the strongest man win," they said. Another favorite maxim was, "To know and to act are one and the same."

Training in Bushido began in babyhood. If a child cried over a hurt, his mother would exclaim: "What a coward to cry for a little pain! What will you do when your arm is cut off in battle, or when, for the sake of honor, you must rip your stomach open with your sword?" [14] For discipline and experience young children were set all sorts of difficult tasks. They were sent far off to deliver a message among strangers. Often they were made to rise before the sun to do some chores, to go on a long errand barefoot in winter, or to visit execution grounds at night and leave some evidence that they had been among the heads exposed there.

A story is told of a famished little boy talking to his companion. "See the little sparrows open wide their yellow bills. How eagerly they eat the worms their mother brings, but for us when our stomach is empty, it is a disgrace to show hunger."

Samurai children were taught to endure suffering and control their faces, so as not to disturb anyone else by their expressions of pain, but they were also taught to be sensitive to the distress of others, and to have a sympathetic regard for others' feelings, even for blossoms and birds.

Cherry blossoms were great favorites with the samurai. Not showy in color or heavy in fragrance, not bearing thorns beneath its beauty, nor clinging to its stem after its beauty was gone, the cherry blossom appealed to them for its simplicity and modesty and its readiness to depart life while still in its prime.

Trained never to shed the blood of an opponent of unequal strength, or of unequal rank, samurai yet felt called upon not infrequently to sacrifice their own wives and children for the sake of the lord whom they served. There are many stories of loyal samurai who, when an enemy was trying to wipe out all the sons of their lord, if there was any resemblance between them, gave their own sons to the sword. And if their lord or one of his family had been treacherously killed by an enemy, they felt it a matter of principle and personal honor to wreak vengeance on the offender. In such an event any sort of trickery was justified, for they were acting in accordance with their code and fulfilling the will of heaven.

CHAPTER 9

DUAL DYNASTIES, DILETTANTI AND DISORDER

(FOURTEENTH THROUGH SIXTEENTH CENTURIES)

FROM 1300 to 1600 were three long centuries of change and confusion in Japan—an age of fighting farmers and merchant priests, of pirates and turbulence; an age when the lower classes of society came to the top; an age when shoguns with foreign trade monopolies built gold and silver pavilions, and emperors made their living by selling autographs.

The Hojos who had given Japan a hundred years of thrifty law and order, reasonably impartial taxes and prompt economical justice were undone by the Mongol invasion; the priests had claimed the victory was theirs and had been generously rewarded. Then the southern landowners, who had fought for the defense of their own lands, claimed the victory was theirs, and resented the intrusion of the northerners. The northerners in turn, with equal justice, claimed they had left their lands in the north and spent everything they had in coming to the assistance of the south. All over the country people were dissatisfied and unsettled. They turned first to this side, then to that in the political struggles which ensued, fighting wherever and whenever they saw something to be gained.

At the beginning of the fourteenth century the imperial court, which had long been in the dim background of government affairs, thought to take advantage of the ill-feeling toward the Hojos, and, with the help of armed priests from Mount Hiei, Mount Koya and Nara, led a revolt against Kamakura, the capital of the dictators. The Hojos, no longer fortified with

strong military leaders of their own clan, ordered an able warrior named Takauji from a district called Ashikaga in the north
to put down the imperial uprising. Ashikaga Takauji's followers, descended from the Minamoto family, inherited resentment toward the Hojos for the way they had treated the illustrious Yoritomo's sons and appropriated his lands and power.
Instead of attacking the emperor, therefore, they joined causes
with him and, turning against the Hojos, soon brought about
the surrender of the Kamakura government.

The emperor, Go-Daigo-Tenno, then thought he was through
with military rulers and directed his efforts toward reestablish-
ing the supremacy of the court. The estates which Takauji had
helped him to win from the Hojos he awarded not to the soldiers who had fought to restore him to power, but to the
priests, nuns, musicians and writers who had been his companions in less prosperous days.

Angered at this turn of events, Ashikaga Takauji set up his
headquarters on the old site of Yoritomo's and began to rule the
northeastern part of the country on his own responsibility.
When the emperor sent troops to put him in his proper place,
Takauji escaped from them and fled to Kyushu. There, many
of his kinsmen had gone at the time of the Mongol invasion,
and had remained to enjoy the profits of seaport trade. With
their support and the friends he made by giving away lands,
Takauji was able to return to Kyoto and set up an emperor of
his own choosing. His was called the Northern Court. The
Northern Court demanded from Go-Daigo-Tenno the imperial
sword and seal, emblems of the right to rule.

Unwilling to yield his position, Go-Daigo resorted to strata-
gem and turned over only replicas. With the real sword and
seal still in his possession, he escaped from the capital through
a broken fence, and traveled in woman's clothes to the hills of
Yoshino, where he set up the Southern Court. The next year,
however, he died and Takauji was appointed shogun by the
emperor of the Northern Court.

Fighting still continued. Both courts had their sympathizers and supporters and both continued to exist about sixty miles apart for about sixty years. The period from 1331 to 1392 is known in Japanese history as the period of the dual dynasties.

One of the most able and loyal men of this period was a soldier, scholar and politician named Chikafusa. Chikafusa was Go-Daigo's friend. It was he who by feats of arms had won possession of the Yoshino region and prepared for the Southern Court there. And after Go-Daigo's death, he set out with a fleet of ships to go to the assistance of Southern Court sympathizers residing in the Kwanto district around Kamakura. Having been the center of administration for a hundred and fifty years, Kamakura, with its harbor and propinquity to the fertile rice fields of the Musashi plains, the broadest in Japan, was now a more desirable location than Kyoto. Though most of his ships were lost in a storm, and he never succeeded in taking the recently fallen capital of the Hojos, Chikafusa kept the Ashikagas so busily engaged in the Kwanto for several years that the Southern Court was allowed to enjoy some peace.

What has since proved to be Chikafusa's chief claim to fame, however, was the writing of a political thesis entitled *A History of the True Succession of the Divine Monarchs*. This was designed to defend the imperial line against the ambitions of military dictators who would base the right to rule on might and merit, rather than on the divine descent from Amaterasu set forth in the Kojiki and Nihongi. Chikafusa wrote:

> Great Yamato is a divine country. It is only our land whose foundations were first laid by the divine ancestor. It alone has been transmitted by the sun-goddess to a long line of her descendants. There is nothing of this kind in foreign countries.
>
> It is the duty of every man born on the imperial soil to yield devoted loyalty to his sovereign, even to the sacrifice of his own life.
>
> The principles of statesmanship are based on justice and mercy, in the dispensing of which firm action is requisite.

Firm action is displayed first of all in the choice of men for official positions. Japan and China both agree that the basis of good government consists in the sovereign finding the right man and bestowing favor on him . . .[1]

Though by Chikafusa's time learning had become more popular in military circles, and all leaders kept priests in their employ as advisers and tutors in the art of managing people, little if any attention was paid to his scholarly essay. Sidelight on the position of the imperial household during this period is given by the fact that though there were four printing centers in the country in the Ashikaga period—at Kyoto, Nara, Mount Koya and the seaport city, Sakai—the *History of the True Succession* did not appear in print until more than three hundred years after it was written. Though in the nineteenth century, when the national integrity of Japan was critically threatened by the flood of Western influence, Chikafusa's thesis came to play a very important part in restoring the dignity of the imperial family, making the emperor the rallying center of all factions and saving the country from being parceled out to foreign interests, during Chikafusa's lifetime it had practically no effect. The country was under the domination of Ashikaga shoguns and their Zen priest advisers.

Since the influence of Zen on Japanese culture was so profound, it is rather interesting to trace its history. For centuries after it was introduced into China the Buddhist sect called Zen had remained protestant and obscure in the southeastern provinces, unable to make headway in the capital and urban centers. But when with the downfall of the T'ang Empire the Chinese were driven by the Mongols out of the northwestern part of the country, a new dynasty, the Sung, grew up around the mouth of the Yangtze River. This was the time when the Arabs were opening the sea-trade route along the southern littoral of Asia. Seaports along the coast below the Yangtze began to develop and replace inland cities as centers of civilization. The Chinese began to change from agrarian to mercantile interests. The Zen sect, long established in this coastal region, became the official Buddhism of the Sung regime.

Zen had been introduced to Japan in Kwammu-Tenno's reign, when Kyoto was being built and Saicho's temple center was started on Hieizan. It continued to be practiced as an adjunct of other sects, but as in China did not flourish while rulers of the people were enjoying an easy-going, prosperous life. Zen emphasis was not on a merciful deity, but on self-control, meditation and the development of will power. Zen's time in Japan did not come until the Fujiwaras' long neglect of the provinces led to the rise of the practical military families.

Japan's first Zen temple was built in the early Kamakura period by a monk from Mount Hiei who had been converted to Zen on his second visit to China. Legend has it that Eisai let the men building his temple sing his name in rhythmic unison, "Eisai, Eisai, Eisai, Eisai," to help them pull the heavy timbers, and in Japan today, laborers raising a large post or beam may be heard chanting something like "Eisai, Eisai."

Contemporary with the decline of Kyoto and the establishment of the military dictators in Japan came increasing pressure on the Sung Dynasty in China from Genghis Khan and his Mongol Tatars. In 1232 the Sung were forced to an alliance, and fifty years later Kublai Khan was ruler of all China. During these troubled times many important political figures from the Sung court, in the guise of Zen priests, sought refuge in Japan. The Hojo regency, lacking the cultural guidance which Kyoto with its many temples had enjoyed, was very ready to welcome these able refugees. Five monasteries were built for them in Kamakura and they were treated as government guests of honor. Their advice was sought and followed in both political and religious matters and especially concerning international relations.

Undoubtedly it was Sung-Zen hatred of the Mongols that prompted the Kamakura government's defiance of Kublai Khan's envoys. Zen influence also played a large part in the supplanting of the Hojos by the Ashikagas. The Hojos had refused to carry on foreign trade, but the Ashikagas in Kyushu found it very profitable. In their mercantile endeavors the Ashikagas discovered, however, that the Chinese studied by scholarly Japanese courtiers and priests of the older Buddhist sects was a very different language from that currently spoken. The Chinese of the courtiers and priests of the older sects was the form which had been learned prior to the cessation of official relations with China four centuries before; but Zen priests were familiar with the present-day spoken and written language and very well informed on current conditions in China. Their assistance seemed essential to foreign trade, and foreign trade seemed essential to replenish the nation's treasuries.

It is said that when Ashikaga Takauji first heard opportunity knocking at his door he turned for counsel to a Shingon priest, who advised him to act under cover of imperial prestige and set up the northern branch of the imperial family, since he could not get his way with the southern. As the power of Takauji's leadership became apparent, however, Muso, the greatest Zen Master of the age, became interested in him. Having been successively in the employ of the Kamakura shogunate and Go-Daigo-Tenno, Muso now became political and spiritual adviser to this promising Ashikaga general.

When Go-Daigo passed away and Takauji was busy organizing a new regime, the worldly-wise Muso recommended that he build a temple in the capital in honor of the late emperor to whom he had never, to put it mildly, shown an abundance of respect. And Muso also recommended that a For-the-Peace-of-the-Nation Temple be established in the most strategic location of each province. The one in honor of Go-Daigo was called Tenryu-ji (Celestial Dragon Temple) and the furnishing of it was the occasion for beginning the regular overseas trading monopoly of which Takauji had dreamed since his stay in Kyushu.

The Mongol invasion doubtless had curtailed trade for a while. People in Kyoto in those days had nothing to spend and they could see little sense in trade. Only a few years before, a courtier, turned hermit, had written: "We could do without anything from China except medicine. As for books they are spread all over this country and we could copy them. It is a foolish thing for ships from China to make the perilous journey over here crammed with cargoes of useless things."[2] But the Zen priests knew what profits there were in mercantile enterprise.

The boats in which they plied back and forth were called after the new temple Tenryu-ji Bune (bune or fune means boat). Since they were boats of only three to five thousand cubic feet, not much investment was involved. Going, they carried chiefly swords, sulphur, timber, fans, lacquer ware and an attractive malleable alloy resembling gold which was popular for temple decor. Returning, they brought books, gold, silver and copper coins, scroll paintings, tea, silk, porcelain, pottery and other works of art. The profits on the round trip were sometimes as much as a hundred times the initial investment.

This overseas trade under the direction of Zen priests was the economic foundation of the Ashikaga shogunate. This it was that enabled Takauji and his successors who resided in Kyoto near the emperors to adopt their superior attitude toward the imperial family and build gold and silver pavilions with gardens so beautiful that people called them Flower Palaces. It was this that enabled them to retain their power in Japan until the middle of the sixteenth century, when piracy rivaling the Ashikaga mercantile monopoly became so prevalent that China finally closed her ports and refused to trade.

What with plagues and droughts, wars, fires and famines, life was scarcely worth living for the farmers and officials, dependent on the yield of the soil, who made up the bulk of the population. But for those who saw beyond the narrow confines of their own islands and extended their interest and efforts to foreign seas and ports, it must have been thrilling to be alive.

The all-conquering Mongols, who had struck terror in the hearts of people all the way from eastern Europe to the islands of the Pacific, had flourished and declined. While the Ashikagas were rising in Japan, a new dynasty called the Ming (Brilliant) was developing in China. The Mings were more familiar with graces and refinements than the Mongols had been, and more amicably inclined toward their island neighbor. They were also materialistic and practical. Their art consisted chiefly of architecture, porcelain and lacquer ware, and their paintings lacked the radiant quality of spirit shown by earlier T'ang artists, still their country was very attractive to adventurous Japanese. Pirates flourished and prospered.

As time went on, larger and safer ships plied back and forth at more frequent intervals. The shogunate in return for a financial consideration, certified the right of certain temples, shrines and wealthy officials to charter ships to make a number of trips to China each year. These were tributary ships; all others were pirates. The imperial court itself did not find it convenient to collect merchandise for such trade, but one great landlord sent fifty tributary ships a year and established settlements for more than sixty Japanese in three different ports in Korea.

Pirate ships no doubt operated in greater numbers, but naturally did not preserve incriminating documents. It is about the officially sanctioned tributary ships that most records have been found. Zen priest envoys were usually in charge of these and carried gifts to the Ming court, in addition to articles for trade. The Chinese ruler sent presents in return for the shogun's offerings. Once, ladies of the shogun's palace journeyed in palanquins the fifty miles from Kyoto to the port of Hyogo to welcome a tributary ship returning home. It must have been exciting to talk with the witty priests about their experiences in China and on the sea. Then to examine and open the endless boxes, baskets, bundles and rolls, and find the gauzelike silks patterned with flowers and clouds, brought specially for the favorite of the shogun!

It is recorded that the *Tara Maru*, a tributary ship, on one voyage carried a chief envoy and party of eleven, twenty-four agents for temples, and fourteen agents for landlords.[3] There were also on board eighteen owners of merchandise, three chief mariners, thirty-five ordinary passengers, five interpreters and servants, three clerks, fifty-two sailors, four actors, one horse breeder and four horses. In addition to the cargo for tribute and trade, provisions had to be taken along for a hundred and twenty-nine days, from January to May. These included beans for the horses, rice, oil, salt, soy, tea, fish, vinegar, half a bottle of rice wine per person per day and ten candles and ten bundles of charcoal per person for the voyage. Among the expenditures recorded for the trip are two kwan mon for a special festival celebrated at the first sight of Chinese land, ten kwan mon for festivals on the first day of every month and the five annual feasts, ten kwan mon for rice cakes and sake for sailors on New Year's Day, a three-kwan-mon fee for prayer, ten kwan mon for festivals and offerings of swords and sacred dances at various shrines on the coast of the Inland Sea, six hundred and eighty-eight kwan mon for food, four hundred and ninety for wages, and other items totaling two thousand and sixty-five kwan mon.

One Zen priest envoy wrote in his diary for August 1 and 3, 1451, that the Chinese people

> treated Japanese travelers as subjects of a tributary country and wanted to train them in the proper ceremonies to attend the birthday celebration of the Ming emperor. The Japanese, however, thought of nothing but trade and were annoyed at the idea of these formalities.

For August 25:

> The village headman on hearing of the approach of our party of three hundred ran away and provided no lodging for us.

For October 9:

> On seeing me composing poems the Chinese officials said that there were about five hundred countries paying tribute to the Ming court, but only the Japanese are able to read.

Though the Ming sent several envoys to Japan who were always well received by the shogun, it was many years before they accomplished what they came for, and succeeded in getting an agreement from Yoshimitsu, the third Ashikaga shogun, to suppress the overseas activities of his countrymen. Perhaps keen competition with his rivals finally persuaded Yoshimitsu to send with a delegation of priests to the Ming court a gift of a thousand ryo of gold, ten horses, a thousand leaves of silver, a hundred fans, three gold-foil folding screens, one suit of armor, ten lances, one sword, one ink stone and one ink-stone box. Thereafter he was hailed as the King of Japan and favored with a present of a thousand ryo of silver, fifteen thousand kwan of copper coin, ten hiki of brocade, fifty hiki of hemp cloth, twenty-eight hiki of blue cloth, three thousand hiki of woolen cloth. And at a maple-viewing party in the capital in the early fifteenth century Yoshimitsu appeared in an elaborate Ming costume riding in a Ming palanquin.

As a soldier hero, and the proud husband of a court lady, Yoshimitsu had great influence in the palace. In 1392, he brought about the reconciliation of the northern and southern branches of the imperial family, rewarding them handsomely for appointing him chancellor. With the further honor and revenue from the Ming court, Yoshimitsu cut a very grand figure. Like the Ming emperor in Peking, he repaired old temples and built new ones in Kyoto. For himself he had erected a palace in a spacious park and, on the side of a lake in the park, a pleasure pavilion ornamented with gold leaf. Naturally endowed with personality and tact, he succeeded in calming agitated clan leaders and restoring peace to the country for several decades.

Yoshimitsu's favorite diversion was a sort of dramatic per formance. From very early times, Yamato people had had Noh. Noh were held in the rice fields in autumn to celebrate the harvest; Noh were held on the hillsides in spring when love was in the air; Noh were held at court on ceremonial occasions when orchestras were assembled and noble youths danced and sang. At first the word was used indiscriminately for exhibitions of talent.

Both courts and temples had trained troupes of musicians and dancers. In early Ashikaga times four troupes were especially well known. One of these was at Isé, and another among the old temples which remained at Nara. The common people were eager to get a glimpse of court and temple life, both of which for centuries had been kept a mystery from them. When public performances were put on, therefore, both rich and poor flocked to see them. When Yoshimitsu attended a program given by the Nara group, he was so impressed that he invited the actors to come and entertain at his court. One of them became a great favorite with the third Ashikaga shogun and was always with him. His name was Seami.

All Seami had to do was to please his patron. He wrote and performed several Noh especially for Yoshimitsu's court. These took on a rather different form from the Noh given on the temple grounds. They had fewer characters, and were more refined in every way. Seami's Noh combined beautiful music, exquisite costumes and the recitation of verse and fine-sounding speeches with a certain grace and perfection of pantomime which was supposed to touch the observer as profoundly and unobtrusively as might a flower blooming at its proper time.

The stories acted as Noh were not new; they were familiar ones for the most part, incidents from the old annals, Kojiki and Nihongi, bits of shrine and temple legends, episodes from real life in other days, from the tales of Prince Genji and of the Heike. They were intended to express a real truth of life, not baldly or emphatically, but delicately, by means of idealistic

NOH STAGE

ER PAVILION

EXCERPT FROM MORI SCROLL

SCREEN SHOWING ARRIVAL OF PORTUGUESE SHIP

THOUSAND MAT ROOM, HIDEYOSHI'S PALACE

symbols. The meaning was hidden beneath the surface with superb esthetic restraint. The chief characters were usually supposed to be not real persons, but their spirits. Often there were no properties on the stage, only a few pine trees painted on the back wall.

Seami never taught actors exactly what to do, but he told them to observe nature closely. When they were acting pieces about the gods, he said, they ought to have pine trees thoroughly in mind. When doing exotic scenes they ought to think of red maple and autumn leaves; cherry blossoms were to be thought of while acting love scenes; and winter forests while doing Noh based on tales of Heike. There were nine kinds of flowers, he wrote, in his notes about the Noh,[4] and actors should be familiar with them all. The lowest kind of flower was a rough and heavy kind like the tulip; the supreme kind was the delicate wild orchid. In between came the strong but slender lily, the lotus, wide open, but still having style, the light blossom of the cherry and the solitary narcissus. Writers of Noh were sometimes described as "friends of the moon and flowers."

Several schools of Noh are currently performing. Some include Americans among their members and plays by contemporary writers in their repertoire. Some still cherish and, on special occasions, wear beautiful silk brocade robes which have been handed down from great actors to their most gifted pupils for centuries. Their program usually includes a variety of Noh, three perhaps, interspersed with short, humorous folk plays called Kyogen (foolish words).

Another popular pastime associated with Noh was Cha No Yu (Tea Ceremony). Tea drinking had an interesting history in Japan. According to tradition tea was first served at a party which Shomu-Tenno, the emperor who opened the eyes of the Nara Daibutsu, gave in his palace for a hundred and twenty monks. Both Saicho and Kukai are said to have brought tea seeds from China, where Zen priests drank the beverage in order to keep awake through long hours of meditation, and to have planted them in Japan in the early ninth century. The son of Emperor Kwammu, who founded Kyoto, having tasted the pale-green beverage in a monastery, was so delighted with it that he issued a proclamation ordering the planting of tea in various parts of the country. The greatest event in tea history, however, occurred in Kamakura, when the son of Minamoto Yoritomo and the able Hojo Masa became ill from drinking too much sake and was cured by drinking tea. The Zen priest-architect, Eisai, had just returned from China with a fresh supply of tea and prescribed it as a cure for his drunkenness. Eisai also wrote an essay, which came to be a classic, describing the healthful influence of tea drinking. He had brought new tea seeds with him from overseas, and arranged for them to be planted and cared for in a temple garden near Kyoto. The leaves from shrubs at Uji are still thought to be the best tea in the world.

From its early use by Zen priests to keep them awake through their meditations, and its later use as a sort of medicine, tea drinking in the fifteenth century became a very fashionable diversion of society. Men in high positions upon occasion gave a small jar of tea leaves as reward to a follower who had performed some noteworthy service. Such a gift was greatly prized, and the recipient invited his best friends to come and share in tasting the tea with him.

In such gatherings the Zen priest Shuko saw interesting possibilities. With a well-cultivated taste for painting and for pottery, the two chief arts of Sung, he was a keen collector of Chinese imports. Shuko no doubt perceived that if a sort of ceremony were made of tasting tea it would be profitable in more ways than one. He encouraged the serving of tea with beautiful utensils in a small room spotlessly clean and surrounded by a miniature landscape garden. Passing their time in this way, men would perhaps develop a love of purity and repose of manner which would mean much to them, and greater appreciation for rare works of art would be developed also.

Shogun Yoshimasa of the Silver Pavilion, patron of Shuko

and the arts, was the first to take up this idea, and tea ceremonies came rapidly into vogue. Soldiers seemed to enjoy them
as deeply as did men of gentler vocations. The greatest military
ruler of the sixteenth century summoned all tea lovers of the
country to bring their choicest teas and utensils to a party
which lasted ten days. And then, in the seventeenth century
when the country became unified and peaceful once more, tea
drinking became a nationwide institution and cultural discipline.
Even powerful governors were very proud to become masters
of the ceremony and poor people earnestly tried to imitate
them.[5]

As the Ashikaga shogunate continued, conditions in the
countryside of Japan went from bad to worse. Individuals participating in overseas trade were very wealthy and indulged
themselves in all sorts of extravagances, but the masses who
tried to squeeze a living from the soil were desperately poor.
While the shogun was spending fortunes on gold screens for
his palaces, on porcelain and painting, eighty thousand people
in the capital died of plague or famine within two months.
The streets and rivers were blocked with unburied dead.

Then the shogun ordered some temples to give doles, but
continued to levy taxes several times a year. Small farmers
found it impossible to raise either the tax rice or food for themselves, and so left their land. Since order and justice for the
people were far removed from the thoughts of the shogun's officials, local chieftains found it greatly to their advantage to take
large numbers of landless unemployed into their own service.
And since estates were of little value without farmers to work
them, wise landlords treated their peasants fairly enough to
make them want to stay. Others built barriers and toll gates on
their roads to prevent the free movement of peasants. In this
way many families became quite independent of the shogunate.

Some sought to obtain official favor by making presents to
one or more of the scores of court ladies with whom the shogun

was surrounded, but these ladies were rather well occupied striving to obtain favor for themselves.

Rivalry within and between the great families became so intense that riots broke out again in the capital; the imperial palaces and most of the important buildings were burned to the ground.

One shogun's wife made the best of this situation by taking the management of many public affairs into her own hands. She saw to the reinstallation of toll gates at the seven entrances to Kyoto on the pretense of rebuilding the imperial palace and then kept all the money herself. Struggles and fighting between great families continually increased and spread from the capital to the provinces. For over a century it went on. Not until about 1600 was peace finally restored.

The merchants and guilds called za added to the disorder of the country. From earliest times, in villages and ports, at temples and shrines, there had been merchants trying to sell their goods wherever people congregated. At first these merchants simply stood with their wares in large baskets and trays strapped to their bodies, or suspended on poles balanced over their shoulders. Then gradually markets had grown up in more populous centers where the merchants had a little sheltered space for doing business, which they called their za (seat, as a seat on the stock exchange). With Hojo orderliness and prosperity, many people had found it profitable to become merchants, and naturally the ones who sold the same kind of things were interested in one another. Some who sold oil at a certain shrine claimed that since they supplied the oil to keep the shrine lights always burning, the right to sell oil should be peculiarly theirs.

It was not until the Ashikaga period, however, when central authority was nil and everyone had to defend his own interests, that the zas came to be powerful organizations. Then in each large city the well-established salt dealers, for example, got together and formed a salt za. By paying a certain fee to the temple or government this group was given the exclusive right to sell salt in a definite area. Anyone else who tried to sell salt in their district was persecuted.

The privileges of the za were handed down from father to son. In Kyoto at this time there were zas of merchants selling silk, charcoal, rice, oil, fish, salt, timber, horses and many other things. There were also pawnbrokers and rice or money lenders. If any za thought another was infringing on its monopoly, a riot was started and the city was thrown into confusion. Some zas had rights in fairly large areas, and had to pass several toll gates in the course of delivering orders. If the tolls mounted high enough to make it worth while, the members of the za arrived armed en masse and tried to destroy the barrier. When they were successful they usually took charge of the barrier themselves and allowed their own members to pass through free, but collected taxes from all others, or forbade others to pass. Many of what were supposed to be public highways were usurped in this way and travel from one part of the country to another was both dangerous and expensive.

The elaborate entertainments and lavish spending of the shogun and of the officials and landlords, who tried to keep pace with him, filled the coffers of the za merchants with one hand but emptied them, for taxes, with the other. Gambling was a favorite pastime, and the pawnshops did a rushing business. When a group of samurai in the service of some great lord felt that too much of their equipment was being held for loans, they often attacked the warehouses, and by force rescued what they wanted. When a number of important officials and courtiers became too involved in debt, or when the populace were so hopelessly behind with taxes and obligated to the rice lenders that they rose up in active protest, an act of benevolence was declared and all accounts were canceled.

Even the shoguns had great financial difficulties. They were described as very wealthy by contemporary writers, who marveled at the splendors of their gold and silver pavilions, but this in itself is evidence of how poor the rest of the people must have been. Kinkaku-ji and Ginkaku-ji may have seemed superb in comparison with other homes of the day, but they are simple indeed compared with such palaces as the Vatican in Rome, the Alhambra in southern Spain and the Ducal Palace in Venice, which date from about the same period.

Court nobles now had to turn their arts and accomplishments to practical use. They joined with the priests as educators and entertainers of the people, commercializing their knowledge of etiquette by producing textbooks, their skill in writing by becoming secretaries to rich merchants, and their musical talents by acting in Noh plays.

Emperors now lived in ruined mansions surrounded by nothing but a bamboo fence. Children made mud toys at their gates, and sometimes peeped behind the blind that screened the imperial apartments. There were no abdicated emperors, because of economic conditions. At one time an emperor's burial had to be postponed until sufficient funds could be found for the funeral ceremonies. Groups of traveling minstrels were sent out to collect small gifts for the imperial court; emperors sold their autographs, and empresses wove little pouches of rice straw and string to exchange for rice.

An emperor who had no means for holding a ceremony when he succeeded to the throne left this advice to his son:

> You have been brought up as if there was no one to be afraid of. Though it may be all right while you are a child to act as if you were of highest position, if you behave so later, people will jeer at you. You must spend much time learning how to act before the people. Do not criticize others. Do not be short in temper; impatience will win you only contempt or hatred. Act always so as not to attract others' censure. These are my last words; keep them as a guide all your life.[6]

The court ladies who had found life so free and easy and full of opportunities in Fujiwara days now could find but little security. Many of them entered nunneries at an early age, or retired to the temples where princesses resided. Others who clung loyally to their husbands were the pioneers of Japanese womanhood as it is known to the world today. They were called the "wives who carefully wash the hulls off rice," [7] and willingly served their husbands with true domestic virtue.

Many priests in these days acted little differently from soldiers. The larger religious bodies like the more powerful landlords were continually struggling among themselves for first place in the capital. Throughout the provinces minor sects were constantly rising and falling, while major ones succeeded in establishing fortified strongholds in many places. As colleagues of the shoguns the Zen sect perhaps had the more favorable position.

During the Hojo regency Zen influence had grown in Kamakura and spread in all directions, but it had not become a real power until the Ashikaga shoguns moved their headquarters back to Kyoto. Though the long-established orders of Mount Hiei strongly opposed an invasion of their sphere of interest they could not prevent it. Five Zen monasteries were established in the ancient capital which served as radiating centers for a new cultural development.

All art forms were refined and simplified. Zen artists did not indulge in elaborate decoration with lavish use of gold and color. Their materials were unpainted wood, black ink and white paper. In architecture they made the most of beautiful proportion and the arrangement of spaces, including in their design the surrounding scenery and creating landscape gardens. Their temples gave a pleasant impression of economy which was distinctly esthetic; they had an air of functional efficiency which other temples lacked. Their teahouses and pavilions seemed almost like the works of nature itself, so well did they harmonize with their environment. Instead of the richly colored and ornamented sculpture of Fujiwara days when the deities Amida and Vairocana were supreme, Zen followers carved simple wooden portrait statues of men like themselves.

In place of the gorgeous pigments and exquisite detail of the classical Kyoto schools, Zen painters achieved their desired effects with a few clever strokes of black ink; the fewer and simpler the strokes, the greater the art. As in the Noh, great truths were represented by impressionistic symbols.

Perhaps a still greater contribution than their guidance in politics, economics or art, however, was made by able Zen priests to Japan in the realm of popular education and character building. In the social upheaval and hardships of the Ashikaga period they set an example for courageous enterprise and inspired self-confidence. Learning and spirituality, they demonstrated, are useless if they do not lead to practical attainments. "Face nature and man, and learn." "Fear nothing, get results." "Wherever you go, be master." This they taught, along with reading and writing, in their many schools. They would not blame environment for failure or wrongdoing. "Eels live in foul water," they said, "because they like it. The heart and environment are one. If your mind is clean and orderly, you will make your environment clean and orderly also. Do not be controlled; be master of every situation."

The line between cause and effect is often hard to draw. It may be that Zen teaching not only had an effect upon the spirit of the times, but was also in part a product of this spirit. The decline of imperial authority and the rise of a succession of military lords gave hope and confidence to many. Yamato farmers who for twelve centuries had seen only their own rice fields began to catch a larger vision. Yamato leaders who for eight centuries had thought chiefly of the supremacy of China had successfully withstood the Mongols. Chikafusa in his obscure essay had written, "Great Yamato is a divine country." The seeds of national consciousness were sown.

CHAPTER 10

CATHOLICS AND CASTLES

(1550–1600)

WHEN things stick together it is usually the result of pressure, and when nations become unified it is more often due to external than to internal forces. The sixteenth century in Japan is often called the Age of Unification, and three great military heroes are usually given the credit for consolidating the score or more of jealously contending clans and temple strongholds into the semblance of a nation. But what really gave impetus to Nobunaga, Hideyoshi and Iyeyasu was the arrival in Japan of Portuguese traders and Jesuit missionaries.

Japan, it seems, was discovered by storm-driven Portuguese adventurers early in 1542 and in September of the same year a ship's crew of a hundred arrived on the large southern island, Kyushu. Strange demons the Japanese thought the Portuguese —with their great stature and blue eyes in florid red-bearded faces. But when a Chinese in their company, writing Chinese characters on the sand with a stick, explained to the headman of the village where they landed that they were engaged in trade, all were given lodging in a Buddhist temple. They had one article with them which the Japanese regarded as a most extraordinary thing. The son of one of the welcoming natives later wrote:

It was about two or three feet long, straight, heavy and hollow. One end was closed and near this end was a small hole through which fire was to be lighted. Some mysterious medicine was put into it with a small round piece of lead, and when one lit the medicine through that hole the lead piece was discharged and hit everything. Light like lightning was seen, and noise like thunder heard; bystanders closed their ears with their hands and flying birds and running beasts fell before them. One day my father asked the foreigners to teach him its use and he soon became so skillful that he could nearly hit a white object placed a hundred steps away. He then bought two pieces of these things, regardless of the high price asked, and kept them as the most precious treasures of his house.[1]

With conditions as they were in Japan, firearms were exceedingly desirable, and local leaders from the various provinces of Kyushu vied with one another in trying to control the importation and production of them. First the lord of Satsuma seemed to have a monopoly on the traders and their cargoes —then the lord of Bungo attracted many of the Portuguese to his domains, but when another young lord offered still greater inducements, the ships all harbored in his port, Hirado. For many years Hirado was the center for foreign trade with Japan and in this trade firearms was the most important item. A few local blacksmiths went so far as to learn to make guns and powder, and devised cannon of large pine trees, hollowed out, and bound with iron hoops. Within very few years after the introduction of firearms, changes began to appear in both the social structure and the architecture of the country. Soldiers became more than ever a class by themselves and leaders had to devise new plans of fortification for their castles and strongholds.

In addition to firearms, such things as leather, glassware, woolen cloth and velvet, highly prized for collars, were included in the cargoes brought from Europe. Sugar, medicine, ceramic wares, cottons, silks and old Chinese coins were picked up by the Portuguese at various ports along their ocean route and traded in Japan for natural and fabricated products—gold, silver and especially copper, which afforded handsome profits.

The islanders also benefited materially from this trade, for the merchants spent freely while ashore and paid well for supplies and ship repairs. The apparently unlimited demand of the Portuguese for Japanese goods caused a marked rise in the price of everything native. The Japanese, unaware of the high value of copper in India and of the great profits to be made by converting copper into cannon, did not understand how the Portuguese could gain by their dealings, but were impressed by their achievements.

Soon after the Portuguese traders came the Jesuit missionaries—Father Xavier (later Saint Francis) arriving in Satsuma in 1549 was the first of these. Though it seemed to him that the Japanese language was invented by the devil to prevent his preaching, Father Xavier, after some success in Satsuma, proceeded to Hirado. From there he worked his way over to the main island of Japan and headed toward Kyoto. On the way he stopped at the court of the Ouchi clan, where, thanks to profitable mining, fishing and trade, and a recently successful display of authority in the capital, this family and its followers were enjoying a rather gay and carefree life. Sneered at for attacking their morals, the poorly clad Jesuit continued on his way, sometimes serving as baggage bearer for mounted merchants in order to make a living, and often sleeping in outhouses, or under the winter stars. His experiences in the capital were not encouraging either; it was a desolate place ruined by fires and fighting and deserted by courtiers. Since those who remained with the emperor would grant an imperial audience only in return for gold, Xavier in great disappointment retraced his steps. In Hirado merchants now advised him that he should dress himself better if he wished to make an impression on upper-class Japanese. Acting upon their suggestions, and representing himself this time as an envoy from the Viceroy of India, he went again to the court of Ouchi taking with him a clock and harpsichord such as had never been seen there before.

Now he created quite a sensation. The Ouchi chief was delighted with the presents and offered gold in return, but Xavier would not accept it: what he wanted was the gift of freedom to preach in the Ouchi domain. His lack of greed must have been very interesting to one familiar with the grasping hands of Buddhist priests: his request was granted with the gift of an old temple and some land for a church.[2]

Face of Japanese clock

The Japanese, who had always associated with religion and government a knowledge of the weather and the movement of heavenly bodies and regarded such knowledge with high esteem, were very much impressed with Xavier's discourses on astronomy. He proved to them that the world was round and explained comets, thunderbolts and showers. They were, therefore, inclined to think that a person so wise in science could not be far wrong in religion. Besides, this religion coming as it did, via India with shaven-headed priests, unintelligible rituals, rosaries, incense and images, to all of which they were accustomed, was thought by many Japanese to be merely a superior kind of Buddhism. Teachings about a personal creator of the world, of whom they had heard nothing from Chinese sources of knowledge, seemed less credible, and the idea that beloved ancestors as heathens were doomed to pass eternity in hell was greatly distressing. Japanese did admire, however, the missionaries who, though pelted and spat upon, merely wiped their faces and continued to preach. Seeing that the Fathers were admired also by the Portuguese traders whom they were eager to favor, many Japanese listened to the Christian doctrines with the same respectful attention they had given to new teachers from Korea or China. But when Jesuits began to argue with Buddhist priests that the Christian God and saints were the only true ones and that Buddhist deities and doctrines were mere fiction, trouble was in the wind.

After a stay of two and a half years in Japan, Xavier resolved to make China his chief goal and wrote: "If the Chinese adopt the Christian religion, the Japanese will also." [3] On leaving the country he took with him a keen young convert with the adopted name of Bernard. Though Xavier succumbed to an illness a year or so later, this youth, probably the first Japanese to set foot in Europe, finally reached Rome and Lisbon. Joining the Society of Jesus, he entered the College of Coimbra and ended his days in Portugal.

In the course of the next thirty years the Jesuits went through many ups and downs in Japan. One daimyo or feudal lord whom they converted turned the administration of his estates over to his son and devoted the rest of his life to preaching and charitable work among his vassals. Even when banished as the result of political complications he continued in exile to live as a Christian missionary. Some converts became fanatical, burning shrines and temples and ordering people to give up Buddhist altars in their homes. Others became Christians and made their vassals adopt the new faith also—only to keep in the good graces of the Portuguese merchants. Some Buddhists persuaded the emperor to sign a letter ordering the Jesuit in the capital to be driven out, but Nobunaga was the power of the throne, and the missionary in question, named Froez, managed to find favor with Nobunaga and win the great hero's protection.

When Froez first saw Nobunaga, the latter was on the drawbridge of the new castle he was rearing, surrounded by a numerous court and seven thousand men under arms. Froez saluted Nobunaga in Japanese fashion but was requested to rise and cover himself, for the sun was hot. Nobunaga then inquired of the Father his age, how many years he had studied, how long he had been in Japan, and whether if the Japanese did not become Christians he would return to India. In reply to the last question, Froez declared: "If there were but one Christian in Japan I would remain to instruct and fortify him in the faith, but I am not yet reduced to that position, for there are a considerable number of believers in the empire." [4]

"But why have you no house or church in Kyoto?" Nobunaga went on, and Froez returned: "Your Highness, it is because of the Buddhist priests who have driven us out of those we had."

Though Nobunaga seemed to be favorably inclined toward the well-bred and learned Jesuits, who approached important people in the capital with polished diplomacy and guarded their safety against Buddhist intrigues, it was not until twelve years later that he bestowed upon them a site near his castle with timber and furnishings for a thirty-four-room house. The chief work of the Jesuits in this grand establishment was the training of twenty-five young noblemen in Portuguese and Latin, Catholic doctrines, painting, drawing, carving and vocal and instrumental music. When Nobunaga paid them a visit, it is said he was delighted with their performances.

In 1580, the Jesuit's annual letter from Japan to the pope reported that Nobunaga had asked the missionary to show him on a globe the way he had come from Europe, had commented seriously that those who undertake such voyages must be great-minded men and with a smile had added: "Perhaps this gospel of yours is really some fine thing." [5]

In 1582, the annual letter reported that the number of Christians in Japan was a hundred and fifty thousand, of whom many were nobles; a hundred and twenty-five thousand of these were on the island of Kyushu, while twenty-five thousand were scattered on the main island, and altogether there were about two hundred churches. The visitor-general of the Jesuits in the East who made the survey for this report caused the Japanese much surprise on account of his great height and the Negro slave he had with him. They had never seen such a tall man or such a dark one before. At first sight of the Negro, Nobunaga burst into laughter and tried to rub the black off. Then, because of his interest, the slave was given to him and remained with him until his death.

On the same ship that carried the visitor-general and his report to Europe it was decided that an embassy of four Japanese should be sent to bear friendly messages from three Christian lords in Kyushu to the pope in Rome, and Philip II of Spain. (Portugal had passed under his rule in 1580.)

After almost two years of strenuous voyaging, according to a contemporary account, these envoys were welcomed at Lisbon in 1584; at Madrid they were received with great distinction by the king himself; at Leghorn a de' Medici duke was waiting to attend them and escort them to the carnival at Pisa and thence via Florence to Rome, where Pope Gregory XIII (to whom we owe our calendar) provided for them a marvelous reception. The procession formed to escort them to the Vatican was headed by the pope's Light Horse, followed by the Swiss Guard, the officers of the cardinals and the carriages of the ambassadors of Spain, France, Venice, and the Roman princes. It also included the whole Roman nobility on horseback, pages with trumpets and cymbals, and officers of the palace all in red robes. Then followed the Japanese on horseback in their national dress, three silken gowns of a light fabric one over the other, splendidly embroidered with fruits, leaves and birds. In their girdles they wore the two swords, symbols of Japanese gentility. Their heads, shaven, except the hair round the ears and neck, which was gathered into a queue bent upward, had no covering. Their whole expression and manner, modest and amiable, but with a conscious sentiment of nobility, impressed the bystanders very favorably. The appearance of these young men, who had essayed so many dangers and fatigues to pay their homage to the Holy See, drew tears and sobs from the audience, and the pope himself, when they prostrated themselves at his feet, hastened to raise them up and embraced them many times.[6]

Following the death of Gregory XIII, the Japanese ambassadors assisted at the coronation of the new pope, Sixtus V, and were given gold chains and medals and shown many favors by him. They declined an invitation from Henry III to visit France and started their return voyage in 1586, after twenty-one months in Europe.

The year this embassy left Japan Nobunaga was assassinated. Having succeeded to his father's estates in Owari province, east of Kyoto, in the same year that Xavier landed in Satsuma, Nobunaga, though only sixteen, had soon shown himself to be a man of inflexible will, resolved to subdue all rival leaders and to create a new central government. In carrying out this purpose Nobunaga was the nearest to an iconoclast that Japan has ever produced; he demolished Buddhist monasteries for materials with which to rebuild the emperor's and the shogun's palaces, and allowed no temple bell to ring lest it interfere with the gong summoning his workmen. When its militant priests fought against him, Nobunaga did not hesitate to order burned to the ground even the great temple center on Mount Hiei which dated from Saicho's day, with all its beautiful old paintings and sculpture and its countless historical documents. He welcomed the Jesuit Fathers on more friendly terms than he

did many of his own vassals and favored them more than the
long-established Buddhist priests, but he actually gave the newcomers only just enough to keep them hoping that he would
give more. Though he did not live to accomplish his purpose,
when Nobunaga was assassinated by the same good Buddhist
retainer whom he had ordered to destroy Mount Hiei, he had
under his control thirty-two of the sixty-eight provinces of
Japan, and these compactly situated around the capital.

Nobunaga was succeeded by his general, Hideyoshi. Born
the peasant son of a foot soldier, Hideyoshi as a lad had been
so wild that his parents could not train him. They sent him to a
temple school, but he hated the sight of books, and, whenever
he could manage it, armed his fellow students with bamboo
rods and got them to fight under his generalship.[7]

"You priests are all a set of beggars," he told his teachers.
"There is no reason why a brave child born in a world of com-
motion and strife should become a beggar."

At twelve, he beat and smashed with candlesticks the image
of Amida before which he was directed to place an offering of
food. Then he was expelled from the temple, and subsequently
dismissed from thirty-eight jobs in succession. Uncannily quick-
witted, resourceful, and a match for anyone in talking, he
usually managed to get where he wished to go and to meet
whom he wished to meet. Having picked Nobunaga as the
most promising of many militant landlords, Hideyoshi quickly
raised himself to a trusted position in this leader's service and
helped to promote him to first place in the nation.

Hideyoshi is described by the historian Murdoch as the sort
of man who endeavored not to kill two birds with one stone,
but to disable many fowls with a single missile, catch them and
use them to provide eggs for his own table. All of his outstanding achievements show this characteristic. He was not so much
a destroyer as Nobunaga was, but rather a builder and organ-
izer on a colossally daring scale.

In the brief span of ten years after the assassination of Nobunaga, Hideyoshi extended and consolidated his power over the whole of Japan. With heroic force and tactful negotiation he won the allegiance of all the great leaders of the country, initiated a national land survey for purposes of tax assessment and organized at Osaka a central administration noted for its efficiency. He conciliated the militant Buddhist clergy who had been Nobunaga's strongest enemies, and used them to help him win over the Kyushu clans. He disarmed all the civilians of the country by ordering them to turn over their swords and weapons for the building of great religious statues. With equal cleverness he invited all the chief daimyos of the country to his magnificent new palace for a royal reception and there, in the presence of the emperor, made them swear their loyalty to the Son of Heaven and to his chief minister, Hideyoshi, the Taiko. It was agreed that any who broke their oaths should be punished by their fellows. He also embarked upon the conquest of Korea and China.

While visiting the shrine of Yoritomo near Kamakura, Hideyoshi is said to have patted the image of the first shogun familiarly on the back and remarked: "My friend, only you and I have been able to take all the power under heaven. You, however, were of illustrious descent, and not like me, sprung from peasants. But after conquering all the empire I intend to conquer China. What do you think of that?"

There are many interpretations of Hideyoshi's Korean expedition. Some say that he was afraid of the Kyushu daimyos because of their relations with the Portuguese and Spaniards, and wanted to test their loyalty, drain their resources and get them out of Japan. Some say he had to find active employment for all the soldiers of the country, and some that it was intended chiefly to satisfy his ego and immortalize his name. It is also said that this campaign was not the result of one man's ambition, but an attempt at colonization and trade expansion inspired by the example of the Portuguese and undertaken as a cooperative venture on a profit-sharing basis. Undoubtedly there is truth in each of these explanations, for Hideyoshi's projects were usually devised to accomplish many ends, but the fundamental fact that Japan was poor in natural resources must not be overlooked.

Agriculture was the mainstay of the nation, but when earthquakes, droughts, storms and pestilences destroyed the crops, or when unsettled conditions in the country gave farmers cause to take up arms, so that planting and harvesting was interfered with, there was always a great depression, from which the only escape was profitable overseas trade. In the midst of the disorders signaling the end of the Fujiwara regime, Taira Kiyomori had come to power on a program of trade expansion. After the wholesale migration of farmers from northeastern to southwestern Japan when the Mongol invasion threatened, even the Hojo government, the most thrifty and economical one the country ever had, could not escape bankruptcy. Then, while the rest of the country remained in poverty, the Ashikaga shoguns with their Zen-priest trade advisers had made their way to gold and silver pavilions through mercantile adventures based on wider experience than Kiyomori had had at his disposal. But just as waves never wear their gleaming crests for long—as snow melts and flowers fade—so is it with the affairs of men. After Ashikaga Yoshimitsu's peak of prosperity came a gradual decline into the miserably disorganized state in which the first Portuguese found Japan.

Reared in the best farming part of the country, familiar with its possibilities and problems, Hideyoshi, when Nobunaga sent him down along the Inland Sea, saw clearly how limited were the opportunities of agriculture as compared with those the growing ports offered. Swiftly his imagination created a Japanese empire with vast continental resources and markets from which to draw wealth.

Though he was warned by the Korean king that the project of trying to conquer China was "like a bee trying to sting a tortoise through its shell," and though he was unable to persuade the Portuguese to sell or rent him two large vessels as he had hoped they would, Hideyoshi was not dissuaded from his purpose. The maritime daimyos were ordered to supply a number of ships in proportion to their revenues, two ships for each hundred thousand koku of rice. Every fishing village had to send ten sailors for each hundred houses. Troops to the number of a hundred and thirty thousand were carried overseas and, in Korea, captured castle after castle in rapid succession.

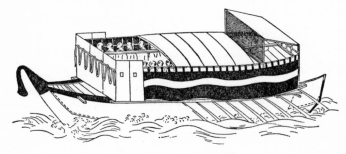

Sixteenth-century warship

A very short time was sufficient for the armies from Kyushu to march the whole length of the peninsula and threaten the Chinese border. Like their European brethren they were none the worse soldiers for being Christian. But then Chinese troops came to help the Koreans. Supplies and fresh troops for the Japanese armies sent out from home had a more difficult time getting through. The Koreans, reinforced by the Chinese, were now prepared for them and shot fire arrows into the small wooden Japanese boats; they also had a ship which looked like a tortoise covered over with iron plates and with spikes at the water line. In this they would pretend to retreat before a Japanese boat until the latter was pursuing them at full speed; then they would suddenly turn their oarsmen round and ram the pursuers' boats with their spiked armor. With ships destroyed and supplies cut off in this manner, the armies could not hold out, and so a truce was declared.[8]

Hideyoshi had envoys present demands to the Chinese, asking among less significant things that permits for commercial intercourse be sent to Japan, and that half of Korea also be ceded to her. After long-drawn-out parleys in which the Taiko thought of himself as victor, the Chinese emperor, instead of agreeing to the Japanese leader's demands, sent an envoy to present him with a gold seal, gold headpiece and robe of state. The coming of the envoy raised Hideyoshi's hopes very high; he expected to be appointed King of China. When at the elaborate ceremony of welcome held in Osaka Castle the envoy read his official message, however, it was only to appoint the Taiko King of Japan. This made the great one so furious that he issued orders for a new campaign. The same Kyushu generals went to Korea again, but this time met with less success, and in 1598, just before he died, Hideyoshi ordered that they be recalled.

The prospects of the Jesuits under Hideyoshi had continued, now bright, now dim. On one occasion he had signed a paper granting them the right to preach throughout Japan and ordered a copy sent to Europe that it might be known there how greatly he favored Christianity. But after his experiences among the Christian daimyos of Kyushu, whom the Buddhist priests had helped him to bring into submission, Hideyoshi sent a set of questions to a Jesuit official.

Why and by what authority, Hideyoshi inquired, did he and his priests constrain Hideyoshi's subjects to become Christians? Why did they overthrow temples and persecute Buddhist priests? Why did they eat animals useful to man, such as cows and oxen? And why did they allow Portuguese merchants to buy Japanese and sell them as slaves in India?

When satisfactory answers to these questions were not forthcoming all Jesuits were ordered to leave Japan, but the order was not enforced and they carried on their work under cover. Three years later, in 1590, the four Japanese envoys, returning from their trip to Rome, brought with them maps, globes,

clocks and watches, musical instruments and new kinds of
armor and weapons which interested the islanders greatly.
These young travelers attracted large crowds to see and hear
them wherever they went, and they helped to make many
converts among fashionable people. In Hideyoshi's own household a tea master and a consort became Christians. Courtiers
who cared nothing for the religion of the Portuguese began to
wear tunics, balloon trousers, long cloaks and high-crowned
hats. They even carried rosaries and crucifixes and learned to
recite pater nosters, so as to be in fashion. Bread, spongecake
and shrimps fried in batter (called as they were by the Portuguese pan, kastera, and tempura) began to appear on the small
lacquer trays and tables of the Japanese elite. Playing cards
were also introduced, and those who used them in imitation of
the Portuguese called them karuta. Aesop's *Fables* were translated into Japanese by an ex-Zen monk, a leper and Jesuit
convert, and this book was printed in the Latin alphabet by a
mission printing press in 1593.

The same year that Hideyoshi had dispatched his first expedition to Korea, Spaniards of the Franciscan order had come
to Japan from Manila and established themselves in Kyoto to
the great annoyance of the Jesuits. From that time on there was
continual rivalry between these orders. In 1596, the *San Felipe*
was shipwrecked on the coast of the island Shikoku. Thinking
perhaps to frighten the Japanese into treating him well, the
captain of this vessel pointed out all the Spanish and Portuguese
possessions on a map and explained: "Our kings begin by sending into countries they wish to conquer, missionaries who
induce the people to embrace our religion, and when they have
made progress, troops are sent who combine with the Christians. Then our kings have little trouble in accomplishing the
rest." [9]

This outspoken boast was quite in line with what Hideyoshi
had long been suspecting, and so, for the sake of what he considered to be the safety and best interests of his country, he

ordered that the missionaries be put to death. Twenty-three Franciscans and three Jesuits were crucified at Nagasaki in 1597. Of a hundred and twenty-five other Jesuits in Japan, eleven sailed away—the rest remained to work surreptitiously and without interference in Kyushu under the protection of influential converts.

In 1598, Hideyoshi died. Though he is justly famous as a great military hero, strangely enough, his most lasting influence was on art and architecture. The results of his patronage in these fields may still be enjoyed today.

From very early times Japanese clan leaders had built their so-called castles in easily guarded mountain passes and other naturally fortified places, usually surrounding them with ditches, embankments of earth and bundles of rice straw and bamboo. Nobunaga had introduced a new style of castle. He chose a site near Lake Biwa with excellent transportation facilities. Establishing there a well-protected settlement of officers and soldiers, he also encouraged merchants who did not belong to any za to come there and enjoy the privileges of free trade. Hideyoshi himself, in 1583, exchanged a piece of property in Kyoto for the best commercial site on the main island of Japan and started to build Osaka Castle. But it was not until his generals returned from their Korean expedition that this castle began to assume the proportions of a veritable walled city.

The Koreans had had some knowledge of wall building ever since the days of the Han Empire. During internal struggles and successive invasions of their peninsula by Sui and T'ang armies and the hordes of Kublai Khan, they had good reason to put this knowledge to use. Then all the principal towns were surrounded with great stone ramparts and within the walls were built towers, not with sides rising several stories high under one roof, but with a number of single-storied and roofed sections seemingly piled one atop the other. These were the models for the tremendous and beautiful castles which appeared in Japan toward the end of the sixteenth century.[10] It has been said that Japanese castles were the result of Portuguese influence, with the implication that they were copied from European architecture. They were the result of Portuguese influence, yes, but there was nothing Portuguese about them. They were simply a natural reaction of Japanese feudal lords to the growing use of firearms and fire-throwing devices which came with the Portuguese. With graceful curves of wall and roof to lighten their serious solidity, they were a typically Japanese response to Portuguese advances.

For the building of Osaka Castle, Hideyoshi ordered materials to be brought from thirty provinces. A hundred boats a day plying the three rivers surrounding the castle carried the huge granite blocks for the walls and the stout timbers for the building. Sixty thousand men were employed three years in constructing its moat twenty feet deep, its enormous walls ten miles around, its nine-storied tower and grand halls. Newly worked mines in Sado and Kai produced abundant gold for decoration. On the outside, the roofs were covered with richly gilded tiles, and on the inside, ceilings, pillars, doorframes and hardware all were plated with gold. Hideyoshi's bedroom was fifty-four feet square, and his bed, five by eight feet, had poppy-colored bedding and gold ornaments at the head. Near by usually stood the great black-lacquer box containing the Taiko's armor and on this, when he was not wearing it, usually lay his sword.

In addition to his Osaka Castle, Hideyoshi had a Palace of Assembled Pleasures, Jurakutei, in Kyoto. This also was surrounded by a stone wall, three thousand paces on each side, and the roof tiles were made to look "like jeweled tigers breathing in the wind and golden dragons intoning in the clouds." [11] When this palace was completed and Hideyoshi moved in from Osaka, several hundred gilded and silvered boats carried the procession up the River Yodo, and five hundred carriages with five thousand coolies transported them from the river to the palace itself. Nobles and populace flocked to meet him and remained for days and days celebrating at his gates. In the garden almost five thousand loads of earth were carried to build an artificial mountain, and there, too, a dancing stage was erected with music rooms to right and left where elaborate performances were given. The utmost skill of artists of all kinds contributed to the Taiko's pleasure. When in 1588 the emperor set aside a century-old tradition and came to Jurakutei in his ox-drawn carriage accompanied by scores of courtiers to be the guest of Hideyoshi, he was so delighted with the place and entertainment, it is said, that he stayed five days instead of three.

The last decade of the sixteenth century found Kyoto in high and exuberant spirits. Perhaps these were the best years the capital ever had. Certainly they were the best since Michinaga's heyday around the year 1000, and the three centuries to come were to bring it little to boast of. Even with the Chinese and Korean situation on his mind the Taiko gave one grand entertainment after another, fetes in the melon garden, nationwide tea-ceremony celebrations, excursions to Mount Koya for visiting his mother's memorial temple, to Yoshino for viewing the cherry blossoms, to Daigo Temple for disporting himself with his friends in the beautiful gardens he had planned. At times he had Noh performances every three or four days, and being very enthusiastic about these had special plays composed in which he acted himself. Hideyoshi was fairly generous with the court. He treated the farmers well who tilled the fields near the capital. Foreign missionaries and traders continually afforded new interests to citizens of Kyoto; merchants flourished there; gold and silver mines began to supply new wealth, and artists had opportunities such as they had seldom enjoyed before.

The peasant son of a foot soldier was drawing revenue from the whole country; he had risen to the chief place in the nation and aspired to be King of China. Nothing was too magnificent or grandiose for him, nothing too rich or colorful. There were interior walls and doors of extravagantly spacious proportions to be painted in glorious and energetic designs. There were heroically splendid gates to be lacquered and carved with peacocks, tigers, lions and peony blossoms.

Eitoku and Sanraku were the foremost artists of the age. Their work is in stunning contrast to the Zen-style paintings of Sesshu, the greatest artist of the Ashikaga era. Sesshu was subtly spiritual and restrained in the use of color. Many of his masterpieces are but a few strokes of black ink on a piece of white silk or paper, serene harmonious strokes in some, explosive strokes in others, excitingly intersecting at right angles, but always his work seems to portray dignity maintained at desperate odds—the dignity of winter, of storm-cleft rocks and struggling gnarled old pines.

There were no odds for the arts of the late sixteenth and early seventeenth centuries. They are heroic in spirit, but they show the power and glory without the struggle and conquest, the blossoming forth of vigorous life without any counteracting forces. They are spring and summer, without autumn and winter. The subjects include Portuguese galleons in full sail, richly clad merchants in scenes teeming with life and exotic splendor; maps of the whole world together with Chinese legendary figures; tigers in bamboo groves symbolizing heroic lords with associates bending to their will; all-powerful dragons with eyes that look in eight directions; monkeys which signify unconventional character and originality; life-size cherry trees in full bloom with birds flying through their branches.

In his early childhood Eitoku studied painting with his grandfather, the famous founder of a great school of Japanese painting. While still very young he excelled the work of his own father and was taken as official painter into the service of Nobunaga. A story says that Eitoku sometimes painted with a monstrous brush of straw but, however that may be, his work

NOBUNAGA VISITING ARTIST MOTONOBU

NAGOYA CASTLE

HIDEYOSHI'S GARDEN AT GO-DAIGO TEMPLE

INTERIOR AND EXTERIOR VIEWS OF NIKKO SHRINE

is full of life and animation, done with bold and vigorous strokes and brilliant colors on backgrounds of gold leaf. Among his masterpieces is a pair of folding screens, each eight feet high by sixteen long, one painted with fabulous lions, the other with hawks on a pine tree.

The second great painter mentioned above as representative of the heroic period was Sanraku. As a boy Sanraku was made page to Hideyoshi and carried the general's cane when he went to supervise the building of Osaka Castle. One day while Hideyoshi was busy Sanraku began intently to draw a horse in the sand. Hideyoshi returning, and observing the boy's concentration and talent, asked him if he would like to be an artist. As a result of this incident, he came to be the adopted son and pupil of the great Eitoku. Sanraku reached the climax of his achievement in painting for Hideyoshi in his prime. Whole walls he covered with backgrounds of gold leaf and over them painted blossoming trees and flowers of all seasons, blooming together in luxuriant profusion, like joyful gardens of eternal paradise.

After the passing of Hideyoshi, the great artists who had served him were eagerly sought by powerful feudal lords and provincial nobles throughout the country. As they scattered from the capital to the castles of their new patrons, a keen appreciation for works of beauty developed far and wide. In another hundred years, even the common people had their cheap but artistic prints, their beautifully patterned silks and household wares of exquisitely decorated porcelain and lacquer.

When the Taiko came to the end of his days, he had only one child, a boy of seven years whom he loved very dearly. In order to preserve for this son, Hideyori, the supreme place he had won for himself, Hideyoshi appointed from among his trusted and able associates five senior ministers to govern the nation jointly until the lad should come of age.

It is recorded that upon his deathbed Hideyoshi summoned

to him Tokugawa Iyeyasu, the ablest and wealthiest of these five senior ministers and said: "After my death you alone will be able to keep the empire tranquil. I, therefore, bequeath the whole country to you and trust that you will expend all your strength in governing it. My son is still young. I beg that you will look after him." [12]

CHAPTER 11

AN OLD SOLDIER ORGANIZES FOR PEACE

(SEVENTEENTH CENTURY)

AFTER two centuries of almost continuous feudal strife for mastery of the capital climaxed by the Taiko's enormous overseas campaign, what Japan needed more than anything else in 1600 was peace. And peace Tokugawa Iyeyasu was determined to establish.

Like Nobunaga and Hideyoshi, his seniors by a few years, Iyeyasu was a son of the soil from the Mount Fuji region. Like them also he had risen to prominence and power through his own military prowess, sound judgment and tenacity of purpose. He had been a loyal ally of Nobunaga and after the latter's assassination had fought against Hideyoshi who was trying to take the control of the country away from Nobunaga's heirs. Recognizing Hideyoshi's real greatness, Iyeyasu later had submitted to him, but yet had shown himself sufficiently great to command the Taiko's honest respect. Hideyoshi had considered it a good bargain to give the Tokugawa leader, in exchange for five small provinces in central Japan, eight large ones in the northeast out of range of capital activities.

Iyeyasu loved and believed in the soil as the true foundation of national prosperity. Unlike the lords of the lands in the southwest whose interest was largely in overseas trade, he concentrated on developing mining and agriculture in the Kwanto. Consequently, when the Kyushu daimyos—owners of fiefs yielding ten thousand or more koku a year—returned from their unsuccessful overseas adventure with both troops and treasuries exhausted, Iyeyasu was the lord of lands yielding about two and a half million koku of rice each year.

Since Japan at this time was comprised of over two hundred individually owned estates, some idea of Iyeyasu's relative importance is given by the fact that the total annual yield of all these, including Iyeyasu's, was estimated at between nineteen and twenty-eight million koku (approximately five bushels) of which about forty thousand were reserved for the imperial court.[1]

With his influence already strong when the Taiko passed away, Iyeyasu did not overestimate his own power. He was determined to give the country peace under Tokugawa domination, but he did not press the issue. A popular folk tale contrasts the characters of the three great heroes of sixteenth-century Japan in verses supposedly written while they were listening for the first cuckoo's song in the spring. Nobunaga's poem went:

> The cuckoo—
> If it does not sing
> I'll put an end to it.

And Hideyoshi's:

> The cuckoo—
> If it does not sing
> I'll show it how.

The verse supposed to be typical of Iyeyasu is:

> The cuckoo—
> If it does not sing
> I'll wait until it does.

Among the maxims supposed to be favorites of Iyeyasu is this: "Life is like a long journey with a heavy load. Let thy steps be slow and steady, that thou stumble not."

Nobunaga had become acting shogun of Japan at thirty-five; Hideyoshi had succeeded him at the age of forty-six. When his turn came Iyeyasu was fifty-seven and he had had time to consider well the difficulties that threatened his ambitions. In the first place, there was China, which might be expected at any time to send an expedition in retaliation for Hideyoshi's invasion of Korea. Then, with their center in Osaka, were several other leaders only slightly less important than himself, who had ships and men all over the Far East and meddled in politics in the Philippines, Thailand and India. The interests of this group were apt to conflict with those of the Tokugawas. Another difficult group was the imperial court in Kyoto, still made up largely of Fujiwaras and not very potent in practical affairs, but regarded with a sort of religious respect. Moreover, in Kyushu and flourishing centers such as Kyoto, Osaka and Sakai on the main island, there were the increasingly aggressive groups of Christians, both native and foreign, whose loyalty was directed to God, the pope and the holy fathers rather than to an old soldier like Iyeyasu. All four of these were potential sources of national disturbance and menaces to Iyeyasu's plans for peace.

Happily, the situation with China was smoothed over without great difficulty by the priests who under one ruler after another had served the government as advisers in foreign affairs. The most immediate opposition Iyeyasu had to face came from the rival leaders who were his colleagues in the regency appointed by Hideyoshi. As soon as the Taiko passed away, Iyeyasu began to fortify his position by marrying his numerous sons and daughters to various prominent persons scattered throughout the country. An objection was raised at once by more loyal supporters of the Taiko's heir, Hideyori, and came to a head in the battle of Sekigahara. In this encounter Iyeyasu took long chances—the Osaka confederates had a hundred and thirty thousand men in the field against his eighty thousand, but by a coincidence of good luck and good management he won. This victory enabled Iyeyasu to obtain surrenders and oaths of allegiance from the majority of the nation's leaders, and after this one battle his foremost position came to be generally recognized. So impressive was this victory that even today in Japan the word Sekigahara is used proverbially for a decisive struggle.

In 1603, by a new road which he had constructed from the Kwanto, the Tokugawa leader, with great show, marched into the capital ten thousand soldiers a day for seventeen days. Soon after this the emperor named him both Minister of the Right and Sei-i-Tai Shogun and presented him with an ox-drawn chariot to ride in. When Iyeyasu appeared at the palace to render thanks for this appointment, it is said the emperor with his own hands proffered a cup of wine and expressed his gratification that wars no longer convulsed the nation and that the foundations of peace were laid.

Osaka sympathizers, however, were still a strong force to be reckoned with and Iyeyasu was content to let those who wished to, think that he was only holding in trust and consolidating the power of the Taiko to turn it over to Hideyori when he came to manhood. The same year that he was appointed shogun, Iyeyasu arranged a marriage contract between his granddaughter and this twelve-year-old boy, and took up his residence for a while in the palace which Hideyoshi had built near Kyoto.

With his own son he discussed the possibilities of setting up their shogunate in Osaka, but Tokugawa interests and Tokugawa strength were centered in the Kwanto. In the Kwanto, therefore, at Yedo castle, twenty miles farther from Kyoto than Minamoto Yoritomo's former capital, Kamakura, Iyeyasu soon established the administrative headquarters of his government. This castle, if such it might be called, had been built by a poet soldier more than a century before and described by him in the verse:

My dwelling adjoins a fir tree plain;
Hard by rolls the sea;
The lofty peak of Fuji-san is seen from below the eaves.[2]

When Iyeyasu first saw Yedo (having been transferred there by Hideyoshi's maneuvers) the wooden walls were weather-stained, the thatched roofs leaked and the entrance steps were made of three planks from the hull of an old ship. A most trusted adviser, thinking it ill befitted the dignity of his lord, suggested: "We may leave the interior for the present, but the entrance really ought to be rebuilt."

Iyeyasu, it is said, laughingly called this an extravagant idea and replied: "Our retainers must be seen to before anything else." [3]

His thirty-two chief supporters were assigned villages and fields roughly in the shape of a horseshoe surrounding Yedo, and each was advised to build as quickly as possible a simple house for his family and come up to the castle for duty. While quarters were being prepared for them the more fortunate retainers enjoyed the comforts of lodging in a Buddhist temple; some stayed with farmers in the neighborhood, or raised temporary barracks, but others had to be satisfied with shelter several miles from the castle. Houses were built and the castle repaired, and a town grew up, which served as a center of government for the Tokugawa estates in the Kwanto.

When Iyeyasu was appointed shogun of the whole country, however, and chose Yedo as the seat of his government, great improvements were made. Landlords from Kyushu, who only recently had acknowledged his supremacy, were ordered by the new shogun to supply labor and materials to reconstruct the city and to build a really worthy castle. Hundreds of vessels which had been built for the Korean expedition were now used for transporting workmen and huge blocks of stone. Hills were leveled, moats dug and marshes filled in. A bridge built over a canal in Yedo at this time was called Nippon-bashi (Nippon Bridge) because, it is said, all Japan had a hand in making it.

When the daimyos from the southwest became exhausted from the enterprise, those in the Kwanto were asked to take it up. There were miles and miles of canals and walls. The castle itself was three castles in one protected by a network of moats and stone ramparts. The white-plaster buildings were roofed with dark tiles and had gold ornaments on the ridges and corners. But though it suggested the power of Iyeyasu, it also, if compared with Osaka, gave evident proof of his thrift.

In 1605, to preclude the possibility of interruption of the Tokugawa peace program should he himself pass away, Iyeyasu had one of his many sons appointed shogun. This enabled the son to become well experienced and established in his position while the father was still alive to guide him. Though the aging hero moved to a castle in his favorite region farther west, Yedo remained the chief center of government in Japan and, with its name changed to Tokyo, still enjoys this honor today.

Iyeyasu paid frequent visits to Yedo, indulging on the way in hunting with hawks, a sport which was his lifelong enthusiasm. Hawking he defended as an excellent means of keeping up horsemanship and other military disciplines in times of peace. It also afforded an opportunity, he said, for getting intimately acquainted with the country and country people. He often let his ladies ride along on such excursions, saying it gave them a good chance for exercise and a natural life such as they were unable to enjoy in their usual formal surroundings.

The Yedo government was designed to establish and perpetuate peace throughout the nation under Tokugawa supremacy. It was a centralized feudalism. Chief in command was the shogun and reporting to him were two groups of officials, the Tairo, Great Elderly Men who were superior soldiers, and the Roju, a group of political advisers chosen from among the well-tried supporters of the ruling family. From among the Roju was appointed one as governor of Kyoto, whose duty it was to watch the activities of the court and make sure that no reactionary movements started there. One was also appointed later as superintendent of Osaka Castle.

The Tairo and Roju met together to discuss and decide upon affairs of state, and under their supervision were five important offices: the shrine and temple administration; chief executives of the treasury and of public utilities, buildings, communications, etc.; the very important administrator of Tokugawa-controlled towns such as Yedo, Sakai and some Kyushu ports; and the great watchmen or spying elders who were supposed to keep close watch on all happenings and to report their findings at meetings of the Roju. Under the administrator of towns were lesser municipal officials, each responsible for and kept informed by those from the next rank below. Among these were the representatives of the leading merchants, the landowners, the house owners or family heads, and of the five-family units into which the population was divided. A similar organization was set up for controlling rural domains. Not all of the country was under the shogun's direct jurisdiction, but most places of political, commercial and industrial importance, comprising about a quarter of the total land area, belonged to him. The daimyos of other fiefs, having sworn allegiance to Iyeyasu, were allowed independence in regulating the internal arrangements of their domains in such matters as finance, justice, education and industry. The shogunate reserved the right to declare war and peace, to coin money and to make roads for the whole country.

If a daimyo died without a direct male heir his estate became the property of the shogun, and if his allegiance wavered there was constant danger of his being transferred to a smaller domain. So long as he was faithful to Tokugawa interests, however, he was allowed to adopt heirs and to rule his own followers and farmers without interference, and was entitled to all the taxes that he could collect from them.

In addition to his carefully designed government organization for preserving peace, Iyeyasu devised a further pre-

caution. Along lines of communication and in the districts
of greatest economic and military importance—such as the
broad, fertile rice fields of Owari between Kyoto and Mount
Fuji, in Mito which guarded Yedo from the north, and on
the Kii peninsula which served as a barrier between the Inland Sea district and the new capital—he established members
of his own family. In other important places and between allies
whose loyalty was open to possible suspicion he settled tried
and trusted stalwarts from his ancestral province.

With the wealthy and powerful temples which had been
such a source of worry to Nobunaga, Iyeyasu also dealt in
accordance with his plan for peace. In some of them he caused
divisions, and for others he founded and favored new counter-
balancing centers. A new temple center to rival Mount Koya,
for example, was established near Nippon-bashi; one to rival
Mount Hiei was granted a spacious site northeast of Yedo
castle. Zojo-ji, with its impressive gate (a tourist landmark
drastically changed by the recent bulldozing of Shiba Park)
was supported as a rival to Kyoto's influential and famous
Chion-in. Iyeyasu himself, unlike his two predecessors, was a
good Buddhist.

Though in dealing with the imperial court Iyeyasu watched
cautiously, he was also generous and, superficially at least,
respectful. Previous shoguns had shown the court only arrogance and neglect, but Iyeyasu turned over to it eight times
as much tax rice as Hideyoshi had allowed and some money
in addition. He also invited the feudal lords to help rebuild
the imperial palace, and started the custom of paying an official visit to the emperor each year. The spectacular procession of the shogun and his followers on their way from Yedo
to Kyoto could not fail to impress the populace with the
dignity and splendor of their rulers.

The Christians, also, Iyeyasu treated with tolerance. He
enforced the edict of Hideyoshi that no daimyo should turn
to the new religion, but all others were allowed complete

freedom of worship until 1614. The foreign priests he favored in proportion to the trade they brought. As early as 1598, in an interview with a Spanish priest from Manila, Iyeyasu made very attractive bids for merchants on their way from the Philippines to Mexico to stop and trade in Japan and teach his retainers how to develop their silver mines. The Jesuit Father who built the first church and held the first Mass in Yedo wrote a letter for Iyeyasu to the governor of the Philippines asking him to send ships for free trade in Kwanto ports and naval architects to build large vessels for the shogunate. The Spaniards, however, showed few signs of cooperation and their priests were continually making trouble with the Jesuits.

Just before the battle of Sekigahara an English pilot named Will Adams had reached Japan in a Dutch ship and been taken as a prisoner to Iyeyasu. One of the first questions he was asked was whether his country had wars. He had replied, "Yea, with the Spaniards and Portugals, being in peace with all other nations." [4] Then Adams showed Iyeyasu a compass and a map pointing out the route he had come by and Japan's position in relation to the rest of the world. All in all, he made a good impression on the shogun—a little too good an impression, perhaps, from Adams' point of view, for although he was given a regular income, an estate, and a native wife, he was not allowed to return to his family in England. His advice on foreign relations and his service in shipbuilding were highly valued. One of the boats he built, with a Japanese crew aboard, was welcomed in New Spain (now California) ten years before the pilgrims landed on Plymouth Rock.

Adams was not cordial toward the Catholics. When some Spaniards came to chart the harbors of the Kwanto, preparatory to trading there, he advised Iyeyasu that a country in Europe which attempted to survey another's coast would be considered hostile, and showed him on the map all the conquests of the Portuguese and Spaniards in America, the Philippines and the East Indies. Adams' suggestions were given additional

weight by the conduct of Catholic officials in the shogun's
service and by the report of a man from the flourishing port
of Sakai whom Iyeyasu sent to Europe to investigate the state
of Catholicism in its homeland. Besides, a letter had been received from King James, of Great Britain, Scotland and Ireland,
suggesting friendly trade without benefit of clergy, and the
shogun had signed an agreement granting freedom to visit any
port in Japan and to build houses on tax-free land in Yedo.
Thus, growing suspicion of the Spaniards and Portuguese and
a wider range of commercial opportunities finally led the
shogunate to order that Christianity be suppressed, that all
churches be demolished, that all foreign priests leave the
country and native Christians be exiled.

In the southwestern part of Japan, however, the Christians
were stronger than the shogunate and the order was not
obeyed. Several priests went to Osaka to solicit Hideyori's
protection, suggesting that if he joined their followers miracles
might be worked on his behalf.

Many others who for various reasons resented Tokugawa
domination were prone to flock to Osaka and now Hideyoshi's
extravagant castle became a great center of ill feeling and opposition toward the shogunate. The Taiko's heir, grown to
manhood, gave evidence of becoming a son worthy of his
father, one who would soon find it difficult to remain subservient
to another. In the face of these circumstances Iyeyasu deemed
it expedient for the sake of Tokugawa peace to destroy Osaka
Castle. But though he surrounded it with a hundred and
fifty thousand samurai, many of them with Dutch and English
muskets and devices for shooting fireballs, the great fortress remained impregnable.

After several weeks with nothing gained, Iyeyasu arranged
a truce and negotiated a treaty.

By this treaty Hideyori was granted full dignity and allowed to remain in his castle with all his samurai retainers.
Iyeyasu even consented to supplement their salaries; all he

asked, to save his own face, was that part of the castle's defenses be destroyed. So as not to inconvenience Hideyori, Iyeyasu went so far as to supply the labor for doing this. The man who was ordered to superintend the destruction assembled a great crowd of workers and, before those within the castle realized what was going on, the outer walls were torn down, the outer moat filled up. When an objection was raised, it was found that the superintendent was away for his health and that the work could not be stopped without his orders. When complaint was made to Iyeyasu, he replied, "Peace has now been fortunately concluded. Let us not talk any more about moats and parapets." [5]

Then the Osaka partisans asked for allowances of rice for the samurai in the castle, and when Iyeyasu implied that they ought to be ashamed to accept a donation from one whom they had fought against, they realized how he had gotten the best of them.

The next year Iyeyasu besieged the castle again, and this time had little difficulty in bringing about its surrender. Hideyori, rather than give himself up, committed suicide.

By this conquest, having freed themselves from their only menacing opponents, the shogunate turned their attention again to their program for permanent peace.

In the country at this time were approximately two million samurai in the service of the Tokugawas and of the more than two hundred lesser feudal lords whose incomes were over ten thousand koku of rice a year. In addition to these were twenty-five to thirty million so-called common people. Rigid distinctions were drawn between the privileges of these three classes; the commoners were further divided into farmers, artists and artisans, and merchants. Farmers ranked first, for they produced the necessities of life from the soil; artists and artisans who created beautiful and useful things were a little lower in social status, while moneylenders, brokers and merchants, since they simply made profits on the labors of others, were relegated to the lowest class. Once a farmer always a farmer, once a merchant always a merchant, from generation to generation. The shogunate allowed neither intermarriage between classes nor the chance of working up from one class to another. The common people, divided into groups of five families each, were mutually responsible for the taxes and good behavior of their unit, and for reporting the misdemeanors of neighbor groups.

Soon after the fall of Osaka Castle the shogunate issued codes of laws regulating the activities of all classes of society from the imperial court down to the merchant, and even lower to the slavelike eta who from early times were segregated in special settlements and subsisted by performing such tasks as tanning, butchering and grave digging, which, being concerned with the handling of dead bodies, were regarded as vile.

Of the laws for the imperial court, perhaps the most significant were these:[6]

> Not to study is to be ignorant of the doctrines of the ancient sages, and an ignorant ruler has never governed a nation peacefully.
>
> A man lacking in ability must not be appointed to the office of regent or minister even though he belong to the Five Designated Families, and none but a member of these families may serve in such a position.
>
> An adopted son shall always be chosen from the family of his adopter.
>
> Reports shall be submitted to the emperor only by an official of the shogunate. Any other person who attempts to address the throne direct shall be sent into exile whatever his rank.

The laws for the military houses prescribed:[7]

> Literature, arms, archery and horsemanship are systematically to be the favorite pursuits.

Drinking parties and gaming must be kept within due bounds.

Offenders against the law and persons guilty of rebellion or murder must not be harbored.

No social intercourse is permitted outside of one's own domain with the people of another domain.

Castles must not be repaired nor new structures started without permission; such things going on in a neighboring domain should be reported without delay.

Marriages must not be contracted at private convenience.

When daimyos come to Yedo they must not be accompanied by more than twenty horsemen—only in rare cases may they dress in silk.

Samurai throughout the provinces are to practice frugality.

Laws for the common people, issued later, prescribed the minutest details of everyday life, such as the shaving of beards and the wearing of cotton clothing.

The average farmer with an income of possibly thirty-five or forty bushels of rice a year was ordered not to build a house more than thirty feet long, nor to give more than one present on the birth of a child, a toy spear perhaps to a boy or a paper or clay doll to a girl. The amounts he could spend on a wedding outfit and a wedding feast were also specified, together with many other items.

To keep the people satisfied with their new regime, and to enforce it, the shogunate instituted an official system of education.

When troops were gathered in Kyushu for the Korean expedition, Iyeyasu had met a young Fujiwara with a very impressive knowledge of Chinese philosophy. As it happened, this Fujiwara, Seika, was the first real scholar with whom Iyeyasu had ever talked, and his Chu Hsi philosophy fitted in well with Iyeyasu's conservative ideas. According to it there were in nature two forces, one static and one dynamic, and these took the form of the five elements—wood, fire, metal, water and earth. Each of these elements was associated with a special virtue—benevolence with wood, righteousness with fire, propriety and politeness with metal, wisdom and intelligence with water, and faithful dutifulness with earth. The seed of these virtues was supposed to be in each individual, and persons who by self-culture brought all these virtues to full flower were thought to make the ideal leaders and rulers of men.

This doctrine further emphasized right relationships, loyalty between lord and subject, filial piety between father and son, love between wife and husband, obedience between elder and younger brothers and sisters and kindliness among friends. It taught people to maintain these proper relationships at all costs; not to try to overstep their position, but to be content and satisfied with their lot in life. According to the Chu Hsi teachings, great honor came only from upholding one's principles even unto death.

It seemed to go so perfectly with Iyeyasu's peace plan that schools were established in Yedo as soon as possible for teaching this philosophy and all promising young officials were required to attend them. It was not long before similar schools sprang up all over the country, and for two hundred and fifty years Chu Hsi philosophy was the basis of all official instruction. In these schools the samurai learned something also of the liberal arts, military disciplines, Japanese history and poetry. Under the third Tokugawa shogun, when peace was well established in the country, a plan was devised for teaching military discipline with the idea not of killing others, but of being so skillful as to win a point without endangering life. Then fencing came to be taught with bamboo poles, and swords were forced out of practical use. Less thought was given to the quality of blades and more to the ornamentation of the sheath and hilt, and the sword became again, as it was in Heian days, a decorative symbol of class superiority.

The common people had never been allowed to wear swords. In schools for them no military training was given;

only penmanship, reading, and use of the abacus were taught. But when the thousands of samurai with very little money and very little to do began to accost common people truculently in the towns or on country roads, some means of self-defense was a matter of life or death. For common men to fight back against samurai was criminal, but there was no law against their being pliant, and they soon began to master the method of defense known as jujutsu. The principle of jujutsu is not to overpower another, but by yielding before his force to let an attacker lose his balance and throw himself.[8]

Iyeyasu died in 1616. Though his heirs inherited neither his breadth of mind nor his strength of character, they did contrive to perpetuate for over two hundred years his policy of peace. The methods they used were supervision and suppression of the people, and isolation.

It was an important feature of the Tokugawa government that everyone was watched, from the emperor himself down to the meanest merchant, and everyone was encouraged to report the irregularities of others. Persons who did irregular things were punished.

That a closer watch might be kept on the doings of the daimyos, they were all ordered, no matter where their estates were located, to build and maintain in Yedo a residence suitable to their rank, to leave their wives there all the time like hostages, and to live there themselves, for a while at least, every two years. This helped enormously to promote the building and commercial prosperity of the shogun's capital, and also served effectively the purpose of checking any unforeseen reaction. When any daimyo appeared to be increasing in wealth more rapidly than seemed desirable to the shogunate, this fact was noted, and the privilege of undertaking some expensive public work was conferred upon him.

The project of erecting a mausoleum and shrine at Nikko to honor the memory of Iyeyasu was begun in 1623 and carried on for twelve years. All the lords of the country were required to contribute valuable materials, the artists to contribute their best skill and most heroic designs. The architectural forms of palace, Shinto shrine and Buddhist temple were all combined in this glorious achievement. The gold leaf used, it is said, if spread out in one piece, would cover nearly six acres, and the timbers placed end to end would reach over three hundred miles.[9] There is a popular saying in Japan: "Do not use the word magnificent until you have seen Nikko." The sayings of the daimyos whose fortunes were depleted by this extravagant undertaking were probably not recorded. Some idea of the pressure brought to bear on them, however, is evidenced by the fact that one of their number who had nothing else to offer uprooted over eighteen thousand cryptomeria trees from the forests of his province and supplied the labor for transporting them and transplanting them around this shrine.

As part of their program of supervision and suppression of subversive activities the Tokugawas ordered the Catholic missionaries to leave the country, and forbade them to preach their gospel, but the Christians somehow managed to carry on. This defiance of their authority provoked the shogunate greatly, and after Iyeyasu's death, several Christians, both foreign and native, were martyred for their faith. As usual, persecution intensified rather than diminished zeal. The babies of Japanese Christians were nursed only once a day so that their innocent hungry cries might rise up to God together with the prayers of their elders on behalf of the believers. Though all Spaniards and Portuguese supposedly were driven out of the country, in 1637, a revolt occurred in Kyushu. Some thirty thousand men, women and children, downtrodden and discontented peasants, fought under banners inscribed with red crosses, and shouted "Jesús," "María" and "Sant Iago" (the patron saint of Spain) as their battle cries. Their resistance and endurance struck terror in the Tokugawa generals sent to quell them, but finally they were driven into an old castle and surrounded. A letter shot out of the castle on an arrow to their besiegers explained their motives:

> We have done this not with the hope of taking lands and houses but simply because Christianity has been prohibited by the shogun. Should we continue to live as Christians and these laws be not repealed we must incur all sorts of punishments, and perhaps, our bodies being weak and sensitive, sin against the Lord of Heaven. These things fill us with grief beyond endurance; hence our present condition.[10]

Imprisoned in their castle for two months, still they would not surrender. Finally the shogunate called upon the non-religious Dutch merchants to turn their shipboard cannon against the stronghold of the rebels. But not until food and ammunition alike were completely exhausted was it overwhelmed. Then the shogunate, unwilling to take further chances with Spanish or Portuguese converts, resolved to adopt the Closed Door policy, and prohibited all intercourse except that with the Dutch and Chinese in the port of Nagasaki. This prohibition remained in effect until 1854.

CHAPTER 12

THE GOLDEN AGE FOR BUSINESSMEN
(1675–1725)

FROM the days of the early settlers the headquarters of the chief clan leaders had been the centers of the nation. Close to their dwellings loyal followers had settled, shrines had been established and markets had been held on special days. In Closed Door Japan were two hundred or more such centers of varying sizes and degrees of prosperity. By far the most flourishing of these were Osaka and Yedo, the castle towns of the two great national leaders, Hideyoshi and Iyeyasu.

After the siege of 1615, the citizens of Osaka had quickly restored their city. Only ten years later, according to official records, it had a population of almost three hundred thousand, with twenty-eight mansions occupied by feudal lords, two hundred government officials, thirteen hundred and four rice brokers, a hundred and thirty-two bridges, two hundred and eleven hotels and inns, fifty bookstores, two hundred and seventy-seven druggists, five execution grounds, forty-one brothels, three hundred and thirteen Buddhist temples, eleven Shinto shrines, two hundred and fifty-six teahouses, seven hundred and six breweries, twenty-four bathhouses, six hundred and sixty-seven pawnshops and fifty-four hundred and sixty-three fishing boats, ferries and other small ships plying the Inland Sea.[1] And like Yedo, the political center of the country, Osaka, the great commercial and industrial center, had continued to increase in national importance until it was destroyed by American bombing raids.

This port as far back as the sixth century, when Prince Shotoku, the Father of Japanese Culture, was regent, had been a harbor where newcomers from the continent had been welcomed and where, after worshiping the sea-god, envoys had been dispatched overseas. Its cosmopolitan tradition stretched over a thousand years, but renewed impetus had been given its adventurous citizens by the inspiration of Portuguese and Spanish traders. Some had managed to get ships of their own in which they could sail the high seas, while others had hired passage to foreign ports where opportunity beckoned. All were prompted by their own initiative, carried on their business independent of superior authority, and enjoyed the profits themselves. Hideyoshi had encouraged this sort of enterprise, and kindred spirits from all over the southwestern part of the country had looked to his castle as their capital. How many of them were engaged in this unlicensed maritime trade may be guessed from the fact that when Iyeyasu was anxious to enlist the co-operation of Spanish shipowners in Manila he had tried to make a favorable impression on them by capturing and executing two hundred Japanese pirates, apparently a small fraction of the total number.

Since this uncontrolled trade was not only unprofitable for the Tokugawas, but also a potential source of trouble for them, they tried to put an end to it. When the Tokugawa government became effective in Osaka the mercantile population had to invent new business interests. Some of them scattered to castle towns throughout the country, where they could put their profiteering experience into practice, but many remained and put up a sort of united front against too close supervision and control by the shogunate. A few obtained licenses from the Yedo officials and went to buy goods from the storehouses in Nagasaki where now the Hollanders alone were permitted to import and export. But before long Osaka, with its central location and excellent transportation facilities, had become the rice market of the nation.

Daimyos in general had very little money;[2] their income was in rice, which the peasants from their estates brought in oxcart after oxcart, all hulled and packed in big straw bags, to the granary of their lord. Rice was still the most important medium of exchange and the standard of value, but the Dutch traders were not interested in rice. It was of little value compared to its bulk and it was grown more abundantly in Java and the Indies where the Dutch had their bases than in Japan. They wanted gold, silver and copper. The daimyos, on the other hand, wanted to be able to buy the white raw silk of superior quality which the Dutch traders brought from China, and they were also eager to possess some of the medicines, glass mirrors, telescopes, clocks and other curiosities from Europe. Osaka citizens were quick to see possibilities of profit in this situation.

There was a family called Yodoya which had opened a produce exchange in front of their own house when Hideyoshi's samurai had first started to swell the population of the city. During the Taiko's regime this family had risen to prominence and wealth by their extraordinary ability in transporting, distributing and fixing the price of rice. With numerous other brokers, they went on from speculation in this commodity to speculation in gold and silver, developed a network of swift communications throughout the country and continued to prosper marvelously even under the Tokugawas, until it was realized that they were drawing wealth from all the provinces—more than the Tokugawas themselves could claim. Such a state of affairs could not long be endured. The Yodoya house, the most conspicuous of these multimillionaires, was ordered confiscated by the fifth Tokugawa shogun on the charge that its members were living in luxury ill-befitting their social rank. A complete list of their possessions would fill pages and pages, but a few are enumerated here to give an idea of what constituted a wealthy merchant at the end of the seventeenth century.

In Osaka alone they owned four hundred and twelve houses and, scattered through surrounding provinces, over three hundred houses, farms, fields and woodlands, and seven hundred and thirty storehouses containing beans and rice. They owned almost three hundred large junks for carrying on their business, and among countless other things: one hundred and fifty folding screens covered with gold leaf; five hundred and fifty flowered carpets from the Ryukyu islands; ninety-six sliding doors made of crystal; over three hundred hens, chicks, sparrows, doves and macaws made of solid gold for purposes of ornament; ten dishes and twenty rosaries of coral; rubies, pearls, agates and amber in untold numbers; seventy-five tons of quicksilver; seven hundred and forty-three paintings; five thousand rolls of velvet, two thousand of poppy-colored Chinese brocade, ten thousand of black Chinese silk; a hundred and seventy telescopes and spectacles; a checkerboard of solid gold; thirty-five tons of cinnabar, seventy-seven pounds of the highly prized ginseng root supposed to prolong life, and numberless swords and teacups of great value. All in all, their estate was estimated at a hundred and twenty-two million ryo, about two thousand tons, of gold.

A popular saying of the time went something like this: "August Yedo is the city of the samurai, and Kyoto the city of fine ladies; Osaka alone is the city of the merchants who are daring, self-respecting, faithful to promises, yielding to no threat, broad-minded and brightly dressed." [3] But Yedo was not without its wealthy merchants either. Since all the daimyos were required to maintain mansions there, it afforded an excellent market for both the necessities and luxuries of life. Purveyors to government officials lived in grander style than many feudal lords themselves, and were escorted through the city by a procession of servants. Stores on the principal thoroughfares had open gates like palaces and were continually crowded with samurai and their attendants. One Yedo merchant with a flair for advertising got all the entertainment girls singing a song about the boatload of oranges with which he started his fortune and, after a great fire swept the city, became very wealthy selling lumber. Silkworm dealers from six northeastern provinces held a convention in Yedo in 1672 to discuss methods for promoting their business, and some years later began to publish a yearbook on sericulture. In Yedo, as well as Osaka, the Genroku period from 1688 to 1703 was a time of great commercial prosperity.

With prosperity, as always, came gaiety and a demand for entertainment. The samurai were ordered to be frugal, and the salaries of rice which they received for keeping themselves in readiness to defend their lords were not adequate for much expensive celebration, but many of them had little idea of paying for things. They considered themselves superior to the common merchants and acted as if they were conferring a favor by borrowing money. They boasted of their ignorance of money matters and made promissory notes that read, for example: "In the event of my failure to repay the loan, I shall not object to being publicly ridiculed," or "should I fail to discharge my obligation at the fixed time, I should be considered as no man." [4]

Had not the samurai brought peace to the nation and made prosperity possible? Then let them be treated with respect. But the merchants, while they aimed to copy the costumes, accomplishments and household decorations of the samurai, still could not repress some annoyance at their swaggering attitude, and often repeated the taunt: "Though the samurai has not eaten, he acts as if he were full." Though continually professing an idealistic interest in Chinese scholarship and military discipline, many samurai could not stifle a secret desire to enjoy the realistic amusements of the carnal businessman, and the two classes came in frequent contact. Especially in Osaka was this true, for many of Hideyoshi's samurai had been forced by circumstances to give up their soldierly pursuits and had turned to trading for a livelihood. To Osaka also, before the doors of their native land were closed, had returned many Japanese who had traveled abroad and lived in Korea, China, Thailand, the Philippines, Java and the busiest ports of the Southern Seas. These homecoming adventurers had seen life in great variety and were accustomed to freedom and excitement. Wealthy merchants, talented samurai and these men of worldly experience naturally mingled together and, out of the association, developed what is frequently called the Genroku Renaissance.[5]

Toward the end of the seventeenth century all the arts took on new life. Literature, music, the theater, painting, applied design and poetry all blossomed profusely, with brilliant new blooms which appealed to the common people and won their enthusiastic patronage. Three outstanding figures in this movement were Saikaku, the realistic novelist, Chikamatsu, the romantic dramatist, and Basho, the symbolic poet. Each in his field created a new type of art for the common people to rival the ancient forms which the samurai held as classic. Saikaku wrote novels with common men as heroes to rival the time-honored Heian court tales of princely amours. Chikamatsu created a new type of drama which far outshone the aristocratic Noh performances in popularity, and Basho created a new poetry whose spiritual quality had far wider appeal than the formal verses the samurai practiced writing.

Saikaku was sophisticated to the *n*th degree and held nothing sacred. Defying all traditions and conventions, he identified himself with the gay pleasure quarter, and in vulgarly frank and vivid terms extolled the joys of the flesh. "Why offer money to Buddha?" he wrote. "Is not a land of women, paradise? Give your money to women." [6] Women and money were his theme. His most famous work was a tale somewhat like the *Genji Monogatari* with a common man instead of the Shining Prince as hero. This *Middle Aged Gentleman of Passion* is done in a style which, though much less refined than hers, has a curt brilliance like the *Pillow Book* of the Heian court lady Sei. All of Saikaku's writings, novels, short stories and sketches of contemporary life and manners, being both realistic and humorous and done in the everyday pleasure-quarter vernacular, were very popular with the common people and did not fail to

appeal to the samurai either. Because of the startling and per-
verting nature of their revelations, however, the shogunate had
them suppressed. On his deathbed at fifty-two, following the
ancient custom of all men of distinction, Saikaku wrote a
poem of passing:

> The moon of this floating world,
> I have looked upon two years too long.

In Prince Shotoku's day, music was supposed to bring harmony to men's hearts and make them easy to govern, but
Genroku music did something very different. Much of it was
plaintive and wailing, exciting lovers to despair and even to
suicide. Whereas the favorite instrument of courtier and samurai
was the stately thirteen-stringed koto, the middle-class popular
instrument was the samisen, a sort of three-stringed banjo introduced from the Ryukyu islands where children used them for
toys. A popular form of entertainment in the early days of
middle-class prosperity had been a recitation of some old
romance accompanied by a strumming of open chords and de-
scriptive phrases, but this soon developed into a more dramatic
form.[7]

In 1603, a temple dancer eloped with her lover and started
the show business in a dry river bed in Kyoto. In simple little
acts she took men's parts and he took women's and they created
such a sensation that she was invited to Yedo to perform for
the shogun and the daimyos. Other troupes appeared in imitation of this one and were acclaimed with equal enthusiasm by
the common people. Officials called them Kabuki—off balance,
not quite right. For years these primitive Kabuki stood for
eccentricity and dissipation, and by many were thought to be no
more than publicity stunts for commercialized vice. The son of
a samurai writes in his autobiography:

> During a summer festival there would sometimes be a series
> of plays lasting seven days together when traveling actors set

up a temporary stage in the temple yard. Then there would always be a proclamation that the samurai of our clan should not even go beyond the stone wall of the temple. Many went anyhow, with their faces wrapped in towels, wearing only a short sword so they would look like common people. These disguised samurai broke over the bamboo fence of the theater, whereas the real common people paid their fees. If the management tried to stop the intruders they uttered a menacing roar and strode on to take the best seats.[8]

Because of their demoralizing influence, the shogunate banned all actresses from the stage. Young boys took the place of the girls, and Kabuki went on. So did the demoralizing influence. Then young actors, too, were banned, and only mature men were allowed to act. Without the charms and beauty of youth to aid them it became necessary to improve both the plays and the acting in order to attract an audience. It was then that the real art of the Japanese theater started; costumes and scenery became increasingly gorgeous; Kabuki became "song and dance skill."

Some theaters had puppets instead of men. Here the play itself was most important, and for such a theater in Osaka, Chikamatsu began to write. Though a product of the same age, he was not as irreverent a man as Saikaku. Chikamatsu knew how to enjoy his emotions, but he understood his duties as well. His plays were usually based on the conflict between the two motives, giri and ninjo, which may be translated as duty and sentiment, loyalty and self-indulgence, conservatism and liberalism, the chief conflict of society in his day. Some of his plays dealt with historical subjects and others were written almost in a single night, after a love suicide or a similar piece of news which everyone was discussing. Chikamatsu realized that everyday life was full of dramatic situations and touched commonplace events with his creative genius. No matter how weak his characters, they have their strong moments which command respect —no matter how strong, they have some endearing human

Outdoor theater with musicians at left, dancers on stage, and the audience at right, including two samurai with faces covered

weakness. Samurai, officials, wealthy merchants, and common folk suffering from poverty and government regulations, all are given liberal treatment. Chikamatsu neither praised nor blamed. He helped people to see the hearts and minds of others with understanding sympathy, and the way he did this had a lasting effect on the social ideals of both samurai and merchant. His poem of passing, however, suggests that he did not take himself too seriously:

Last words?
Well, well, I hope the cherry will bloom as ever after I am gone.

About fifty of Chikamatsu's five-act plays are still available for the modern reader,[9] and some of them are still produced in theaters. In the earlier ones there is frequent use of long narrative parts in alternating five- and seven-syllable lines to be chanted by the chorus at the side of the stage. But as Chikamatsu became more experienced in technique, and as puppets of greater and greater accomplishment were devised, dialogue came to play a more important part. Puppets were made about two-thirds life size and fitted so cleverly with machinery that they could roll their eyes, raise their brows, open and close their mouths, move their fingers and even manipulate a fan.

In Yedo, living actors who wrote their own plays had been more popular than the puppets, but now they too began to act the dramas written for puppets. Plays based on historic subjects showing the loyalty and devotion of a retainer to his lord found greater favor in the shogun's capital than those dealing with love suicide. There wisdom, benevolence and courage constituted the ideal character and the samurai were supposed to specialize in these virtues. The common citizens of Yedo, however, being noted for their scrappy dispositions, were especially delighted by comedies in which merchants were shown putting something over on samurai.

The theaters in which the Kabuki were presented also came to be highly developed in the Genroku period. Two- or three-story structures they were, with elaborate stage, pit and galleries. The first-class boxes were hung with split-bamboo curtains and surrounded by gold screens so that the wealthy merchants could enjoy the entertainment in elegant seclusion. The principal approach to the stage was not from the side or back but by a long, narrow platform built aislelike through the pit. This might serve as the veranda of a house, a street in a town scene, or a road in the country, and it afforded the spectators a chance to look closely at the actors. Instead of drawing a curtain for changes of scenery, they had a revolving stage and passed from one scene to the next in full view.

The audience came to the theater in the morning, laden with lunch boxes and sake bottles, and stayed all day, eating, drinking and walking around as their natures directed.

Besides the theaters there were the pleasure boats on the canals and rivers of Osaka. Rich merchants owned their own luxuriously appointed ones and engaged caterers, musicians and dancing girls to provide entertainment on them. Poor people hired less pretentious public boats, took along their own food and drink and did their own singing and dancing.

This picturesque, romantic diversion became so popular that the word which was used to describe the reckless gaiety of life in the pleasure quarters was Ukiyo (floating world),[10] a delightfully carefree drifting on the tide, where no bonds or restrictions could hold one back, where within narrow confines, each man could order life to his own satisfaction.

In former days artists had painted only for temples, palaces or castles, but the colorful and spectacular Ukiyo offered such an abundance of attractive subjects, and the prosperous merchants such a ready market, that a new type of art developed, called Ukiyo-e—pictures of the floating world. At first they were painted in colors, not realistically but by each artist subjectively according to his own taste. Moronobu was one of the

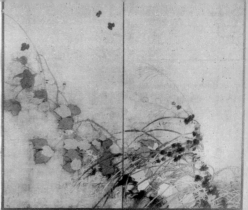

PAIR OF SCREENS

TEA JAR

LACQUER BOX

HANGING SCROLL, PINE TREE IN SNOW

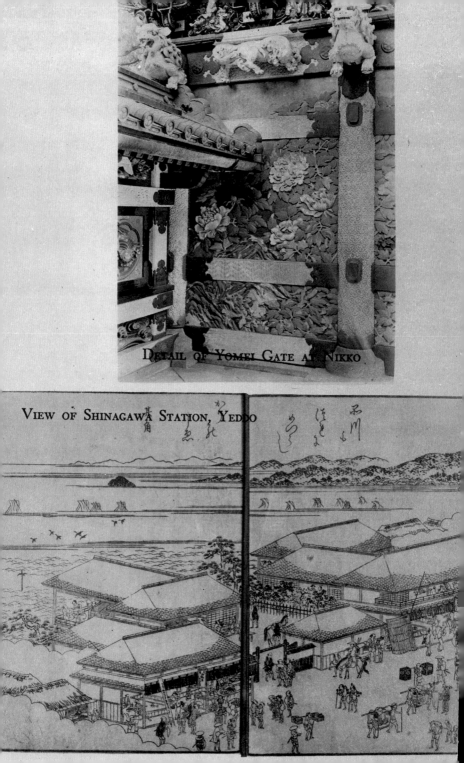

DETAIL OF YOMEI GATE AT NIKKO

VIEW OF SHINAGAWA STATION, YEDDO

early artists to do this. When the demand for such pictures became greater, artists began to cut their drawings on blocks of wood and to print large numbers of copies. These prints could be sold very cheaply and people liked to have them as souvenirs of a favorite actor or beauty in the pleasure quarter, or to stimulate thrills which they could afford only in imagination. It was from penny prints which traveling friends brought as presents from a visit to the city that country people got their notions of urban life.

The earliest prints were done only in heavy black lines on white paper, but the addition at first of two colors, rose-red and green, and then of others made them so much more desirable that eventually an exquisite variety of color and detail was used. Books of pictures which told stories without words of events in the lives of professional entertainers were also printed from wood blocks. Very often these prints and storybooks were obscene and not infrequently they profaned sacred subjects. The name of the old saint Daruma who had sat in meditation so long that he lost the use of his feet, was given to pleasure-quarter ladies who rarely left their silken cushions, and the Bodhisattva Fugen, usually shown in Buddhist paintings riding an elephant and reading a sutra, was travestied by famous beauties dreaming over love letters.

The pleasure quarters were made to resemble as closely as possible the Heian palaces of seven centuries before. The ladies in them wore voluminous robes of gorgeous silks, and cherished gifts of beautiful accessories. For this purpose, as well as for decoration in homes of Yedo officials, daimyos and wealthy merchants, the applied arts blossomed with a multitude of blooms during the Genroku period.[11] Korin and his brother Kenzan are known all over the world for the marvelous designs they created for gold-lacquer writing boxes, small ornamental screens, precious textiles and other domestic furnishings. Both were brought up in Kyoto, and their work is welcome evidence of the continuing and genuine refinement of life in the ancient imperial capital. Many of the silks of the Genroku period were also made in the city of fine ladies, and some are still preserved in museums and private collections. Their exquisitely woven patterns and subtly harmonized colors are beautiful beyond description.

As one can find nothing vulgar or flamboyant in the work of Korin and Kenzan, neither is there anything in the writing of Basho to offend the most gentle soul. He stands in striking contrast to Saikaku and Chikamatsu, the other two members of the famous literary trio of the Genroku period. The noisy brilliance and venality of the floating world were profoundly distressing to him. He longed to create some purifying influence. Sitting alone in midnight stillness pondering the problem, Basho heard a sound, the splash of a frog jumping into a pond. A sudden flash of insight came to him—he would make a fresh sound in the stagnant old pond of poetry.

The oldest collection of Japanese poetry dates from the Nara age and contains many long poems, together with the thirty-one syllable tanka. The latter form came to be used almost exclusively by Heian court versifiers, and the spontaneous expression of earlier days deteriorated into stilted and stylized composition. For pastime, nobles had held contests in which those participating were challenged with the first three lines of a tanka and required to supply two concluding lines at once. From the thirteenth century on, three lines alone, of five, seven and five syllables respectively, came to be used occasionally as a complete form. Such poems are called haiku.

By Basho's day many people were writing haiku, in which frail sentiments were expressed with an attempt at rhetorical dexterity. Someone described these haiku as "slobber," but Basho, adopting the same brief form, filled it with profound and sublime meaning. Not only did he himself become the greatest Japanese poet of all time, but he initiated a great popular movement of haiku writing, which recently has spread even to Europe and America.

The supreme art of haiku writing in the Basho manner consists not so much in what is said as in what is suggested. Basho
was a mystic. He spent month after month wandering through
the country listening for the voice of nature and adoring her
works. The seventeen-syllable notes on his deepest experiences
contain the essential facts for making the experience live again
and for showing kindred spirits the way to gratifying truths.

One day when he and a pupil were going through the fields,
looking at the darting dragon flies, the pupil made the verse:

> Red dragon flies!
> Take off their wings
> And they are pepperpods!

"No," said Basho, "this is not haiku. If you wish to make a
haiku on that subject you must say:

> Red pepperpods!
> Add wings to them,
> And they are dragon flies! [12]

There is another story about Basho which shows how modest
he was and also in how much favor haiku were held by even
the lowliest people.

On one of his many rambles, the story goes, Basho came
upon a group of rustics out enjoying the light of a full moon,
drinking sake and composing haiku. As soon as they noticed
him the rustics thought it would be fun to ask the wanderer
to join them—and Basho could not very well refuse. One of
the number spoke up and said, "Everybody here is bound to
compose a verse about the full moon. You must compose something, too." Basho apologized and said he was a humble man
from a country place, and begged to be excused.

"No, no," they said, "we can't excuse you. Good or bad, you
must compose one verse at least."

"Well then, I will give you one," agreed Basho, and began

> 'Twas the new moon . . .

"The new moon! Stupid fellow, this is the full moon," one
of the rustics exclaimed, but the others bade him let the guest
go on, as it should be very amusing.

Then Basho continued:

> 'Twas the new moon,
> Since then I have waited
> And lo! Tonight!

The whole party was amazed at his aptness and asked the
stranger's name. When he told them they were greatly excited
and sent for all their friends to come and join a party in his
honor.[13]

Basho's last haiku was:

> On a journey, ill—
> And my dreams o'er withered fields
> Are wandering still.[14]

And still his poems are learned by heart and repeated on
suitable occasions in all sorts of Japanese households.

The effect of the haiku movement was sobering and wholesome. People began to take somewhat less interest in the gay
pleasure quarter and to find more enjoyment in the country.
A tremendous eruption of Mount Fuji which occurred in 1707
also startled the people into an appreciation of the awful power
of nature in contrast to the floating world. This eruption, which
was Fuji-san's last, buried Yedo, seventy-five miles distant,
under six inches of ashes and terrified the people with darkness
and thundering noises. It seemed like an ominous expression
of a deity's mighty wrath.

From the days of the Ainu, who gave it the name fire, or
bursting forth, Fuji-san had been famous in Japanese poetry
and lore. Towering almost two and a half miles above the
surrounding lakes and plain, in clear weather it was visible
a hundred miles away, and held in awe because of its outward

pure serenity as well as for its inner volcanic fire. As early as Iyeyasu's time there had been sects of the native Shinto cult which emphasized the spiritual and physical value of mountain climbing, and as travel between Yedo and Kyoto increased, Fuji-san's perfect cone became an increasingly familiar and inspiring sight. In the late Tokugawa period people began to come from all over the country in white robes, with little bells jingling from their girdles and climbing sticks in their hands, to make pilgrimages to the top. Climbing Fuji-san came to be a popular religious practice, as it still is today,[15] and an austere discipline to balance wanton tendencies.

CHAPTER 13

WHEN PERRY CAME WITH U.S. GUNBOATS

(MIDDLE NINETEENTH CENTURY)

SINCE 1635 no Japanese had been allowed to leave his native land and only a few Hollanders and Chinese had been allowed to enter it. Though during the two centuries of isolation there were usually half a dozen or more Europeans residing in Japan to carry on the trade of the Dutch East India Company, they were confined to the tiny island, Deshima, which lay in Nagasaki Harbor and was only two hundred thirty-six paces long by eighty-two paces wide. Most of these traders had little interest in Japan beyond "their ledgers, their guilders and their schnapps," and for this reason enjoyed but slight esteem among the natives.[1] Local families, however, acted as their cooks and servants, providing them with food, drink and household wares, and in this way became familiar with their ways.

Furthermore, the shogunate officially had a monopoly on foreign trade and maintained a staff of interpreters and commissioners, sometimes two hundred or more, who had frequent dealings with the foreigners and came to be fairly well informed not only in the Dutch language, but also in anatomy, medicine, natural history, botany, horse breeding and astronomy as taught in Europe, and in the newly discovered wonders of electricity. When men of high caliber, like Kaempfer, Thunberg, Titsingh and Siebold, were resident at Deshima the tiny island became a great center of learning.[2] Provincial governors sent their brightest young men to Nagasaki to study Dutch sciences so that the prestige of their native places might be enhanced. Some official students opened schools of Dutch learning in Yedo. The eighth Tokugawa shogun established a great library of foreign books there,[3] encouraged the cultivation of tobacco and sweet potatoes as supplementary crops to rice, had an observatory with a telescope erected in Yedo and a rain gauge and sundial set up in his palace park.

Several Japanese artists went to Nagasaki to study Western techniques of oil painting, map making and copperplate engraving. In this way they added not only to Japanese knowledge of Western subjects, but also to the accuracy of Western maps of the Japanese islands and surrounding territories. Some of them specialized in Nagasaki prints, by means of which their fellow countrymen, even in remote districts, were able to get some idea of the appearance of the Hollanders' ships, houses, customs and costumes.[4]

Politically minded students read Dutch news letters and other sources of information about contemporary conditions in Europe, America and China. They learned of the tremendous accomplishments of Peter the Great in modernizing Russia, and of the American and the French Revolution, the Napoleonic Wars, the imperialistic expansion of England in India and Malaysia, of Russia in Siberia and Alaska. They learned of the shame and loss which even their great neighbor China suffered before the guns of the British navy, and of the constantly increasing activity of Americans in the Pacific area. When these students, a few hundred perhaps, thought of the state of affairs in their own country they became very serious and restless.

In 1814, the English seized the Dutch possessions in Java and Sir Stamford Raffles, the English governor, sent representatives of the English East India Company to Nagasaki to ask for trading rights such as the Dutch had. The mission did not gain its point, but it reported, "The Japanese are a nervous, vigorous people whose bodily and mental powers assimilate much nearer to those of Europe than what is attributed to Asiatics in general."

Other English ships which tried to put into Japanese ports about this time, and several attempts by Russians to establish relations with the Japanese, continued to stimulate the latter's eagerness for a knowledge of world affairs. Dutch agents, stranded on Deshima with nothing to trade, on account of the trouble their ships were having with the English, were gladly supported by the Japanese in return for preparing a Dutch-Japanese dictionary and teaching what they knew of international movements. A few Japanese at this time also began to study Russian and English, but these students of Western ways were but a little leaven in a very large lump.

It is estimated there were about thirty million people in Closed Door Japan. To keep them in order and in their proper places, the Tokugawas had perfected the control system of class distinctions introduced by Hideyoshi. Under the shogun and his officials were the local landlords, the daimyos, who held absolute power over the people of their respective estates. The four classes in descending rank were samurai, farmers, artisans and merchants. One was born in a certain class and allowed no change in status either through marriage or personal merit. When Perry came, the bulk of the population was scattered throughout the folds of the mountain ranges in small valleys and plains where sweet potatoes, rice and other cereals and mulberry bushes could be grown, where timber could be cut from the forested slopes and small fish caught in the swift flowing streams, but where few progressive ideas were allowed to penetrate. Of the thirty million about eighty per cent were farmers, seven per cent samurai, three per cent merchants, two per cent artisans, the remaining eight per cent made up by miscellaneous officials, priests, actors, outcasts, etc.[5]

The average family had about two acres under cultivation, not all in one piece perhaps, but in little patches here and there within easy walking distance of one of the sixty thousand villages in which farmers' homes were clustered. If farmers could have used for themselves all the produce of their lands they might have lived quite comfortably, except in times of drought, insect plague, severe storm, earthquake or volcanic eruption, for the country was at peace. The farmers were for the most part hard-working people and their wants were simple. Unfortunately, however, they not infrequently were driven by officials to raise more and more rice for taxes to pay the salaries of the unproductive samurai and other expenses of superiors and government, and their own shares of the harvest were scarcely enough to keep them alive. The farmers' wives dried and salted fish, and pickled vegetables to store on the kitchen shelf. Often they helped along the family income by raising silkworms in spring and summer and weaving the spun silk into cloth in the winter. Sometimes the children helped them make sandals or mats from rice straw, or lanterns, baskets and umbrellas of bamboo, which could be exchanged for food or other domestic necessities.

But when, as sometimes happened in spite of their best efforts, the farmers became desperate and the officials took no measures for their relief, they would rise up in an angry mob, carrying their sickles and long-bladed hoes for weapons and straw mats for banners, beating drums, blowing horns, ringing bells, and shouting their resentment and demands. As they approached the castle where their feudal lord or local officials resided, the samurai outside the walls would run into the courtyards and bar the heavy gates. Then, after a while, representatives would be sent out to negotiate with the farmers concerning their demands. The ringleaders of the rioters were always severely punished, sometimes even crucified, but usually their efforts brought relief for a while.

Artisans and merchants had their troubles too. They swarmed in the few large cities each of whose population numbered nearly half a million, where hastily built wooden houses with open-front shops were crowded close together and fires frequently broke out. Their businesses were strictly regulated and they had constantly to be on their guard against losses from dealings with samurai, whose tastes were high and salaries low. Like the farmers, most of them limited the number of their children for economic reasons to two or three; but though they thus deprived themselves of the ready pleasure in having many babies, they had plenty of diversion as compared with country people.

The chief excitement in the villages was afforded by the eagerly anticipated first nightingale to return in spring, an evening's gossip in the light of a full moon, the festivals of local shrines and temples or occasional wandering acrobats and story-tellers. In the cities, however, interesting things were always happening and life was very much more free and easy. Farmers liked to break away from their fields whenever they could manage it and go to the city to become tradesmen or day laborers, and their daughters found domestic service in large city houses much more attractive than the grueling routine of the farm. Such desertion of the land by peasants was not at all approved by the government and rigid measures were devised to prevent it. Nevertheless, the city censuses continued to show increases in population.

The first accurate geographical knowledge of their country came to the Japanese when one of their able students of Western science, after eighteen years of extensive travel and conscientious measurement by the methods of both astronomy and land surveying, produced an accurate large-scale map of the whole country.[6] This gave men in authority their first true picture of the coast lines of the various islands, the courses of roads and rivers, the contours of mountains and the circumferences of lakes. By 1850, communication facilities between important centers, considering the difficult topography of the country, were fairly well developed.

Roads and transportation had been greatly improved when the daimyos from all the provinces were required to pay regular visits to Yedo. There were five main highways all starting from Nippon-bashi in Yedo. The two most traveled, the Eastern Sea Road and the Central Mountain Road, connected Yedo with Osaka and Kyoto. The other three ran to Nikko, northeastern Japan and the great silk-growing district northwest of Mount Fuji. With a hundred and forty-six daimyos and their long retinues of banner and baggage bearers traveling back and forth from Yedo at frequent intervals, the Eastern Sea Road was very colorful and lively. The great print artist, Hiroshige, took delight in picturing the fifty-three stations where travelers might stop to get fresh horses for the next lap of the journey.[7]

Because of the many narrow mountain passes and the many rivers which had to be crossed, there was little wheel traffic along these main highways. Daimyos and very important people were carried in sedan chairs on the shoulders of their servants, while lesser passengers and baggage were carried on horseback. At rivers one sometimes found bridges of boats tied together or ferries to take one across, but wading or riding across on the shoulders of a porter was not at all unusual. For food and rest along the way inns were available. There, travelers were given small charcoal fires to warm themselves if it was cold, a large tub of hot water was provided for bathing, and thin mattresses, three feet by six, were spread on the straw-mat floor for them to sleep upon. There was a rule that they should stay only one night at each inn.

At intervals on the roads barriers were established where travelers had to pass between six in the morning and six in the evening and show some evidence that they had good reason for making a journey. A significant number of those who passed the barriers were pilgrims visiting famous temples and traveling salesmen for quack medicines. Actors had only to perform to prove their profession; villagers usually had passports from their village head. For anyone taking a side route to avoid these barriers, the penalty was crucifixion.

The fastest travelers on the Eastern Sea Road were the official express messengers. They always ran in pairs, one carrying a small lacquer box containing the documents or money being sent and the other carrying a lantern marked *Official Business*. They had the right of way. All other traffic stood aside to let them pass, and by a relay system they were able to cover the distance between Yedo and Osaka sometimes in as few as fifty hours. Other common carriers for tradespeople made three trips a month between the two cities, taking on the average eight days for the journey. For an extra fee they could do it in five days.

Bulky goods and produce in large quantities were generally transported by boat, and usually sent first to Osaka, then redistributed from there to other parts of the country. Many daimyos maintained warehouses in Osaka and sent the local products of their districts there to be sold. Salt fish and seaweed were brought from northern Japan, silk and lacquer from Kyoto, sake from the island of Shikoku, bleached textiles from Nara, the old temple capital, cotton cloth from Kawachi, candles from a section two hundred miles north of Yedo and rapeseed oil for lighting from central Japan. The three districts which exported rice in large quantities were central Kyushu and the northeastern and northwestern provinces of the main island. Though the building of large ocean-going ships was prohibited by law, over twenty thousand small freighters plied back and forth between Osaka and Yedo and about eighteen hundred shipwrecks are recorded to have occurred in a year between Shimonoseki and Sendai. Boats chartered for official use flew white flags with red discs in the center and the name of the ship underneath.[8]

Japanese homes of the mid-nineteenth century, architecturally, were much the same as Japanese homes today. There are many Western-style houses in urban districts nowadays, but they are by no means in the majority even in the cities.

The outside of Japanese homes in the last days of the Tokugawas varied somewhat in accordance with local conditions of climate, occupation and available materials as, to be sure, the inside did, too, but there were several characteristics common to them all. Country houses almost invariably were only one story high, the walls were built of unpainted wood and rough clay with bits of twigs and straw in it, and the acutely sloping roofs were covered with heavy straw thatch. In cold and windy districts stones were laid on top of the thatch, and firewood, dried vegetables and other winter supplies were piled or hung close to the walls under the wide eaves. The homes of more prosperous country folk sometimes had roofs of gray tile and a coat of lighter plaster over the clay walls. They also had the added privacy of a fence or wall which ordinary farmers did not enjoy.[9]

But whether the house belonged to a rich family or a poor one, and whether it was in the city or country, its floor was raised about two feet off the ground and covered with padded straw matting, and the front of it had not a small door with a lock and key but a very wide opening which could be closed by paper-covered lattices sliding in grooves, or by light panels of wood at night and in bad weather.

In entering a typical middle-class house one did not withdraw from nature and the outside world. Rather, the world outside the door was seen as part of the dwelling; the moon and grasses and singing insects were its decorations. The interior with its natural wood ceilings and pillars, its straw-mat-covered floor and arrangement of a few flowers before a single hanging-scroll painting was simply a refined and sheltered corner of nature itself. Housewives of good taste[10] avoided using conspicuous or new-looking furnishings. The sought-after effect was of emptiness with a very few well-harmonized things long and fondly used.

In addition to their natural simplicity and modesty, Japanese homes also showed ingenious adaptability and economy. In fact, that refinement which is generally thought of as typically

Japanese esthetic taste is undoubtedly due in large measure to the prevailing poverty of the country and the people. Built with the least possible labor from readily available materials, their houses were designed to give great flexibility. Any room might become sitting room, bedroom or dining room, and any number of persons could be accommodated, for chairs and beds were simply cushions spread on the floor when needed and piled up in the closet at other times. Dining tables were individual lacquer trays likewise placed on the floor. Heating was by small charcoal fires in containers, like jardinieres, carried where needed. Water was sometimes led into the house from a stream through bamboo pipes but more often was drawn from a well. Lighting in Tokugawa times was by candle and oil lamp. From very early times Japanese houses have had special bathrooms with floor drains and wooden slat platforms where a large quantity of water was heated in a tub by an attached stove. One could splash freely, relax and luxuriate in the nightly bath as at no other time or place.

Tokugawa education for both boys and girls discouraged all sense of individuality. According to the teaching of the Buddhist temple schools the less one was a willful individual and the more one lost oneself in the harmony of the universe, the better. In the official Confucian schools boys were taught chiefly the importance of conventionally prescribed modes of behavior for maintaining right relationships. They were never a unit in themselves, but always a part of some larger unit which demanded their loyalty—the family, the school, the town. So long as they acted for the good of the larger unit they were respectable members of society, but if they rebelled against existing conditions they would bring disgrace upon their superiors, and rather than do this it was often considered proper to commit suicide. In private schools where a few privileged girls went for instruction from the daughters of well-known men educators the textbook was *The Great Teaching for Women*,[11] which expounded chiefly the virtues of sweet obedience to parents, husband and ruler, controlled speech, gentleness, under all circumstances, constancy, faithfulness without jealousy, and also frugality and thrift.

The religion of the people was closely associated with this same lack of individualism, the same sense of being part of a larger unit, of being bound in personal relationship with the great spirits of their nation's past and also of its future. They were not so much concerned with sin or saving souls as with living everyday lives worthy of their ancestry, knowing reality and being able to face with serenity any experience which life might bring. This knowledge and power was to be achieved by intuition rather than through theological exposition, sermons or lengthy prayers. The profoundest Buddhist teachings were expressed in seventeen-syllable poems—no words can explain what water is, you must stick your finger in it—or in paintings of a few brush strokes—clouds across the moon, a man in a tiny boat on an expansive sea, a patch of green grass emerging from melting snow. The true spirit of Shinto was found not in books, but in the fragrance of the century-old evergreens surrounding and towering over the shrines which were symbols of community pride and prosperity.

Christianity had been almost completely stamped out in the early seventeenth century, and the Dutch, who were allowed to continue trading on the island of Deshima, had carefully avoided religious controversy. Nevertheless, Japanese confidence in the saints of India and the sages of China had been shaken by the Jesuits and Franciscans; and when the nation's doors were closed, many Japanese intellectuals, therefore, turned their attention back toward their native cult and literature.

Because they had had no written language of their own in early days, there seemed to be no basic scripture for a national religion. In fact any purely Japanese literature was difficult to find. The first leader of the National Learning Movement, however, a man named Kamo Mabuchi, gathered together ancient hymns and prayers, the poems of the Manyoshu and legends of the Kojiki and claimed them as Shinto Scripture, "the national expression of our ancient heritage; the voice of our divine land." Composing poems of his own in the same style, which he claimed was designed to make the human heart more gentle and more understanding of all things, he encouraged others, also, to do the same. Gradually clannishness and pride in Chinese scholarship was supplanted by pride in the ancient traditions of Nippon.[12]

In his *Study of the Idea of the Nation,* Kamo wrote:

the Chinese despise all foreign countries as "barbarian"... despite the fact that their country has been torn for centuries by disturbances and has never really been well administered, they think that they can explain with their Way of Confucius the principles governing the whole world ... When these principles were introduced to this country, it was stated that China had obtained good government through them. What an illusion!

Japan in ancient days was governed in accordance with the natural laws of heaven and earth, with never any indulgence in such petty rationalization as marked China, and had, generation after generation, known prosperity, but no sooner were these Confucian teachings propagated here than a great rebellion occurred in the time of Temmu. Later, at Nara, the palace, dress, and ceremonies were Chinesified and everything took on a superficial elegance; under the surface, contentiousness and dishonesty became more prevalent.

People also tell me, "we had no writing and therefore had to use Chinese characters ... every place name and plant has a separate character. Can any man learn all these? In India fifty letters suffice for the writing of five thousand volumes of Buddhist scripture. In Holland, they use twenty-five letters. The appearance of letters in all countries is in general the same, except China's bothersome system ...

Kamo's pupil, Motoori, a merchant's son and friend of im-

poverished Fujiwara descendants in Kyoto, spent thirty years
translating the Kojiki into Tokugawa Japanese from its archaic
original and wrote of the tradition of the Sun-Goddess:

> The True Way is one and the same, in every country and
> throughout heaven and earth . . . But the ways of foreign
> countries are no more the original than end-branches of a tree
> are the same as its root . . .

> The Sun-Goddess casts her light to the ends of heaven and earth
> for all time. Not a single country in the world does not receive
> her beneficent illuminations. However, foreign countries do not
> know the meaning of revering this goddess . . .

> Our country's Imperial Line represents the descendants of the
> Sky-shining Goddess, destined to rule the nation as long as the
> universe exists. In foreign countries dynastic lines do not con-
> tinue; they change frequently and are quite corrupt.

One of Motoori's students cut the whole work on cherry
wood blocks so that it might be printed and made available for
other scholars. Hirata, a practicing physician who had studied
Dutch books, was attracted by it, and determined to strengthen
Shinto by any and all means.

Fascinated by what he had read of Western astronomy, he
pointed out that the Copernican theory confirmed ancient
Japanese traditions exalting the sun; and from Christian theological works written in Chinese by Catholic missionaries in
Peking, which he managed to secure in spite of the fact that
such books had been banned in Japan for three hundred years,
he adapted arguments against Confucianism and made them
into arguments for the supremacy of Shinto.

> Those who pass for Confucian scholars learn only a few Books
> and Classics and rudimentary composition. Buddhist priests are
> of broader learning: they are required to read enough books to
> make at least seven pack loads for a strong horse . . . But

Japanese learning is even more embracing . . . Because of the
diversity and number of the different parts of Japanese learning,
people are at a loss to evaluate it . . . Japanese should study
all the kinds of learning, even though they be foreign, so that
they can choose the good features of each and place them at the
service of the nation . . .

The Dutch have the excellent national characteristic of investi-
gating matters with great patience and have devised scientific
instruments for doing this . . . When they cannot understand,
they say these things are beyond human knowing and belong
to Gotto [God]. Their findings, the result of hundreds of people
studying for a thousand years, have been incorporated in books
which have been presented to Japan. I have seen them . . .

The spread in Japan since middle antiquity of Confucianism
and Buddhism, both exceedingly troublesome doctrines, has
worsened and confused men's minds, and as a result of the
attendant increase in the number of things to worry about,
various maladies unknown in ancient times have become
prevalent.

The National Learning Movement thus had both religious
and political aspects and came to be known as Neo-Shinto. It
resulted in a nation-wide search for historical documents and
other materials from shrines, temples and all possible sources
and in the undertaking of an enormous history-writing project
by a rival branch of the shogun's family in Mito. Eighty thousand koku of rice a year were set aside for this project and
hundreds of assistants worked on it for over a hundred years.
Dai Nihon Shi (*History of Great Japan*) was finally completed in 1905 in three hundred ninety-seven Japanese-style
volumes.

Neo-Shinto extolled the virtues of the imperial family and
emphasized the desirability of making the divine emperor,
whom military rulers, from the twelfth century on, had forced
into the dim background, once more the actual ruler, the cen-

ter of authority and enlightenment. This movement, coupled with the discontent of an oppressed and suppressed populace, and the eagerness of the Dutch scholars to burst the bonds of isolation, constituted a strong internal threat to the Tokugawa regime.

Then Commodore Perry steamed into Yedo Bay with four United States gunboats prepared for action; "black ships" the Japanese called them. Beacon fires spread the alarm from hill to hill, and people ran to and fro in great confusion. Petty officials came in little boats and warned the intruders to leave at once, but instead of withdrawing, the American commodore approached still closer to the capital of the shogun and insisted that someone of suitable rank be sent to receive the letter which he brought from President Fillmore.

Realizing full well the weakness of both their finances and their coast defenses, the shogunate used every scheme they could to avoid making a direct response: they had been successful in turning away several Russians and other Europeans and the American, Biddle, and his warships seven years before, but Perry maintained an attitude of polite but positively unyielding formality, and at last a special pavilion was constructed for a meeting. At the appointed time, with five thousand samurai and several local officials ranged in ranks to watch the proceedings, the commodore stepped ashore attended by three hundred marines and a private guard of two huge and handsome Negroes. In profound silence the governor of Uraga received the vellum letter in its box of rosewood with gold fittings, and the ceremony concluded without a word being spoken. Soon after, Perry, promising to return again in the spring with a larger squadron for a favorable reply to the President's request for "friendship, commerce, a supply of coal and provisions and protection for shipwrecked people," steamed out of Yedo Bay.[13] He wanted to make the most of the involvement of the Russians, British and French in the Crimean War and have the United States be the first to sign a trade treaty with Japan.

Then the shogunate, which had never before deigned to consult any but the most important daimyos, distributed copies of
a translation of President Fillmore's letter to all the daimyos
and invited their opinions. The daimyos went home and discussed the matter with their samurai. Those who had studied
with the Hollanders in Deshima recommended the opening of
Japanese ports, but the large majority thought back to the ag-
gressiveness of the Spanish and Portuguese and the trouble they

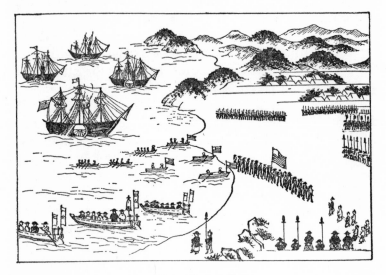

Perry's landing at Uraga

had caused and decided that it was better to keep barbarians
out of Japan.

With "thank money" from Yedo and Osaka merchants, the
shogunate started a cannon foundry and a shipbuilding program to prepare themselves against the return of the black
ships, futile though the effort seemed. They also hoped they
might be able to strengthen their economic position and, since
the copper mines which had supplied their chief medium of
exchange were almost exhausted, they studied various methods

of carrying on trade. They worked out a complete program of government control of horticulture and mining and tried to raise the status of laborers. The visit of several Russian boats to Nagasaki during Perry's absence, however, helped to convince them of the inevitable.

Perry returned in February, 1854, with ten ships instead of four, armed with two hundred and fifty guns, came ashore with a brass band and great parade and made presents to the highest officials of whisky and champagne, standard literary works, rifles, revolvers, clocks, perfume, a sewing machine, a telegraph and a toy locomotive. Officials in their best kimonos strained their necks and eyes to detect something going on in the marvelous telegraph wires. Dignified men rode on top of the toy locomotive and railroad car, laughing nervously as it went round and round its circular track. The pictures of the United States' war with Mexico in two books which they received struck real terror into the hearts of the rulers of Japan, which had had over two hundred years of peace. Remembering the two monstrous Negroes who had served as Perry's guard, however, they thoroughly enjoyed being able to send with the presents they gave in return two enormous wrestlers, an almost unimaginable variety of Japanese, weighing three or four hundred pounds.

After a month of negotiations a treaty was at last drawn up and signed, with copies of it in four languages, English, Dutch, Japanese and Chinese. It provided for:

peace and friendship between the two countries,
the opening of Shimoda and Hakodate to American ships and the supplying of necessary provisions by Japanese officers,
relief of shipwrecked people,
the freedom of Americans in the ports, subject to just laws,
careful deliberation in transacting business,
trade in local ports subject to local regulations,
a "most favored nation" clause,
the residence of United States consuls at Shimoda,

the exchange of ratifications within eighteen months,
freedom of religion to Americans, possible treaty revision after
1872.

Apparently satisfied with the results of his careful planning,
Perry proceeded to inspect the port of Shimoda to the west of
Yedo Bay and to make a trip up to Hakodate, the chief port of
the northern island Hokkaido, in the region frequented by
New Bedford whalers. Before returning to the United States

Perry's men and Japanese wrestlers

he also steamed down to the Ryukyu islands and arranged
with the daimyo of Satsuma in western Kyushu for an open
port there.

The Satsuma fief was rather out of range of shogunate activities: its leaders had been able to carry on a certain amount
of trade and to exert a certain political control over Ryukyu
even during the Tokugawa isolation. This made them oppose
any expansion of the shogunate's trade monopoly and join with
other daimyos, who for various reasons were against opening
the country to barbarians, not because they wished to keep the
country closed, but in order to embarrass the Tokugawas and
further their own position as leaders of the nation.

When Townsend Harris, the first United States consul to
Japan, arrived in Shimoda in 1856 it was a sorry place. Most of
the buildings had just been destroyed in an earthquake, and he

had to put up in a few rooms in an old temple. The annual ceremony of stamping on the cross which had been kept up for over two centuries to prevent any revival of Christianity had just been officially discontinued, but the teaching of "the pernicious doctrine" was still strictly forbidden, and people were urged to have no intercourse whatsoever with foreigners. The common people who constituted over eighty per cent of the population had nothing to say in the matter. They continued patiently to cultivate their little patches of rice and tend their little shops, but daimyos and samurai, especially from the southwestern seacoasts of Japan, kept charging the shogunate with incompetence and cowardice and took up the slogan *Sonno joi* (honor the emperor, expel the barbarians).

For two years Consul General Harris tried in vain to negotiate a treaty allowing the United States unrestricted trade in Japan. He told how the world had been changed by the introduction of steam; how Japan, if she did not do so voluntarily, would be forced to abandon her exclusion policy; how by simply permitting her people to exercise their ingenuity and industry she might soon become a great and powerful nation; how a moderate tax on commerce would soon give her a large revenue by which she might support a respectable navy; that it was better to yield to a consul general than to an armed fleet as China had had to do, and so on.[14] There was a surprising amount of diversity of opinion on the problems the Tokugawas chose to ignore or were incapable of meeting.

After many frustrating experiences with them, Harris discovered that the shogunate was delaying the signing of the treaty until approval of the emperor could be obtained at Kyoto. This was the first inkling he had had of the existence of a ruler other than the shogun, and it put a different light on the situation. The moment the emperor's approval was received the daimyos would withdraw their opposition, shogunate officials assured him. And when Harris inquired what they would do if the emperor refused his consent, they answered promptly

and decisively that the government had determined not to receive any objections from the emperor.

In this, however, they had not calculated well. All the shogun's rivals and enemies had rallied around the emperor and
drafted a document, the purport of which was that the imperial
mind was gravely concerned over the transactions with the
United States, for they constituted a dire menace to the prestige of the nation and involved dangers of a most serious nature which jeopardized permanent peace.

This was the beginning of the end for the Tokugawa shogunate. Neither they nor the emperor nor the outside daimyos
could prevent the signing of trade treaties with Western
nations. Harris' demands were repeated by British, French and
Russian officials, all clamoring for similar rights, with gunboats to render their demands more effective. The ports of
Yokohama, Nagasaki and Hakodate were opened for trade
with these countries in 1859 in accordance with treaties which
the shogunate signed.

CHAPTER 14

OLD JAPAN TANGLES WITH MODERN WORLD

(LATE NINETEENTH CENTURY)

YOKOHAMA in 1859 was a swampy little village of about a hundred houses, except for one hilly strip, cut off from the mainland at high tide. Because of its resemblance to Deshima the foreigners with new trade treaties objected to being settled there, but the shogunate went ahead with the construction of a causeway and the preparation of the ground for building. Soon shops and storehouses, stone jetties, warehouses and a custom-house were ready for occupancy and the newcomers could do nothing but move in. In less than two years the foreign population included fifty-five British, thirty-eight Americans, twenty Dutch, eleven French and two Portuguese—one hundred and twenty-six in all; in five years it had increased to six thousand, had three British bankers, several foreign doctors and civil engineers.[1]

Imports consisted largely of sugar, woollens, cottons and liquor. For exports the Japanese were rather hard put to it; they had so little that foreigners wanted and could so ill afford to lose any of their copper, gold and silver.[2] They offered, however, copper, isinglass, vegetable wax, tea, tobacco, fish and oil and caused the local prices of these consumer items to soar. Though in the flourishing days of Nagasaki they had always imported silk, when they found how the foreigners valued it they began to produce it themselves and developed the silk trade into one of their greatest sources of revenue.

Approximately eighty acres is said to have been the area of the foreign settlement in 1865, but already it included five hotels and a Catholic chapel, a social club and sports field, twenty-four grog shops, bowling and billiard parlors, a milliner, French baker, livery stable and sea-bathing establishment. There was a volunteer fire brigade with three engines, a race track and a park on the bluff, where a missionary had planted American geraniums and where army and navy bands gave public concerts.

The settlement's first newspaper, *Japan Herald,* appeared November 23, 1861. A single sheet folded to make four pages, it carried nothing but advertisements on the front. O. H. Baker, Ship and Family Chandler, carried the largest of these in Volume 1, Number 1, and begged to inform the inhabitants of Yokohama that he kept constantly on hand to offer at the lowest remunerative prices everything from hats and caps to boots and shoes, and from soap to American solidified milk. Lea and Perrins' celebrated Worcestershire Sauce was given a prominent place inside, along with carefully detailed reports of the prices of imports and exports in both Yokohama and Nagasaki markets, and an account of a fire which destroyed several hundred houses in the native quarter of the city. Under the heading, "Latest European News" one read:

> The Secessionist President, Jefferson Davis, is reported to be dead.
>
> Garibaldi is reported to have declined the Commander in chiefship of the Federal Government of America. The Federal Government is preparing to send a large force down the Mississippi from Missouri.
>
> In consequence of the state of the cotton market the Lancashire manufactories are now generally working short time.
>
> Baron Ricasoli is said to have proposed compensation to the pope for the surrender of his temporal authority.
>
> Spain, with France and England, has determined on a military intervention in Mexico.

A project of marriage is reported between the Prince of Wales and a Danish princess.

On another page we read: "The next outward mail leaves Shanghai on Monday next. The following on the 7th December arriving at London via Marseilles January 26th." Three columns of notifications from the British consul general gave warning to British subjects that they were not to ride or drive in such a way as to endanger others, not to discharge firearms except at designated places, nor go in pursuit of game without written permission. Neither were British subjects to intrude into Japanese establishments without invitation, or to assault or offer any violence to Japanese officials. Furthermore, notice was given that since it was neither safe nor expedient in the present state of the country to stray into villages and towns and pass the night away from the settlement, such practice was a serious cause of anxiety to the shogunate authorities and should not be indulged in.

The attitudes of various classes of Japanese toward foreign diplomats and traders differed widely. Townsend Harris, for example, wrote in his diary in 1856:

> The people are of genial disposition and are evidently inclined toward intercourse with foreigners, but the despotic rule of the country and the terror they have of their so-called inflexible laws forbids them to express their wishes.

He saw in the common people such cleanliness, simplicity and honesty, frugality and contentment as he had seen in no other country. And when later, by his own dignified conduct, he had gained the respect of government officials and was received by them in Yedo he found that most careful preparations had been made for his visit. The road to the shogun's capital, though lined with curious spectators all along the way, was kept free of other traffic and especially swept for his procession. As was their custom when some great dignitary of their own country passed, the watching crowds instead of shouting madly kept reverent silence and bowed heads. The quarters prepared for his entertainment within the castle walls, though they had never held such furniture before, were provided with chairs, tables and a bed copied from Harris' own. Even a bathroom and water closet, such as he was accustomed to, were provided for the American consul so that he might be entirely comfortable and favorably impressed by his hosts. Their nervousness, inexperience in Western ways, and consequent vacillation and delaying continually annoyed him, however, and their polite efforts to avoid yielding to all of his requests and yet not give offense he frequently condemned as lying.

When traders began to come in numbers, many complained at first because Japanese merchants were so hesitant to do business by themselves without referring to the officials who had been in charge of all dealings during the isolation. But soon their complaint was that the Japanese had their eyes as wide open to trade and commerce and making cent for cent as any other nation, and would buy no wooden nutmegs.

The ones that made real trouble were the conservative samurai. The earthquake which destroyed fifteen thousand houses soon after Perry's departure, was, they said, like the epidemic which cost so many lives after the introduction of Buddhism in the sixth century, chastening by the deities of the land. They looked upon the foreigners as invaders who had begun by taking a few ports and would soon overrun the country. Though swordsmanship had gone very much out of fashion in Tokugawa times, a number of samurai revived the ancient art and felt they were doing the nation a great service by using it not only on the barbarians but also on their own leaders who, they felt, were weakly betraying them. Dozens of assaults and assassinations were perpetrated by these overzealous patriots, and enormous sums in consequence were paid as indemnities by the government. A group of them, ordered to rip open their stomachs for having killed some French sailors, expressed in several poems the satisfaction they found in sacrificing their own lives for the sake of their country. Perhaps they should not be blamed for feeling as they did, for even Townsend Harris, just after hoisting the first consular flag ever seen in the empire, wrote in his diary: "Grim reflections, ominous of change, undoubted beginning of the end. Query, if for real good of Japan?"

The island nation was in a grave situation indeed. Two centuries of peace had weakened its military defenses, skill and spirit almost to the point of extinction, and now it was threatened by navies representing the fruits of two centuries of continual conflict and conquest. Two centuries of isolation had impaired its posture in international diplomacy and here it was faced by diplomatic giants, wholly different in nature, challenging Japan as a nation. In the ensuing contest the Japanese people revealed their fundamental characteristics: geniality, versatility, durability, qualities of the sun and sea and mountains which they worshiped.

One of the most representative leaders in the Second Great Change, and the one who probably did more than any other individual in making Japan what it is today, was Fukuzawa Yukichi. His autobiography embodies so well the changes which took place in Japan during this transition period that several passages are included in the next few pages.[3] Fukuzawa's theme was: "Young men, poverty and ignorance are hobbling your country; free her by mastering Western science and making money." This was a complete change from the attitude of the old samurai who were inclined to spurn money-making as beneath their dignity and who valued honor and name above all else. "Independence and self-respect" was the motto of Fukuzawa's life. When Perry came to Japan, Yukichi was a poor country boy of nineteen, but versatile and virile. From hearing the talk of the samurai about the need for national defense he resolved to go to Nagasaki and study the science of Western gunnery. To study Western science seriously, his brother told him, one must be able to read the books published in Holland with letters printed sideways, and this he resolved to do. The next time his brother had business in Naga-saki he went along and began his study of the ABC's.

After staying for some time in Nagasaki in a gunnery expert's home and doing all sorts of odd jobs in return for his food and lodging, young Fukuzawa was headed for Osaka where he began to study with a doctor named Ogata who had a school in his home.

No other group of students in Japan at that time could com-pare with us in energy and hard work. For a whole year I had not used a pillow to sleep on but had been studying without regard to day or night, rest or relaxation. I would be reading all day and when night came I did not think of going to bed. When tired I would lean over my little desk or stretch out on the floor, resting my head on the raised alcove floor. All my friends lived in this way. When we happened to have some wine at suppertime I would drink it and go to sleep. I would wake up about ten o'clock and, sitting at my little desk, read on through the night. In the early morning hours when I heard the commotions of boiling rice in the kitchen I took that for a signal to fall asleep again. Just in time for breakfast I would wake up and go out to the bathhouse for a morning plunge. Then on coming back I would fall to at my morning rice and to reading again.

The only Dutch texts the school owned were a few on medi-cine and physical sciences, in all about ten volumes. Each student was therefore obliged to copy every word of the one precious copy. If a student copied ten pages of a dictionary a day he could earn more than his cost of living.

There were then no steel pens in use in Japan and our only paper was the ordinary coarse Japanese kind, meant for brush writing. Some students used to rub this paper with a porcelain bowl to smooth it first and then copy Western writing with a fine brush, but most of us soon learned to size the paper with alum coating and then to use the quill pen. There were several stores that sold birds' quills, usually of cranes or ducks, cut about three inches long, quite cheap. Fishermen were said to use them for catching bonito. When shaved down the quills served for pens very well. For ink—no foreign ink had been brought in—we rubbed the native ink blocks with water and kept the liquid in a pot or sometimes we soaked a piece of cotton in it for ease in carrying.

As this was the only way to have foreign texts we became quite skilled in writing while some friend read the original. Though we were all really good friends, the older ones helping the new students by explaining texts and answering questions, we never helped each other with class preparations. No one ever thought of being so cowardly as to take help in preparing his required work, no matter how difficult. Then each student had to depend on his own ability with the grammars and the one big dictionary the school possessed.

Of course, at that time there were no examples of industrial machinery. A steam engine could not be seen in the whole of Japan, nor any apparatus for chemical experiments, but when we learned something of chemistry and machinery we wanted to try it out. We managed to make chloric acid to use in plating iron with tin when no tin craftsman in Japan could plate anything but copper or bronze with tin by using pine pitch. We tried to make iodine from seaweed and worked till we were black with smoke, but without success. Then we tried ammonium chloride. We learned that horse hoof would serve the purpose. So we bought some fragments of it from a tortoise-shell ware store; it was sometimes used for fertilizer. We covered the hoof with a layer of clay in an earthenware jar and put it over a fire. A smelly vapor came out which we condensed in an earthenware pipe. Our experiment was going very well and the condensed vapor was dripping freely, but the stench was terrible. Our clothes became so saturated with the smell that when we went to the bathhouse in the evening the street dogs howled at us. Then we tried the experiment naked, but our skins absorbed the smell. We endured it without complaint but the neighbors objected and the servants wailed that they could not eat their dinner on account of the sickening gas.

One day a new text in physical science recently translated from English to Dutch was loaned to us for two days. All that

we knew about electricity then had been gleaned from frag-
mentary mention in Dutch readers. But here was a full explanation based on the experiments of Faraday even with the
diagram of an electric cell. We decided to copy the chapter on
electricity—one hundred and fifty pages with diagrams. When
the time came to return it we all handled the book affectionately
in turn and gave it a sad leave-taking as if we were parting
with a parent. When we heard it had cost eighty ryo (about
$80.) we were dumbfounded. Ogata's students soon became the
best informed men on electricity in the entire country.

In Yedo there were constant demands for Western knowledge from government offices and feudal nobility, and anyone
able to read and translate foreign books was rewarded. Osaka,
however, was a city of merchants devoted to internal commerce,
who looked down with contempt on students of Dutch. There
was no living in it for us, but we knew that we alone possessed
the key to knowledge of the great European civilization. However ill-fed or poorly clothed we were, we knew we had something beyond the reach of princes. We were proud of our hard
work.

Of course we were all for free intercourse with Western
countries, but there were few among us who took really serious
interest in that problem. The only subject that bore our constant attack was Chinese medicine; and we thus came to dislike everything that had any connection with Chinese culture.
Our general opinion was that we should rid our country of the
influences of the Chinese altogether. We ridiculed students of
Chinese medicine whenever we met them. "Look at them,"
one of us would begin, "they think they are learning something;
they listen to those crazy lectures of their master, but he simply
repeats the same old mouldy theories handed down for how
many centuries!"

In 1858, Fukuzawa left Osaka and went up to Yedo, and
the next year the port of Yokohama was opened to foreign
trade.

When I went to Yokohama for sight-seeing I found to my

great disappointment that I could not talk with the merchants nor read any of the signboards. I had been striving with all my powers for many years to learn Dutch and now English seemed sure to be the language of the future. So I determined to study English, but there were no teachers.

He therefore bought a book of Dutch-English conversation and after a while managed to get an English dictionary and one friend to study with him. To learn pronunciation they sought out shipwrecked fishermen who had been picked up by foreign ships, and asked them to pronounce English words. Soon they realized that English was not wholly different from Dutch and that their knowledge of Dutch could be applied to English.

In 1859, on the advice of Townsend Harris, arrangements were made for the sending of a Japanese embassy to Washington. Congress appropriated fifty thousand dollars toward this and sent a steamer to carry the envoys across the Pacific. An escort ship manned entirely by Japanese officers and crew was dispatched by the shogunate from Yedo in January, 1860, and on this Fukuzawa managed to take passage.

For a whole month we saw nothing but waves and clouds and one sailboat said to be carrying Chinese workmen to America. It was like being in jail and having earthquakes day and night. . . . I am willing to admit my pride in this accomplishment for Japan, that about seven years after the first sight of a steamship, Japanese people made a trans-Pacific crossing without help from foreign experts . . . Even Peter the Great of Russia who went to Holland to study navigation could not have equaled this feat.

After five weeks they landed in California, which the United States had annexed five years before; thousands turned out to see the strangers. The mission, though not Fukuzawa, arrived in Washington while the Republican National Convention which nominated Lincoln was meeting in Chicago. They were shown all sorts of military installations and public institutions, including Congress in session.

There were many confusing and embarrassing moments, for we were quite ignorant of the customs and habits of American life. When we were taken to a hotel we noticed all over the floors carpets and rugs such as only wealthy Japanese could buy from importers' shops at so much a square inch to make purses and tobacco pouches with. It was astounding to see a whole room covered with it—and our hosts in the shoes they had worn on the street walking on this costly fabric. We followed them in our hemp sandals.

Before leaving Japan I was an independent soul, a carefree student fearing nothing, but on arriving in America I suddenly became shy, self-conscious and blushing. The contrast was funny even to myself.

One evening we were invited to a dancing party. When we arrived we saw ladies and gentlemen hopping about the room together and could not quite make out what they were doing. It struck us as terribly funny but we knew it would be rude to laugh.

At one dinner given for us a whole pig was brought onto the table roasted—head, legs, tail and all. We at once thought of a fairy tale of a cruel witch who indulged in gruesome feasts. Still, it tasted very good! On taking leave our host and hostess kindly offered us horses to ride home on. This pleased us, for a chance to ride horseback again was a relief. We touched whip to the horses and trotted back to our quarters. The Americans stood and watched us with evident surprise.

I was impressed by the enormous waste of iron everywhere. In garbage piles, on the seashore, old tin cans, empty cans, broken tools. Why, in Yedo after a fire there would be hundreds of poor people looking for nails in the charred wood, so valuable was metal in Japan. And we had to pay fifty cents for twenty or thirty oysters—in Japan they would have cost only a cent or two.

One day I asked a gentleman where the descendants of George Washington might be. He replied, "I think there is a woman who is directly descended from Washington. I don't know where she is, but I think I heard she was married." This was a great shock. I could not help feeling that the family of Washington should be treated with great reverence.

When he got back to Japan, Fukuzawa found that the shogun's chancellor who had signed the trade treaties with the foreign powers had been assassinated, and the cry "Expel the barbarians" was everywhere.

Nevertheless, he brought out a dictionary of English which was to serve as a foundation for a series of later books, and when in 1862, while America was involved in Civil War, the British offered to take an official Japanese embassy to Europe by way of Singapore and Suez, he was appointed to go along as interpreter. With the allowance given him for expenses he bought many books in London, the first English books to be imported into Japan and the first to which Japanese students had free access. Leaders who believed in the need for a new educational system, taking Western civilization into account, rallied round Fukuzawa and he became the spokesman of the liberal group which advocated complete renovation of the national life.[4]

The conservative opposition, advocating "reverence to the Emperor and expulsion of foreigners," aligned itself with the Mito School which was compiling the colossal official history of Japan. They aimed to conciliate and unite the various religious, intellectual and political elements in the country against the threat from outside; and to show the barbarians their vigor and contempt.

Their spokesman Aizawa in his *New Proposals* wrote:

In the defense of the state through armed preparedness, a policy for peace or for war must be decided upon before all else. If there is indecision on this point, morale will deteriorate while everyone hopes for peace that cannot materialize. In the days of old when the Mongols were insolent, Hojo Tokimune stood resolute. Emperor Kameyama prayed at Isé and offered his life for the salvation of the country. The men called upon to sacrifice themselves defied death in a body. Their loyalty and patriotism were such as to bring forth a storm that smashed the foe at sea. Put the entire nation into the position of inevitable death; only then can the defense problem be easily worked out.

Loyalty to the emperor and filial piety to parents were basic morality. Only this would unite the nation. "Let the Shogun issue orders to the entire nation to smash the barbarians and everyone will enforce the order. This is a great opportunity. It must not be lost." For subsequent generations this ideology became the "national polity" and before World War II Aizawa's *New Proposals* were acclaimed as immortal.

Between these two extremes was a moderate group, who saw the realities of the situation in a more practical way. To strengthen the nation politically, they urged a closer working union between the Kyoto court and the shogun's officials; in the cultural sphere, they called for adoption of Western science together with preservation of Japanese ethics. Their eight-point program expressed by Sakuma Shozan included: the erection of fortifications equipped with artillery at all strategic points on the coast; suspension of copper exports and casting of guns; building of large merchant ships to prevent loss of rice in coastal shipwrecks; capable official supervision of maritime trade; development of a navy—warships and crews; establishment of schools and modern education so that "even the most stupid men and women may understand loyalty, piety and chastity"; and systems for reward and punishment, and selection of able officials.

Actually, however, the shogun's officials were in immediate contact with the foreign powers and obliged to negotiate with them. Though given a deadline by the emperor for expelling the barbarians, they could do little about it.

Satcho leaders took advantage of the situation for discrediting the Tokugawas and restoring power to the Kyoto court. With increased respect for the West, after a disastrous attack on

British warships, they made technical assistance agreements for English engineers to set up sugar factories, a foundry and machine shop and a cotton mill in their southwestern provinces. They also added several Western-style boats to their Ryukyu trading fleet.

Most leaders came to feel that perhaps, after all, intercourse with the West would not be such a bad thing if only they could manage to preserve their national integrity. This, however, they realized could never be done so long as the country was divided into factions. Only by presenting a strongly united front to the demands of Western nations could Japan hope to survive. Tokugawas and anti-Tokugawas alike began to feel that the situation required the restoration of the imperial dignity. The prestige of the imperial house in ancient times owed much to the fact that it alone was officially recognized by the Chinese court. Though shoguns had later been authorized to take over the internal administration of the country they had had very little to do with overseas affairs. Both Ashikaga Yoshimitsu and Hideyoshi, it is true, in consequence of their relations with China, had been designated King of Japan, but the Tokugawa shogunate had never felt easy about assuming the responsibility for foreign diplomacy.

In 1867, the old emperor who did not want foreigners stepping on the Land of the Gods died, and his fifteen-year-old son succeeded to the throne with the support and ready advice of Satcho allies. Soon afterward the shogun tendered his resignation.

Now that foreign intercourse becomes daily more extensive, unless the government is directed from one central authority, the foundations of the state will fall to pieces. If administrative authority be restored to the imperial court, and if national deliberations be conducted on an extensive scale, and the empire be supported by the efforts of the whole people, then the empire will be able to maintain its rank and dignity among the nations of the earth. Although I have allowed all the feudal lords to state

their views without reservation, yet it is, I believe, my highest
duty to realize the national ideal by giving up entirely my rule
over the land.[5]

The shogun himself was ready to fight when, after peace-
fully resigning, he found that he was treated as an enemy of
the imperial house by the four southwestern seacoast daimyos,
and that they stepped right into the place which he had va-
cated. His loyal supporters were not willing to give in easily
either. The commander of the Tokugawa navy even attempted
to set up a new government on the northern island, Hokkaido,
in defiance of the new powers, and many sincere patriots were
assassinated for their outspoken opinions. The new leaders,
however, were well prepared and qualified for their position.

Because of their geographic location they had always been
in closer touch with foreigners than the northeastern daimyos
had been; first with the Korean countries and China, then with
the Portuguese, Spaniards and Dutch, and now with the English.
When the sixteenth-century hero, Hideyoshi, had managed to
subdue them by employing Buddhist spies, the Satsuma clan
had angrily resolved to do away with all Buddhist centers of
idle, extravagant priests. While in many other parts of the
country, samurai had been detached from the land and formed
a great body of decadent unemployed, in the southwestern
provinces they had worked as farmers and kept up their military discipline even in the years of peace, for they belonged to
the "outside daimyos" and never knew when they might want
to defend themselves against Tokugawa encroachments. The
education and well-being of the people generally had also been
carefully watched. As a result, the leaders of Satsuma, Choshu,
Hizen and Tosa were able to carry on the Second Great
Change with remarkably little friction.

The new regime was designated Meiji (Enlightened Government). Even before the enthronement ceremonies for the
youthful sovereign were held, he had given audience to foreign
envoys and issued an edict granting foreigners full protection

with capital punishment for offenders. The idea of the Son of Heaven face to face with common Westerners was shocking even to many of the Satsuma clan, but it was quite in line with a new philosophy of direct approach and simplicity.

Economic considerations undoubtedly did much to make this philosophy acceptable, for the imperial court, a few days before the announcement of the new regime, it is stated, had only twenty to thirty days' stock of rice and very little money. In accordance with the aims of the new regime, the enthronement ceremony[6] itself, which had been based on Chinese customs of the T'ang Dynasty and in use for a thousand years, was now reformed. Chinese costumes and decorations were abandoned, and Shinto ritual offerings were substituted for the burning of incense. A great globe map of the world was prominently displayed.

Kyoto also was involved in the great change. It was considered to be too out of the way a place for the Meiji capital. Osaka was proposed as a substitute because most of the nation's wealth was concentrated there, and the cooperation of the rich merchants was much desired. The boy emperor was taken to Osaka on a visit and given a chance to review the warships of various clans lined up two miles off shore. But since foreign governments were accustomed to think of Yedo as the center of power, and since Yedo's neighboring port, Yokohama, was flourishing so rapidly, the Tokugawa properties in these two cities were confiscated and the imperial residence was moved to Yedo. Its name was then changed to Tokyo (Eastern Capital).

The imperial cortege left for Tokyo on the Great Eastern Sea Road accompanied by three thousand officials. On this journey, which required twenty-two days, the emperor had the first opportunity of his life to observe the regular activities and living conditions of farmers and common people. He enjoyed stopping the procession and watching the farmers harvesting their rice.

Just before the New Year he was taken back to Kyoto for

his wedding ceremony. An imperial messenger delivered a dress and sword as imperial wedding gifts to the selected lady on the appointed day, and she proceeded to the palace in an ox-drawn cart. There, seated on a platform, she was honored with a repast provided by the court, and by secretary conveyed her respects to her future consort. A special messenger then proceeded to the emperor's presence and announced the installation of the empress and the ceremony was ended.

On his second journey to Tokyo the emperor stopped to pay his respects at the Isé Shrine dedicated to his divine ancestress Amaterasu. This was also an innovation prompted by his Neo-Shinto supporters to impress upon the people reverence for the founder of the imperial house. Popularization of the emperor was not to be carried too far. It was the theory of divine descent that had preserved for him the throne and which would continue to bind the Japanese nation together as a family. A strong Shinto revival was therefore promoted, while Buddhist priests were stripped of their privileges and Buddhist temples throughout the country were ransacked and desecrated. Statues small enough to carry were stolen by marauders for the valuable metal in them, and gold leaf was scraped off wherever it was found.

The new government was designed to give the nation the strength of unity. What unity had been achieved thus far, however, was more sentimental than real. There were still two hundred and seventy-six daimyos with as many separate fiefs. Each daimyo commanded his own samurai, and several of them had navies. Each exercised the right of legislation over his own domains and regulated the collection and expenditure of revenues according to his own ideas. Not more than one-sixth of the land of Japan had reverted to imperial control as a result of the shogunate's downfall. To make the government really effective some means had to be devised for giving the sovereign supreme command of all armaments, armies and navies, for investing him with authority to promulgate laws for the whole land, and, most important perhaps of all, for creating a central treasury.

By 1869, the four southwestern seacoast daimyos had most of the offices of the new government filled by their own men, and most of the policies were entirely of their own making. The Tokugawas had been allowed to retain three of their ancestral estates, but for some time were given no part in public affairs.

Though a really stable government was not achieved until two decades later, immediate steps were taken for the centralization of power. First a group of the strongest daimyos voluntarily offered to return their feudal rights to the court and all but seventeen of the rest followed suit.[7] (This was not unlike the reform for which Fujiwara Kamatari and Prince Naka had set an example by giving up their own lands in 645.) These and the Tokugawa fiefs were converted into seventy-two prefectures and the daimyos were rewarded for their cooperation with positions in the new government and with government bonds which were negotiable as capital for undertaking new businesses and industrial enterprises.

The method of dealing with the land and farmers was very simple indeed. Though theoretically it was claimed that all the land belonged to the emperor, those who were working and living on the land were allowed to remain where they were in return for a tax in money based on the land valuation. They were allowed to buy or sell, will or inherit, and move about as they pleased. What did most to win the loyal support of the farmers for the new government, however, was the granting of uniform laws to all classes of people and the adoption of the principle of universal conscription. To be on an equal footing with the old samurai was a great thing for common farmers and artisans; and it was a great thing for the new government to have the staunch support of this great mass of the population.

Timber and mining lands, and those unfit for cultivation,

remained as the private property of the imperial household and an important permanent source of revenue for them. Urban properties, which had belonged to the Tokugawas in the ports and Yedo, were sold to whoever had courage and money to buy them, in order to raise immediate funds for the new government.

Instead of the regular rice stipends which they had received from their feudal lords, samurai were granted annual pensions payable in bonds as long as the government felt they could afford it. After that the samurai had to shift for themselves. This was harsh treatment indeed, for many who had had little experience in handling money failed miserably when they tried to go into business. Others who had held responsible executive positions on the estates of their feudal lords eventually made great successes in banking, shipping, communications and industry; many eventually became government officials. What seemed to disturb them most was that they were no longer privileged to wear two swords.

During the process of political and social readjustment, the advisers of the young emperor deemed it wise to have some definite assurance themselves, and to enlist the confidence and cooperation of the entire nation in the program of the Second Great Change. An assembly of all daimyos was summoned and a Charter Oath proclaimed to them: all affairs of state were to be decided by impartial discussion; civil and military powers were to be centralized and equal opportunity assured to all classes; all classes were to unite and strive for the progress and welfare of the nation; all outworn customs were to be abandoned; intelligence and learning were to be sought for throughout the world in order to strengthen the empire.

Within five years a postal system such as Fukuzawa had seen in Paris replaced the runners between Tokyo, Kyoto and Osaka. A railroad ran between Tokyo and Yokohama. There were gas lamps at the palace gates. And the new school system on paper called for over fifty thousand primary schools, one for each six hundred persons, feeding into thirty-two middle schools which in turn were to prepare students for eight universities.

Confucianists now became "obstinate, old-fashioned, ludicrous." "Civilization and enlightenment" became the new leitmotiv, symbolized by pocket watches on chains, Western-style haircuts and Western-style umbrellas worn through the sash like swords. Brick buildings sprang up on the Ginza housing Western-style restaurants serving *meat*. Samurai, peasants, artists, merchants, young and old, male and female, wise and fools, rich and poor, so long as they ate meat and were not culturally backward, flocked to them, looking polished and shiny from Western soap and reeking of eau de cologne. Commerce was also a great word. Even rickshaw pullers were caricatured calling to each other in passing, "How is commerce today?" Samurai in government offices became dignitaries in chairs and a popular ditty went:

> A civilization and enlightenment bird
>   flew in from the West.
> Nesting in a chair-tree he sang,
>   "Salary! Salary!" [8]

Such frivolity, however, was more than balanced by the intense seriousness of the new intellectuals. Though the Charter Oath of March, 1868, served as a first milestone for new Japan, little progress seemed to have been made. Imperialists and shogunate were equally corrupt, Fukuzawa thought; withdrawing from public affairs and devoting himself to teaching the young about the West, he wrote books such as: *Conditions in the West* in which he pointed out that the West has two advantages, learning based on mathematics and reason, and a spirit of independence; *An Illustrated Account of the Natural Sciences,* and a *Guide to Western Travels*. In *About All Countries* he pointed out that history advances from savagery and nomadic hunting as in Africa to barbarous feudalism as in

Turkey, China and Japan, and to civilization as in America and Europe. "Civilization comforts man physically, and elevates him spiritually," he wrote in his *Outline of Civilization,* "it advances both knowledge and virtue." He became greatly concerned about Western morals—writing at length about private morals (faithfulness, honesty, modesty and politeness) but more important to him and his followers were public morals such as fair play, honor and courage.

CHAPTER 15

ON THE WAY TO WORLD POWER
(1868–1919)

ENRICHMENT and strengthening of the nation! Enrichment and strengthening of the nation! This was the rallying call of Fukuzawa and the resolute ambition of the new leaders. Those who crossed the Pacific and the Atlantic to observe and study in America and Europe realized that not only in navies and fighting strength, but also in industrial development and public education, the West was vastly superior to Japan. And they suffered, these island people, from a sensitivity that made it most difficult for them to endure being looked down upon.

Undaunted by the herculean nature of their task, the new leaders, having already determined to build up a national defense inferior to none, now determined to remodel completely their education system, and build up an independent self-respecting citizenry.

The young emperor issued an edict which ran:

> During youthtime it is positively necessary to view foreign countries so as to become enlightened as to the ideas of the world. Girls as well as boys should be allowed to go abroad; and my country will be benefited by their knowledge so acquired. Women have had no position socially because it was considered that they were without understanding, but if educated and intelligent they should have due respect.

At the government's expense five girls were sent the following year to study in America; the eldest was fifteen but the youngest one was eight.[1]

A young Satsuma clansman who had been the first Japanese chargé d'affaires in the United States returned home in 1873 full of ideas. In America, he had observed, scholars formed learned societies for the study of arts and sciences, gave lectures and published papers from which the public benefited greatly. With several others who had been abroad, a society called Meirokusha (Meiji Sixth Year Society) was organized to advance Western learning and morality.[2] This group taught government officials Western theories; they also demonstrated that although the formal Tokugawa Japanese language was not at all suitable for intelligible, rapid communication in the modern world, Fukuzawa's newly developed vocabulary made Western style speechmaking and debate possible. And they published the first of many learned Japanese opinion magazines in which Fukuzawa's views were often criticized.

"It is true," one member wrote in effect, "that as Fukuzawa has said the government is still despotic, the people apathetic, powerless and ignorant, but for twenty-five hundred years, oppression and servility have been the usual fare of the people, staples, like rice and pickled radishes. Barely seven years ago learning consisted of such things as Confucian classics, tea ceremony, flower arrangement, skillful use of bow, sword and lance and horsemanship. Intellectuals ought to be steadfast and forbearing."

Articles in the Meirokusha magazine discussed: writing Japanese with a Western alphabet, loving one's enemies, whether intellectuals should be in the government or outside criticizing it, the death penalty, freedom of religion, *The False Evil Ugly Japanese* as well as *The Truthful Virtuous Beautiful Japanese* and equal rights for women as well as new views on keeping mistresses. A few of them had strong Christian leanings and emphasized the fact that Western culture was founded on Christian thought. Activities of the society were eagerly re-

ported by the press, and their influence was of historic importance.

Soon hundreds of students were flocking to the United
States and Europe. Rutgers College in New Jersey alone had
over three hundred in a short span of years because of its connections with the Dutch Reformed missionaries. A few were
specially admitted to Annapolis. Law students went to Cornell,
Michigan, Harvard and Yale. Philadelphia, with its railroad
and locomotive companies and nearby bridge works and State
Geographical Survey was a favorite center for young engineers.
Students of agriculture were scattered throughout the country.
Many received masters' and doctors' degrees. German universities, it was felt, gave better intellectual training, but they lacked
the moral and religious influence of the American, and were
not so practical and wide-awake.

In comparison with these Western institutions, the ones in
Japan seemed very poor indeed, and in the mid-seventies there
was great emphasis on improving education. Compulsory education was increased from four years to six, and a uniform curriculum was introduced which facilitated the molding of the
many scattered clans into a united nation.

For training the army of teachers required by these new
schools many normal schools were established, most of them
for men, but a few for women.[3] Middle schools, special schools,
foreign-language schools, technical schools and universities
were provided for those who wished to continue their education beyond the compulsory level. To hasten the process of reform, experts and scholars from Europe and America were invited to come to Japan as advisers to the different departments
of the government and as professors in the universities.

Frenchmen were requested to assist in preparing a criminal
code and in teaching army strategy and tactics; Englishmen,
to help build railways and lighthouses and develop telegraphy.
Italian sculptors and painters were asked to introduce Western
art; Germans, to train doctors and army officers and to help put

into effect local government systems. Americans served in establishing the educational and postal systems, in carrying out agricultural reforms and colonization projects.

While the chief interest in learning was utilitarian, purer scholarship also developed rapidly under Western teachers. In feudal days it had been considered shamefully disloyal not to uphold everything one's master taught, but now scientific equipment and techniques were introduced and Japanese students for the first time began to search for truth for truth's sake. The search extended especially through the fields of biology, medicine, botany, astronomy, geology and history. Tokugawa scholars had studied history just as they wrote in a vertical column from the top to the bottom, from the present of their own country down to its remote past, but Meiji scholars wrote like Westerners in horizontal lines and they extended their studies into all corners of the world, comparing their own historical documents, stone-age pottery and skulls with those of other countries.

The northern island, Hokkaido, became a sort of frontier to which adventurous spirits turned with all their new ideas. Homesteads were granted to those who would settle there, and many samurai were conscripted to go there and work on farms. An agricultural college was opened with an American as its director, and various crops and breeds of cattle were imported from the United States. This island was not so cut up by rivers and mountains and by dense population as the rest were, and so larger scale farming was possible. Corn and potatoes were grown in quantity; apples and tomatoes and sugar beets yielded very successful crops. Fish canning and the making of fish oil soon developed as profitable industries along with the manufacture of paper. In Hokkaido, also, Japan's first railroad was built connecting some coal mines with a seaport forty-five miles distant. A Pennsylvania Railroad engineer was in charge of the construction and the engines were imported from the Baldwin Locomotive Works in Philadelphia.

More important than these, however, were the industrial developments which the government, by providing land and bonds for capital, had promoted on the other islands. Western methods of extracting and refining ores were put in practice in the copper, gold and silver mines. To supply the needs of extensive foundries and shipbuilding yards, coal and iron mines were opened, and steel industry started. Cotton-spinning, silk-reeling and textile mills and pottery factories were promoted. Steamers and stage lines were operated between several places, and railroads were being built. Yokohama and Tokyo were connected by telegraph, and newspapers were published in several cities. Almost a million people were employed in manufacturing, a million and a half in commerce, before the end of the first decade of Meiji. The total annual value of exports and imports during the same period had risen approximately from thirty million to sixty million yen.

General Ulysses S. Grant visited Japan in 1879 during a trip around the world and reported to fellow Americans:

This is a most beautiful country and a most interesting people. The progress they have made in their changed civilization within twelve years is almost incredible. This is marvelous, when the treatment these people and all Eastern peoples receive at the hands of the average foreigners residing among them is considered. I have never been so struck with the heartlessness of nations, as well as individuals, as since coming to the East.[4]

The ambitious and able young samurai from the southwestern seacoast regions who had been instrumental in founding the new regime, however, had by no means reached their goal. The financial burdens involved in converting a disunited feudal country into a modern nation were enormous. The cost of building a completely new school system, training and equipping a new army and navy, and subsidizing the development of industries, railroads and shipping had imposed a great strain on everyone. There were many who had little enthusiasm for the new government. Particularly difficult in this respect were the unemployed samurai of other than Satcho clans who had been given few opportunities by the new leaders. The restoration of the emperor had done little to restore the power which had long been passing from their hands. The vulgar merchants' money controlled their destiny. Instead of the impartial discussion, equal opportunity, justice and righteousness which the Charter Oath had led them to expect of the new government, they found a dictatorship very similar to that they had known before, and the same humiliating trade treaties of 1858, granting to foreigners extraterritorial rights and control of tariffs on goods imported by Japan.

To allay dissatisfaction and unite rival factions the new government sent an embassy to the United States and Europe to arrange revision of these treaties, but met with no success. As a result, there was a split within the new Meiji government, with Okubo leading a group devoted to continuing peace and political reform, and Saigo leading a group with militant ideas.[5] Russian fortifications and acts of violence on Sakhalin and other Western aggressions must be stopped. Saigo, who had been Chief of Staff for the imperial armies which overthrew the shogunate, thought that by diverting the attention of the entire nation toward war the position and spirit of Japan would be strengthened, but the support of China and Korea must be won first.

"Grounds for starting a conflict with Korea might be found in international law," Saigo suggested, "but the Japanese people would not accept them. If, however, an envoy were sent to the Korean government to reproach them for weakening relations with Japan and asking them to strive for improved relations in future," the popular field marshal went on, "the contemptuous attitude of the Koreans will reveal itself. They are certain to kill the envoy. This will bring home to the entire Japanese nation the necessity of punishing their crimes." Such a scheme was calculated to divert attention from civil strife, and thereby to benefit the nation.

"I cannot claim to make as splendid an envoy as the foreign minister recently returned from China," Saigo wrote the prime minister, "but if it is a question of dying, *that* I assure you I am prepared to do. I beseech you to send me."

When his plan was rejected, Saigo withdrew from the government, prepared to retire quietly, but his hot-blooded samurai followers clashed with government forces, and loyalty impelled him to join them. With generations of military tradition behind them, they presented a grim challenge to the new citizen-conscript army. This rebellion was crushed in 1877, and Saigo's life was given up for his friends. Because of his earlier services, however, he was posthumously pardoned by the emperor and became a martyred-samurai hero of later generations.

Okubo, on the other hand, with the natural gifts of a talent scout, enlisted capable young men from other clans to assist him in the internal development of the nation, and when he, too, within a year was assassinated, his protégés were well prepared to carry on his plans.

Though the victory of the new conscript army over the Satsuma samurai increased the confidence of the government in the ultimate success of its reforms, the cost of it caused a crisis in government finance.

Prefectural councils then were created to assist in local financial administration and collection of taxes. Industries which the government had been supporting were now transferred to the private ownership of wealthy families who had made possible the founding of the Meiji regime. The Bank of Japan was established with the right to issue paper money and do business directly with the imperial treasury, a peculiarly Japanese system of state-controlled finance. Rich merchants and industrial development notwithstanding, the country was intrinsically poor; the loyal, hard-working farmers were still the greatest asset in the national accounts.

As Japanese grew more aware of the European trend toward constitutional representative governments, following the American example, it became clear that the Meiji regime would also have to have a constitution, a rule of law, if it aimed to win the respect of Western nations. Political parties formed and a critical press voiced widespread opposition to the control of Japan by a few clan leaders. These pressures resulted in an imperial decree that, though European civilization must first be more widely spread and firmly rooted, "in the twenty-third year of Meiji, 1890, a parliament shall be opened. Let the officials and the people prepare for it."

An extensive study of constitutional systems was undertaken by Okubo's protégé, Ito, and a group of loyal young supporters of the emperor.[6] Bismarck, then the chief figure in Europe, they found, had started with conditions not entirely unlike those in Japan, and had built up a unified nation with far-reaching international influence.

It was evident to Ito from the outset that mere imitation of foreign models would not suffice; the historical peculiarities of Japan had to be taken into consideration; for example the Crown was an institution deeply rooted in Japanese sentiment and history; also centuries-long traditions of family loyalty and inertia had made of Japan a vast village community where cold intellect and calculation of public events were often hindered by warm emotions between man and man; free discussion so necessary to a representative regime was apt to be smothered; the attainment and transfer of power, a matter of family honor. Deprived of safety valves for giving vent to discontents, differences of opinion were apt to degenerate into passionate quarrels.

The Meiji Constitution when promulgated therefore was "the gift of a benevolent and charitable emperor to the people of his country." It began "The Empire of Japan shall be reigned over and governed by a line of emperors unbroken for ages eternal. . . . The emperor is sacred and inviolable."

A popular assembly called the Imperial Diet was provided for, but the Cabinet was to exercise all powers, executive, legislative and judicial, which were vested in the Crown by the Constitution. The Cabinet of nine ministers, appointed by the emperor, was responsible in the name of the emperor, for the operations of nine departments: Home Office, War Office, Board of Education, Foreign Office, Admiralty, Board of Agriculture and Trade, Treasury, Department of Justice, Board of Communications and Public Works. A Privy Council of men who had previously rendered distinguished service were to be the emperor's specially appointed advisers for life. The Supreme War Council was also under direct imperial command, not answerable to the Diet. The chief and practically sole function of the Diet was to discuss the budget presented by the Cabinet; if the Diet did not approve, the Cabinet could resign, but it could also dissolve the Diet. All matters were trusted to the judgment of the Cabinet ministers, and the emperor, indeed, "could do no wrong."

The first general election of Diet members took place from July 1 to 3, 1890. Every man who paid a land tax of fifteen yen or over was allowed to vote. They were urged to exercise their new political rights as the duty of an indispensable element of the nation. Still the populace was politically uneducated and irresponsible, and the Satcho advisers appeared better entrenched than ever in their positions of influence. If the little island empire was to be enriched and strengthened, if it was to become independent and self-respecting, people could not be flying off on German, Russian or American tangents; many forces would have to be held in dynamic balance; all their energies and limited resources would have to be concentrated and centralized in a unified program.

What everyone was really interested in was reduction of land tax and revision of the foreign trade treaties. Several Diets were dissolved and a Cabinet had to resign due to impasses on these

issues, before England in 1894 conceded treaty revision and
other nations followed suit.

Now that Japan had some experience in Western techniques
of education, transportation, industry, agriculture and government, she realized how limited were her own resources and
horizons as compared with those of the Western nations who
were close neighbors. She could no longer endure the restricted
living of her cramped little islands. She had to expand. She,
too, had to develop her strength by military activity. With the
rest of the world left to Western influence and competition,
East Asia, it seemed, might rightfully be her special province.
Though China shared little of Japan's ambition and energized
readiness to change, she had much more in common with the
Japanese than with Europeans.

To become a great power on the Asiatic continent, like the
Western nations from whom she had learned so much, now
became Japan's chief ambition. China's lack of interest in
international trade and her supine attitude toward the West
irked Japanese excessively. They felt that they had much more
in common with China than Europeans had, and that to develop status they must expand and demonstrate the quality
of their new army and navy.

The Sino-Japanese War developed successfully for Japan.
China ceded to Japan the Liaotung Peninsula and the islands
of Formosa and the Pescadores. She also agreed to the complete
independence of Korea and the opening of the Yangtze for
navigation. Then Japan had a disappointing experience with
European diplomacy. Russia, Germany and France, in the name
of the peace of the Far East, made Japan renounce her claims
to any territory on the continent and, together with Britain,
proceeded to establish themselves in strategic places in North
China and Manchuria. This continued foreign aggression finally
aroused bitter feeling in Peking, and the Boxer uprising occurred. Japan, being nearest, was able to send the first relief to

the besieged legations, and her troops gave an excellent impression of efficiency, discipline and good behavior. The outcome was the Anglo-Japanese Alliance which recognized:

> the independence of China and Korea, the special interests of Great Britain in China, and of Japan both in China and in a peculiar degree, politically as well as commercially and industrially, in Korea, and the rights of both parties to take such measures as may be indispensable to safeguard those interests either against the aggressive action of any other power or in the case of disturbances in either country.[7]

According to Sir Charles Eliot:

> One result of the Boxer troubles was that Russia remained in military occupation of Manchuria and this created a position most dangerous for Japan's interests. Japan undoubtedly desired peace, and while realizing that war might be inevitable, did her best to avoid or postpone it. She acted in concert with Great Britain and the United States, and Russia was induced to sign a treaty pledging herself to withdraw her troops from Manchuria in three installments. Russia did not withdraw her troops from Manchuria at the dates fixed, and the Japanese Government opened direct negotiations at St. Petersburg. They proposed that Russia and Japan should each recognize the other's status in Manchuria and Korea respectively; that both powers should respect the territorial integrity of China and Korea and be parties to an engagement that all nations should have equal commercial and industrial opportunities in Korea and Manchuria. The negotiations lasted for five and a half months, but Russia proved unyielding and unconciliatory.

In the war which followed, the Japanese army and navy achieved a series of brilliant victories and piled up an enormous national debt. Both Japan and Russia, therefore, were very willing to accept President Theodore Roosevelt's mediation, and the United States' interest in halting Russian advances was served as well. By the peace treaty signed in Portsmouth, New

Hampshire, in 1905, Japan acquired supremacy in (and subsequent annexation of) Korea, a lease for the Liaotung Peninsula and the South Manchuria Railway, together with mining and other pertinent rights, and the southern half of the island, Sakhalin, where there were oil fields.

A few years later, when the Chinese Republic was in the making, its guiding spirit, Sun Yat-sen, spent much time in Japan, and its president, Yuan Shih-kai, a more practical politician but also under Japanese influence, signed an agreement to: grant special privileges to Japan in Shantung, Manchuria and eastern Mongolia; engage Japanese advisers; concede land for Japanese shrines, schools and hospitals; introduce Japanese advisers into the Chinese police force; buy about half of their munitions from Japan; concede three railway lines in the Yangtze valley and the right of priority to Japanese capital in Chinese railways, ports and mines. Included among the Japanese demands [8] was one for the right to carry on Japanese religious propaganda.

By this time, World War I had broken out in Europe and Western attention temporarily was concentrated there. Japan, however, joined the Allies and, as called upon to do, took action at once against the German leased territory in Shantung and German island possessions in the Pacific. Having succeeded in capturing all these by the end of 1914, Japan next assumed responsibility for convoying Australian troops and protecting Allied shipping in the Mediterranean against German submarines. She did not send troops to Europe, but joined with England, France and the United States in the Siberian expedition of 1918. With the wartime boom in transportation and industry Japan enjoyed unprecedented prosperity.

Now Japan felt that she had done well. In one brief half century of strenuous effort she had transformed herself from a bankrupt feudal state to a modern nation almost twice its original size. The explanation of this miracle was to be found in her well-organized educational system and the diligent, hard-

MEIJI MEMORIAL HALL MURALS

IMPERIAL PROCESSION TO DIET BUILDING, 1937

ROOM IN MODERN JAPANESE INN

CHILDREN ON SCHOOL PLAYGROUND, TOKYO

working students devoted to the progress of the nation. Even elementary-school students were familiar with the heroes of the West, the history of Western governments and scientific inventions. And in the universities, scholars and experts were developed whose knowledge was not confined to their own hemisphere but extended to the whole world.

Japan felt she had earned the right to propose at the Paris Peace Conference in 1919 that the principle of racial equality be accepted, that the League of Nations grant to all nationals of the member states equal and just treatment in every respect with no distinction either in law or fact on account of race or nationality. There were six dissenting votes out of seventeen, however, and Japan had to give up this cherished ideal. Still, she was now a member of the League of Nations and one of the great powers of the world. The terms of the Versailles Treaty gave her a mandate over the Caroline and Marshall islands and certain rights in Shantung.

The last of the Satcho advisers still held great influence. Yamagata, who was chiefly instrumental in establishing conscription in 1872, and who in the Imperial Precepts to Soldiers and Sailors had expressed what were probably his own views, also played a large part in initiating local self-rule in 1887. In 1917, he directed his attention to the evils of the Japanese two-party political system:

> Even the World War, in relation to this struggle for political advantage, has become like a fire on the far side of the river. Hardly a thought is given to the fate of our neighbor China. The parties seem smugly unconcerned over the danger to our country of having to stand alone and without support in future among the powers of the world.

His suggested solution was a third party of impartial and moderate men, possessed of intelligence and a sincere concern for the well-being of the country in contrast to the common run of politicians pursuing politics as a livelihood.

Further, with respect to foreign policy Yamagata lamented the fact that China was not strong enough to stand beside Japan in resisting the coalition of the white races against the yellow. He pointed out:

> a striking fact that the Turkish and Balkan wars of former years and the Austro-Serbian and Russo-German wars of today all had their inception in racial rivalry and hatred . . . The anti-Japanese movement in California and the anti-Hindu, in British Africa . . . When the present conflict in Europe is over . . . the rivalry between white and non-white races will become violent . . .[9] if the colored races of the Orient hope to compete with the so-called culturally advanced white races and maintain friendly relations with them while retaining their own cultural identity and independence, China and Japan must become friendly and promote each other's interests.

Yamagata believed that Japan's dominance of Manchuria was as vital to protect weak China against Russia as it was for Japanese growth and security. Tactful diplomacy, he thought, could make the Chinese recognize this, whereas the petty bullying of the Twenty-one Demands would only alienate them.

> But we must also realize the need to negotiate with America. Our politicians must be sternly warned against raising the issue of racialism.[10]

The way to world power was rough.

CHAPTER 16

UNEASY JAPAN

(1919–1941)

In spite of her conspicuous achievements, Japan could not rest. Her politicians were uneasy. Yuan Shih-kai had died a few months after signing the Twenty-one Demands and his successors had not been compliant. Russia in the throes of revolution had concluded her separate peace with Germany before the other Allies, and the new Soviet regime, the avowed enemy of imperialist colonial policy, was soon making overtures to Chinese leaders, many of whom were susceptible to these advances, for treaties on terms of full equality. Communism was becoming rampant in China. Huge Czarist Russia with her slow but steady movement toward the Pacific had for a century been a source of uneasiness to Japan; but now Soviet Russia added to the old economic threat a new one of revolution and destruction of family loyalty, the very foundation of the Japanese polity. Japan could not tolerate the extension of Soviet influence in China, nor could the West, it seemed, understand Japan's special interests in East Asia. Now that Japan had become a power, the United States no longer treated her as a friend but seemed rather to be stirring up feeling against her.

The internal politics of Japan were equally disquieting. Though, according to the Constitution of 1888, the emperor was sacred and inviolable, and the Japanese people had been indoctrinated with the idea that their greatest glory was to be achieved in laying down their lives for him, actually their divine ruler was given little opportunity for leadership. He was used as a front by the most powerful groups in the country. The politics of Japan down through World War I had continued to be controlled by the Satcho clans. These leaders had been helped in a financial way by the Mitsuis, Mitsubishis and Sumitomos, old families of money lenders and merchants. The latter had been rewarded by government subsidies and tax immunities but had remained subordinate. The line of great Satcho leaders now, however, had come to an end, and there was no strongly consolidated group to take its place. Immediately following World War I, military leaders lost favor.

Large numbers of men were dropped from the army; military appropriations were drastically cut. Priests sold charms to ward off conscription; insurance companies sold policies against it and the classes in military schools were very small.

Big Business demonstrated the value of world trade and world good will. Under its prospering leadership, there was a renaissance of interest in Western literature and learning. Liberalism, democracy and internationalism appeared on every editorial page. In 1918, the precedent was set for commoners to become premiers. A universal manhood suffrage bill was passed in 1925, giving the vote to thirteen million men over twenty-five years of age. The government voted to refund to China its share of the Boxer indemnity [1] and make an effort to quell the public resentment against the United States Exclusion Act. Industrialization and colonization of its own territories was sponsored rather than aggressive expansion. Those in authority wanted to make their country the equal of the great Western nations in every way.

The new leaders, however, did not have direct access to the throne. Unlike the heads of the army and navy whom the constitution fortified with this privilege, they had to work through the Cabinet and patriarchal advisers appointed by the government, the Lord Keeper of the Privy Seal, the Minister of the Imperial Household and the Grand Chamberlain. In addition there was the Privy Council, organized in 1888, which shielded the emperor from responsibility for direct action or failures.

The army, on the other hand, was almost free from civil control. If the Diet limited its budget, the army could dissolve the Diet. If the Foreign Office did not cooperate, the army could make independent statements and create "incidents" by sending troops where it wished.

The upstart navy was not in accord with the old army and avoided political entanglement. The rise of middle-class men and peasants to high rank in the rapidly expanded army had created moderate cliques in conflict with extremist samurai officers. The new capitalists of heavy industry were not of the same temper as the older raw-silk merchants. The bureaucrats of permanent civil service had the backing, now of one group, now of another, and the resulting government, to outsiders as well as to Japanese, appeared irresponsible.

The conservative members of the military group had been incensed after all three wars, the Sino-Japanese, the Russo-Japanese, and World War I, to find what they thought their rightful winnings pared down by stronger Western powers. The Washington Conference and the Exclusion Act aggravated their resentment. The samurai had always held the merchant class in some contempt; and army officers now were inclined to feel that there was more self-interest than patriotism in the international dealings of those in control of the government. The prestige of the army rose after the terrible earthquake of 1923, when it brought order out of confusion, rescued the injured, disposed of the dead, restored communication and transportation, and in three weeks' time erected barracks to shelter the homeless.

Communist organizations sprang up in opposition to the capitalistic government. They even went so far as to attack the person of Hirohito, then prince regent, in protest against the continued restrictions on people's liberties and the continued spending of the nation's substance for foreign good will, while millions at home with no social welfare program were inadequately clothed, fed and housed. Many discontented factory workers were mildly of the opinion that the government could well afford to legislate better compensation for them. Army leaders pushed farm relief measures through the Diet and won the good feeling of a large part of the agricultural population. Factory wages were better than the returns farmers got for their labor but, as foreign trade expanded, brought little rise in home standards of living. As more low-priced goods from Japan were rushed into world markets, more tariffs and quotas were set up against them. There was graft, and scandal after scandal in high places. The army claimed big business lacked the moral stamina to defend the nation's best interests.

Several men of means and international sentiments were removed from public office by the expedient method of assassination. The commanders of army detachments guarding the South Manchuria Railway, as commanders in the field were constitutionally privileged to do, took matters into their own hands and called for additional troops to suppress local disturbances threatening Japanese interests. By such maneuvers, Manchukuo was developed as the headquarters of the military faction, and soaring appropriations for military use were justified. Out of range of interference by civil authorities, the army experimented with new tactics and matériel, with government administration and industrial management, and integrated cherished schemes.

Greater than Japan's political insecurity, however, was her economic uneasiness. Her limited resources had always been a matter for concern. During the Tokugawa Shogunate, when Japan was isolated from the rest of the world, the hard-pressed farmers and fishermen could feed only about thirty million mouths—the population had to be kept at that level—even though to do it required infanticide.[2] Now comparison of her own resources with those of her Western neighbors aggravated

Japan's sense of poverty. Though the traditional mainstay of the nation was agriculture, only about fifteen per cent of the country was arable: half of the country was forested but much of the timber, inaccessible. Attempts at trade in previous periods of history had depleted the country's mines to a point of imminent exhaustion. Japan had a population over one-half that of the whole United States to be maintained on a group of islands about the same size as the single state of California. Her chief resources were well-bred silkworms, the potential hydroelectric power of her rivers, and the energy and skill of her loyal people.

With these resources, industries had been developed and enormously expanded, but almost all the raw cotton and rayon pulp basic to the textile industries, the largest of all Japan's manufacturing enterprises, had to be imported and transported thousands of miles. Manufactured exports for several years had mounted rapidly, but this could not be expected to continue.

Japan's success in trade competition depended on her ability to maintain low prices. These were made possible by several factors, chief of which, perhaps, was the steadfast loyalty of her workers toward paternalistic leaders and employers. Then too, Japan had entered the industrial world after techniques and machines were fairly well developed, and her factories had the advantage of modern equipment. A large percentage of her manufactured goods, furthermore, was produced by what amounted to home industries, in which whole families co-operated and the capital investment was practically nil. Another factor was low wages—not as low as in the rest of the Orient, but so low that food prices had to be kept at a level which scarcely met the actual costs of agriculture.

So long as the people felt that they were all working together for the enrichment of the nation they did not complain. Farmers' daughters were glad of the chance to work for a few years in a city textile mill to earn and save money toward marriage. Thrifty country people seized opportunities for producing raw

silk and welcomed industries in their villages which supplemented their meager earnings from the land. The old feudal
loyalties persisted in many places for several generations and
though wages were low, if the employer gave a little bonus on
special occasions to show his good intentions, workers did not
think of finding fault. They were as well off as they ever had
been.

With the World War I industrial boom, however, changes
began to occur. Some men made millions overnight and, with
abounding optimism, expanded buildings and equipment,
loaned large sums to Europe and China,[3] and were satisfied
with themselves. Others saw prosperity only afar off: salaries
rose slowly, but food and commodity prices rocketed. The old
bonds of loyalty began to rankle on all. Strikes broke out. Dock
and mill workers, printers, street-car motormen and conductors,
letter carriers and many more occupational groups forced demands on their employers. Fisherfolk rioted because the price
of rice was out of all proportion to the price of fish, and farmers
formed cooperative unions. The whole populace, the greatest
natural resource of the country, was in a state of agitation.

Then in the great earthquake of 1923, the Tokyo and Yokohama region, the very citadel of new Japan, tumbled into
smouldering ruin. A hundred and fifty thousand lives were
taken, hundreds of thousands were homeless, without food,
water or means of transportation. Property losses were estimated at almost three billion dollars. The local bank panics
and failures which resulted were followed and rendered more
acute by the world-wide depression.

Japanese industrial magnates, however, had remarkable business acumen. Realizing that the limited resources of Japan
made concentration of capital necessary for favorable competition in international trade, they consolidated small operators in
a unified program, and were able to increase their production
and profits while the factories of other nations were operating
at a loss. Total British textile sales were topped. Indian cotton

mills were undersold in India. In Kenya and Uganda, Japanese sales soared to six times the British. The Dutch were losing native customers much too fast in Java—the United States saw its South American markets slipping. Very exasperating these Japanese who had been forced to open their doors and trade with the West!

And very uneasy too! The Zaibatsu responsible for almost three-quarters of the Japanese national income could be counted on the fingers of two hands. Ninety-three per cent of Japan's families were living on an income amounting to less than three hundred and fifty dollars a year and were unable to contribute anything much toward the national budget. The Zaibatsu paid the taxes and bought the bonds, but in spite of all their efforts the national debt was mounting by leaps and bounds. The army's doings in Manchuria were frightfully expensive and furthermore they were destroying the good will that businessmen had so painstakingly built up.

"We know what we want, let's take it," urged the army.

"Yes," agreed the Zaibatsu in effect, "but gradually, so as not to get people upset."

By November, 1935, though most government officials still sympathized with their revenue producers, the Zaibatsu were belabored relentlessly by the army. In an effort to curb military spending, Finance Minister Takahashi publicly declared that Japan was secure from challenge to war from any quarter, and his government opposed the appropriations which the army demanded. An impasse was reached on this issue and the government decided to dissolve the Diet and hold a general election in order to have an expression of public confidence.

Its campaign slogan was: "Which shall it be—parliamentary government or fascism?" [4] The returns indicated popular approval of the government, but within a week three of its leaders, including Finance Minister Takahashi, were assassinated in what is usually referred to as the February 26 Incident. A group of young army men in an excess of zeal had attempted to murder in their beds the key men of the government and to occupy strategic government buildings. Their averred reason— the emperor was being misguided by these advisers who preferred personal profits to the honor of the nation. Tokyo was under martial law for several months and, with army backing, Hirota became the first of the line of totalitarian premiers. Though in practical Oriental fashion, efforts at compromise were made by various pressure groups, extremists persistently overruled moderates and liberals.

The psychology of the Japanese aggravated their uneasiness; they were basically insecure. Even the adventurous migrants who brought bronze swords and mirrors to stone-age settlers seem to have been well aware not only of their own cultural superiority to the more primitive inhabitants of the islands, but also of their own deficiencies and limitations when they compared themselves with established continental peoples. This awareness seems to have been inherited by their descendants who reacted strongly to progressive influences from abroad, not with a defeatist attitude as might have been expected under such enormous odds but with a passion for heroic attainment. Time and again, the Japanese have found at their door foreigners whose powers it seemed impossible to equal. Time and again, their fortitude and diligence have surmounted the greatest difficulties.

In the days of Prince Shotoku, men of Yamato, encountering foreign Buddhist priests of very superior attainments and political ambitions, learned to read and write themselves and developed their own scholars and politicians. When the great T'ang Empire loomed in all its glory threatening eclipse of the Heian court, the Heian court set up its own bureaucratic government and outlived the T'ang by two hundred years. From the encounter with the Mongol Armada, Ashikaga leaders turned their minds to profitable overseas trade. Spanish ship captains, who pointed with pride to maps of their widespread possessions, served as inspiration for Japanese expansion through the seacoasts and islands of the southwestern Pacific. And when, from the long Tokugawa isolation, Japan opened her door and beheld Western civilization, she accepted it as a challenge to proficiency in yet another culture.

Like the Chinese script and institutions which she had adopted at the time of her First Great Change, modern Western civilization which impelled her Second Great Change was little suited to Japanese conditions. Western civilization seemed based on free competition; the Japanese, on controls. Western civilization was sustained by large-scale industry and commerce but Japan lacked the natural resources for these. Still the West offered a stimulating challenge which the Japanese by nature could not ignore, and having accepted could not lay down, even though, as they came to view the West more closely, they were somewhat disillusioned.

With a close-up view of conditions in the West, the costly efforts of Western educators, clergy and politicians to develop a healthy social and economic order seemed not entirely success-ful.[5] Western diplomatic methods, which Japan watched closely at Versailles and in Washington, increased her insecurity rather than her respect.

The old Tokugawa idea that it was safer to keep Western nations out of Japanese affairs began to gain ground. Japan had studied the whole West rather thoroughly, but the West, it seemed, had never been interested in really knowing Japan. They regarded her superficially with romantic sentiment but with little understanding of her character or her problems. Furthermore, Japanese thought Westerners insultingly legalis-tic, binding each other with so many laws and treaties, harping on rights and seldom mentioning duties. In Europe, it seemed to the Japanese, most calamities were caused by men envious of each other's rights. It was in the faithful performance of duties that Japanese were concerned. They preferred to think in terms of character rather than laws, to deal with each case on its own merits, and make changes in agreements as situations changed. The Western way of taking matters to court and public hearing seemed not only undignified but impractical; differences were better settled by persons immediately concerned through the mediation of friends or sympathetic parties rather than by professional lawyers.

Of greater influence still, perhaps, was the realization that Western ways were very expensive. Piped water, sewerage systems and central heating were costly to install and during earthquakes, potential sources of great danger. Telephone lines were also expensive and dangerous in a country visited by at least one typhoon each year. Automobiles required roads and gasoline—gasoline had to be imported and roads had to be carved out of the farmers' rice fields. Western clothes for men, with tight collars and sleeves and trousers, were less comfortable than kimonos though more convenient for business and, therefore, quite generally adopted, but Western clothes for women which had to be fitted to the individual, which continually changed in style and required suitable hats, gloves, shoes and handbags, were much too costly for most family budgets. In the Western diet, meat, milk and butter played a prominent part, but Japan could afford little pasture land for grazing cows or goats. There were the additional problems of Western conveniences destroying stamina and depriving many people of jobs.

Japan's change of feeling toward the West was eloquently stated in a lecture by Mr. Yusuke Tsurumi, a Diet member and roving ambassador at Williamstown, Massachusetts, in 1924:

> Japan is discovering that Western civilization, dominated by the machine and the passion for comfort, offers no solution to the great problems of inherent permanent national stability, serenity of spirit, and man's greatest achievement, the conquest of himself. Triumphant man may not be revealed, in the end, adorned in a top hat and attached to a telephone. Asia has a civilization of her own. To restore and develop the best in that civilization is a fine work worthy of the noblest endeavors.

When the imperial-minded extremists began to assert themselves loudly in 1930, they carried on this same line of thought. Skepticism and disillusionment activated defense mechanisms. Once again, with fervor, the people were exhorted to turn their backs on the West and to look upon their own past—to study The Way of the Gods and practice it—to develop in themselves the characteristics of their ancestral heroes—loyalty, subservience, simplicity, frugality, hard work, self-restraint.

Though there had long been, among thoughtful Japanese, those who felt that what their country needed for sound development as a modern world power was a national, practical reinterpretation of history, doing away with the Sun-Goddess myths and the divinity of the emperor, the totalitarian leaders now felt they needed divine ancestry more than ever. Their people must be made to feel that they were a very superior race, a race of gods, immortal gods, with a very special mission to fulfill.

American-educated Yosuke Matsuoka, who would later lead the Japanese delegation out of the League of Nations, proclaimed:

> The mission of the Yamato race is to prevent the human race from becoming devilish, to rescue it from destruction, and to lead it to the world of light. The hidebound, material-minded civilization of the present generation has finally plunged the whole world into its present welter of confusion . . . our Yamato race has a peerless tradition . . . Providence calls on Japan to undertake this mission of delivering humanity from the impasse of modern material civilization. Back to the Japanese spirit!

Frequently one read or heard public speakers using old slogans like: "the highest hope of a member of our race is to die for the emperor" or "duty is weightier than a mountain; death, lighter than a feather." Words like these confronted the people everywhere they turned—in school, the newspapers, the radio, the movies—training the imperial subjects it was called. The new Commission of Education and Culture was going full blast. No one was allowed to escape its indoctrination. And should there be any bold enough to question it, wherever two or three were gathered together, there was a "thought policeman" in their midst. Independent thinkers, taken into custody by ubiquitous investigators and police, were sometimes not heard from again.

The first step in the process of indoctrination was the elementary school. Children entered school at the age of six or seven, as full of their own little characteristic quirks as any children in the world, for all Japanese babies were pampered by their parents. By the time they came to the end of their six-year compulsory education, however, they were all buttoned into identical uniforms, with identical textbooks strapped in knapsacks on their shoulders and their heads crammed with identical ideas of Japanese history, rightful attitudes and dutiful conduct.

In addition to the Way of the Gods and the Japanese destiny, elementary-school students were taught to keep their senses keen and bodies fit. There was great emphasis on gymnastic exercises, hiking, climbing and swimming. Each elementary school had its own "olympic" teams and contests. Enjoyment of nature was also encouraged; children were taken out in sketching classes to train their eyes to beauty and were taught to appreciate the music of water, wind and insects. "He who is master of his mind," they were frequently told, "is happy even if he has nothing."

The elementary schools were coeducational. Only about ten per cent of the children went beyond this compulsory level. Those who wished to continue their education had to pass very rigid examinations. Higher education was too precious to be wasted on mediocre students. Going to school was not a social pastime; it was a serious business. It prepared students not only for the keen competition and rigorous demands of the process of earning a living, but also for the distinction of representing the intellectual life of Japan to intellectuals abroad. Standards of attainment in the technical schools and universities were very high, but most youths would rather sacrifice eyesight and health than fail to pass. Everyone had to live up to what was expected of him or be disgraced. While engineering schools could not turn out graduates fast enough to fill all the places waiting for them at salaries far superior to those of other professions, less than half of the graduates in other fields found employment the first year out, and they were grateful for a salary of sixty yen a month. (In the 1930's, the yen in Japan was supposed to have the buying power of the dollar in the United States.) Higher education commanded such respect, however, especially among country people, that they frequently banded together to provide funds for the brightest boy among them to attend a city university.

In the way of adult education, it was forbidden to publish anything "subversive of public morals, provocative of disorder, disturbing army discipline, confusing the financial world or subverting the public mind." Temporary bans were frequently issued on the mention of certain topics. Most publishers hired special "jail editors" to serve sentences imposed for offending articles.

Journalists and fiction writers exerted an especially significant influence in modernizing Japan. With new techniques and a new spirit derived from English and American literature, they produced innumerable translations and creative works of their own. Freedom was their favorite theme—individual freedom of action and thought, freedom from encumbering Japanese traditions and social customs. They were not in the least nationalistic. Those interested chiefly in Russian literature released a flood of psychological novels. French, German, Italian and Scandinavian writers also had their devotees who not only wrote like the Western authors but also enjoyed living as they lived, to the extent afforded by the cafés and restaurants of various nationalities on Tokyo's Ginza.[6] These men were ac-

customed to being read and re-read and quoted; they wanted
to stir up powerful currents of thought. Totalitarian restraints
were particularly disheartening to them.

In religion, art and entertainment the same sort of restraints
were imposed. Everyone, no matter what the faith of his heart,
had to perform certain Shinto rituals. Though Christians numbered only a fraction of a per cent of the Japanese population,
their influence was out of all proportion to their numbers;
suspicion was always being cast upon them, and they were
very closely watched by the thought police. Restraints were
applied to Christian schools and the teaching of Christianity.
In 1940, the government assumed control of all religious institutions and compelled all Christians to merge into one organization. Several months later the Catholic Church, in return for its
recognition of Shinto, was given separate official recognition.

Western art and music had become very popular among
educated young Japanese. The rich oil colors and free use of
human forms afforded so much more emotional satisfaction
than black ink landscapes and classical Japanese subject matter.
Exhibitions of the contemporary painting of the 1930's reflected
every Western art movement from the Old Masters through
Surrealism and Dada.

Many young Japanese were familiar with the best of Western
music. When Western symphonies or solos were played on the
radio or phonograph, they listened with closed eyes—inwardly
contrasting its richness and harmony with the thin monotonies
of Japanese music. They were turning more and more to
Western orchestras and instruments, and creating compositions
which combined occidental with oriental musical traditions.
But such forms of art and music were denounced by totalitarian
agents, as wanton extravagances undermining morale.

For many years, a popular escape from everyday repression
and inhibition was offered in large cities by Hollywood movies.
Japanese movies, like Japanese life, were frugal. They employed
neither large crowds nor elaborate stage sets. They had little

of the gaiety and glamour of Hollywood films, and abounded in close-ups of agonized faces. Their usual theme was the triumph of loyalty and duty over personal desire. When love themes were treated, more often than not, it was in a way to ridicule or discourage romantic adventures. But real life in Japan was full of that sort of thing. Most marriages still were arranged by parents for their children. Mates were chosen with an eye to family stability rather than to individual liking. Identifying themselves with the lighthearted, carefree lovers they saw in American movies, was therefore a source of satisfaction for Japanese young men and women. For them, American movies afforded, at much less expense, the escape which geisha provided for their fathers. They defended their frequent attendance at American movies to their consciences and their elders by saying that talkies gave excellent training in the use of spoken English.

In 1937, the importation of Hollywood films was banned. For a brief period this gave Japanese movie producers an open field for experimenting with new styles of comedy and of poignant realism.[7] *Five Scouts* released at about this time, resembled *All Quiet on the Western Front,* it showed common humanity, with little sense of heroic mission, caught in an inevitably disastrous flow of events.

The skirmish at Marco Polo Bridge in July, 1937, however, followed in August by fighting in Shanghai and the blockading of the China coast put an end to films of this sort. In 1938, the Home Ministry published a code:

> Do not make light of military matters or exaggerate the horrors of war; do nothing to lower morale or fighting spirit; avoid excessive merriment; eliminate individualism; develop the beauty of the family system and of sacrifice for the nation. Banish insincere thoughts.

Films divulging the techniques of spying began to appear and to reflect suspicion on foreigners. Worse villains than foreign enemies were Westernized Japanese, not whole-heartedly cooperating with the war effort. English teachers were pictured patriotically serving as interpreters; working girls, marrying and supporting disabled soldiers. The nation needed heroic *little* people.

More and more houses displayed the rising-sun banners with which friends expressed their good wishes to new conscripts.[8] Station platforms now were frequently crowded with school children waving farewells to troop trains. Consumer goods were becoming scarce. There were blackouts and air-raid drills, and women's patriotic societies being organized. Foreigners were more and more closely watched and discouraged from traveling. Women walking along the street, in both city and town, found other women every few hundred yards thrusting toward them pieces of white-cotton toweling, each piece marked with places for a thousand French knots to be embroidered in red by a thousand women and sent to some soldier to wrap around his stomach and give him courage.

Social gatherings were called off. Occasionally there was a Red Cross train returning the wounded; or mourners carrying white cloth-covered boxes of ashes. Japanese newspaper headlines played it down; this was an incident which would soon be over, but to Western leaders, looking forward hopefully to an era of relaxed international tensions and firmer economic opportunities, it was very disconcerting.

In Chicago, in October, 1937, President Roosevelt made a speech about quarantining aggressor nations. Chiang Kai-shek appealed for help to the League of Nations. Nineteen Western nations, meeting in Brussels a month later, agreed to stay out of the conflict and public opinion polls in the United States showed that a majority of Americans felt no threat to their security and wanted to remain neutral. Such public sentiments, however, did not prevent the Japanese Imperial Army from setting up the Provisional Government of the Chinese Republic in Peiping and the Manchurian Industrial Development Corporation which facilitated use of the natural resources of North and Central China for military purposes. To exert more rigid control over the Japanese economy a National General Mobilization Bill was pushed through the Diet.

Almost two years later, when nearly a third of China was under Japanese domination and a further expanded Co-Prosperity Sphere in Greater East Asia was being proclaimed, the United States nullified its 1911 commercial treaty with Japan and thus cut off access to raw materials necessary for Japanese industries. Hitler, by making a nonaggression pact with Russia, relaxed the latter's attention to her western neighbors but increased Japan's uneasiness over the Siberian-Manchurian border. A mutually-supporting treaty which Japan soon managed to make with Germany and Italy, and a neutrality pact with Russia, brought a sense of greater security.

After the Germans had invaded France and attacked Russia, Japanese troops took advantage of the situation to move into Indo-China, within striking distance of British and American bases in Malaya and the Philippines. This move was countered by the confiscation of Japanese holdings in the United States; the British and Dutch took similar steps with Japanese investments in their countries.

Now, in effect, Japan could obtain imports only from the territories which she occupied and, for her military operations, she must have bauxite and oil—large quantities of oil. The situation was becoming critical.

Army and navy chiefs, worried over what concessions they could make for the privilege of buying oil from the United States and the Dutch East Indies, finally submitted to the emperor the opinion that it was unwise to waste time in unavailing talks with the United States; better to prepare for immediate, direct action. The whole of the South Seas, they informed His Imperial Majesty, would be subdued, and desired areas would be occupied, within three months of the start of hostilities.[9] Naval chiefs explained that by capturing the oil reserves of the South Seas, Japan would vastly enhance her strength for further fighting.

Not satisfied, the emperor insisted that the Cabinet also be included in such considerations. Prime Minister Prince Konoye convened a Council before the throne on September 6, 1941. The nation was split between the Supreme Command of the Military and the Civil Government. It was decided to proceed with both military plans and peaceful negotiations, and if, by October 10, they could get no relaxing of the embargo and of the United States demand for withdrawal of Japanese troops from China, the army and navy chiefs would be ready for total war.

Gazing around the assembly, the emperor, it is reported, produced a poem composed by his grandfather, Emperor Meiji, which he read out from the throne:

> The seas stretch to all quarters from our shores
> And my heart cries out to the nations of the world.
> Why do the winds thrash the seas
> And disturb the peace between us?

After this conference, Prince Konoye proposed to President Roosevelt that they meet together in person to discuss the mutual problems of their countries, but since he was able to give no guarantees of military backing for his proposal, it was not accepted. Prince Konoye was succeeded as prime minister, in October, 1941, by General Tojo,[10] whose long military experience with the army in North China led many Japanese to think him well qualified for dealing with their problems. Westerners, for the same reason, suspected Tojo's government was committed to war; continuing negotiations seemed futile.

Uneasiness grew still more in Japan at this time, because of the international activity of the Communist party. Prince Konoye later commented: "I had my plans and both army and navy professed to approve them, but they never seemed to work out as I expected." This was presumably explained in part by the fact that a member of the brain-trust in the Cabinet office was a former Osaka newspaper correspondent named Ozaki, who put great confidence in one Richard Sorge, adviser to the German ambassador in Japan. The Sorge Spy Case was disclosed by the Japanese Ministry of Justice in 1942. Upon his arrest, Ozaki said, "My hair has gone white from the struggle, but my campaign to make a Red Japan has succeeded. Japan is plunged in the Great War; the country is in chaos and revolution is just around the corner. Nine tenths of my work is done."

On November 5, 1941, Combined Fleet Top Secret Order No. 1 was sent to all Japanese fleet and task force commanders. Still, diplomatic negotiations were continued in an effort to have the United States withdraw support of Chiang Kai-shek and cancel its embargo and fund-freezing order. United States intelligence agents had cracked the Japanese diplomatic code and were able to keep Secretary of State Hull informed of the orders from Tokyo to the Japanese ambassador in Washington. An attack was expected on the Philippines.

When a personal appeal to Emperor Hirohito from President Roosevelt reached the palace in Tokyo on December 6, radio operators of the task force, only several hundred miles from Pearl Harbor, had already received the go ahead signal, "Climb Mount Niitaka"; and the following morning Japan's undeclared war against the West opened with a devastating blow.

Japanese radio-newsmen announced the outbreak of war and read an imperial decree. Citizens listened respectfully, breathed a sigh of relief from suspense and resolved to go through with it to a victorious end.

CHAPTER 17

STRUGGLE FOR SUPREMACY IN EAST ASIA

(A Review 1895–1942)

WESTERN nations had got such a head start in imperialistic expansion in Asia and the Southwest Pacific that at first no one even thought of Japan entering the struggle. So tremendous, however, was her suddenly released energy that in the course of one generation Japan converted herself from an isolated feudal state to a very respectable nation, with transportation and communication systems, compulsory education, a constitution, an elected Diet and a modernized army and navy eager to test themselves in the scramble that European nations were making for spheres of influence in China. Japan did so well in her first engagement with China that after it was over Russia, Germany and France in the name of "the peace of the Far East" stepped in and made Japan renounce her continental gains, later proceeding together with Britain to establish themselves more securely in strategic places in North China and Manchuria.

In the early days of the China trade the United States had enjoyed her full share, but with such boundless undeveloped natural resources as she had at home, she felt little urge to seek territorial concessions in the Far East. In the last decade of the nineteenth century, however, she had joined the push for political and economic expansion. She bought Alaska, established a certain control over the Samoan Islands, seized Guam, acquired the Philippines by defeating the Spanish fleet in

Manila Bay, annexed Hawaii and became a contender in the transpacific struggle.

After half a century of experience in East Asia, it should have been clear to all concerned that China could not possibly continue to be the bonanza they had at first thought, but it appeared to the United States that the decline in her China trade was due chiefly to the special privileges other nations had acquired. In March, 1900, therefore, the Open Door policy was announced as an accepted solution of the China problem, guarding primarily against European encroachment in general, but especially against Russian expansion in Manchuria. For this reason and the fact that it might help hold China together until her turn came, Japan at first welcomed the Open Door. But as the Japanese became more intent on expansion in Manchuria as vital to their national life this policy caused conflict after conflict.[1]

At the turn of the century, Japanese efficiency, martial spirit and ambitious pride appealed greatly to Theodore Roosevelt. He studied everything he could about Japan. When Japan began her war with Russia he hoped she would win, but he had not anticipated such a show of military potency. "I wish I were certain," he wrote a little later, "that the Japanese down at bottom did not lump Russia, England, America, Germany, all of us, simply as white devils, inferior to themselves not only in what they regard as the essentials of civilization but also in courage, and forethought, to be politely treated only so long as would enable the Japanese to take advantage of our various national jealousies and beat us in turn."[2]

Still, he was glad to be able to arrange the Portsmouth Conference for peace negotiations between Japan and Russia because he believed that Japan's policy was the one that would most effectively strengthen America's position in the Orient and safeguard her trade and commerce.

American public opinion had been strongly with Japan all through the war, but after the Portsmouth Conference it began to change. It was reported that the Japanese had become "insufferably overbearing and insolent" since their victory over the Russians. Japan was definitely now a power to be reckoned with. She could no longer be expected to accede quietly to United States policy. Her defeat of Russia put her in a position to expand. The United States navy saw her casting covetous eyes on the Philippines.

As such opinions began to appear in American newspapers, Japanese newspapers began to say that Japan might have had more rewards for her victory had not President Roosevelt intervened. They suspected the possibility of the United States trying to thwart their future expansion. Each now began to envision the other not as trusted friend but as potential rival.

Certain journalists finding the suspicion and hostility of Californians toward the Japanese in their midst highly profitable to newspaper circulation, encouraged the passing of a law specifically prohibiting Japanese from owning any land in that state. Popular reaction to this in Japan was violent. Our suspicions of Japan's aggressive intent were not allayed by the publication of her Twenty-one Demands on China.

In 1917, Japan proposed sending troops to Siberia to protect Allied interests from the dangers of the Russian revolution. President Wilson agreed to the sending of Allied troops, but only for as long as the current emergency lasted. The Japanese contingent numbered not seven or eight thousand as expected, but seventy thousand, and stayed on for years until they got full control of North Sakhalin. The civil government in Tokyo was embarrassed by this, but the hard-riding military were stubborn.

European delegates to the Versailles Conference had given little consideration to Far Eastern problems. As far as they were concerned, Germany was the issue. But the Japanese delegates came with two vital objectives: they wanted to have the principle of racial equality incorporated in the covenant of the New League of Nations, and they wanted legal recognition of their claims to all German rights and territory in Shantung and the

Pacific Islands north of the equator. On the first point they won a majority vote (not including America's) but when the question was raised of unanimity being necessary on such a point, President Wilson, as presiding officer, again dashed Japan's hopes by ruling that it was. Convinced that safeguarding the League was the paramount issue in the very complicated cir‧ cumstances, however, he conceded Japan the material gains which she had claimed as her right.

Thus, in addition to Formosa and the Pescadores—with their rice, tea, and camphor which she had won by the Sino-Japanese war—Southern Sakhalin with its fish and petroleum, and special rights in the railroad and coal mines of the Port Arthur region which she had won from Russia, and Korea with its rice, which she had annexed by Treaty in 1910,[3] Japan now included in her empire the Mariana, Caroline and Marshall islands with their cotton and copra, and special commercial privileges in Shantung. Japan was gaining in her struggle for supremacy in East Asia and American suspicion grew more tense.

Both Japan and the United States continued to expand their navies. The United States was fast becoming the world's greatest naval power, and as statements were frequently made that the next war would be upon the Pacific, the Japanese were striving to compete in what amounted to a race between the navy departments of both nations. Civil officials and the public on neither side viewed the prospect of war with favor.

The existence of the Anglo-Japanese Alliance became a subject of unfavorable criticism in the United States, especially by the navy. In the event of war between this country and Japan would the British have to fight on the Japanese side? Entered into originally, in 1902, to dissuade Germany and France from joining Russia in a possible Russo-Japanese war, the alliance had had the tacit approval of the United States government until after the Japanese victory, in 1905. But with only three great naval powers left after World War I, and two of them in the alliance, it seemed to the third a potential menace.

Because of the American attitude, the British government of

its own accord, in 1920, gave its ally a year's notice of the termination of the treaty. Before it was abrogated, early in 1921, President Harding invited Great Britain and Japan, France, Italy, Belgium, Holland, Portugal and China to a conference in Washington to deal with naval and Pacific problems, and to establish a new international order in East Asia.

The New York *Tribune* suggested editorially that since Japan was being called upon to surrender her claim in almost every controversy, she "might be placated for concessions by agreement among the Powers to withdraw objection to her exploitation, say, of Manchuria," but others resented such aspersions on our altruistic idealism in holding to the Open Door.

American individuals of influence voiced opinions to the effect that disarmament in the Pacific was dependent upon political agreement and that such agreement would have to provide for the increasing population of Japan and its necessary economic expansion without involving the exploitation of any other people or the sacrifice of the integrity of China or the policy of the Open Door. Most of the delegates to the Washington Conference assumed that this could be done.

The confident optimism with which Secretary Hughes presented his plan for reduction of naval armaments on a five-five-three ratio for Great Britain, the United States and Japan was so dynamic that Japan agreed to accept the plan in principle, insisting, however, that neither the United States nor Britain build any more naval bases in East Asia. As a graceful way out of the Anglo-Japanese Alliance the United States, Britain, Japan and France signed the Four Power Treaty agreeing to respect each other's insular possessions in the Pacific and to consult together should a threat to the status quo arise. A third treaty, the Nine Power Treaty, was also concluded at the Washington Conference in 1922. This treaty pledged the signatories to

respect the independence and territorial and administrative integrity of China;

provide the fullest opportunity to China to develop a stable
government;

maintain equal opportunity for the commerce and industry of
all nations throughout the territory of China;

refrain from taking advantage of conditions in China to seek
special rights which would curtail the rights of other states.

The United States had shown a streak of diplomatic genius.
While setting high standards for maintaining peace and good
will in the Pacific, she had thoroughly protected American interests. Refusal to sign these treaties would almost have con-
victed Japan, before the world, of aggressive designs. Japan
signed. She was commended for imitating the best of the West
instead of the worst as she had been doing. These were the
heydays of Japanese liberals, bright and hopeful days for the
most part, throughout the world.

Deeper rooted than liberalism in Japan, however, was the
ambition to be inferior to no nation. This intense urge to keep
up with her neighbors had been shown in the earliest Japanese history. The Washington Conference had failed to acknowledge this realistically. By summarily refusing to recognize Japan's historic aspirations, her right to continental
expansion and her need to control sources of raw materials, the conference imposed a tremendous burden on the
liberals without acceding anything to help sustain their
strength.

Adding insult to injury, came the Exclusion Act in 1924.[4]
Public resentment arose in Japan; there were official statements to the effect that her primary concern was not whether
a few thousand or a few hundred Japanese immigrants were
admitted to the United States, but whether Japan was to be
accorded the courteous treatment due her as a civilized Power.
This tended to calm some of the people. When the world-wide
depression struck, however, resentment against exclusion by
the West revived and strengthened the determination of the
militarists to expand in Manchuria. The Chinese revolution,

with boycotts and antiforeign feeling, played directly into their hands.

Japanese national interests clearly were not to be defended by diplomacy—they had to depend on the force of arms. Baron Shidehara, Commoner Hamaguchi and Viscount Kato, Japan's great liberal diplomats, were nevertheless able to stand up under the blows from without and the opposition from within for several years. The climax of the era of good will did not come until 1930.

At the London Naval Conference, Japanese delegates agreed to naval reductions without the consent of the Supreme War Council. This was defying precedent, and for his insistence that the civil government had the right to direct the foreign policy of Japan, Premier Hamaguchi was assassinated. Politicians, the militarists pointed out, did not maintain the integrity and the efficiency required for national defense. Thanks to the weak-kneed diplomats, trouble was brewing for the third time in Manchuria. There had been continuous treaty violations along Japan's billion-dollar South Manchuria Railway, and something should be done before it was too late.

A four-months' struggle between the army and the Foreign Office ended in the Mukden Incident, in September, 1931. Simply ignoring the Foreign Office seemed to the army such a satisfactory procedure that it was adopted as a regular technique. Trying to justify the *faits accomplis* of the army and to present them in palatable form to the outside world became the major activity of the Foreign Office.

In the Kellogg-Briand Pact, the nations of the world had pledged themselves to outlaw war as an instrument of national policy, and the United States, though not a member, determined to act in concert with the League of Nations to effect a settlement between Japan and China by negotiation or other peaceful means. As time went on, however, it became evident that Japan could be prevented from winning Manchuria only by superior military force, and this they were not prepared to use. When China carried her grievances to the League of Nations, therefore, neither economic nor military sanctions were applied.

Japan saw no reason to halt her advances. She was convinced that justice was on her side and was prepared to maintain her stand. She had to have wider fields of activity in order to survive. Her interest in East Asia was a vital interest. Some Japanese might say that there was too much banditry and official extortion in Manchuria, too many war-lord-broken treaties, but the man in the street felt that his government should adopt a strong policy for overcoming these difficulties.

Matsuoka, an official spokesman at the League of Nations, expressed another point of view:

> We do not take. We are in a position to give. Japan has taken all she needs from the West, assimilated and naturalized Western mechanism and materialism. That much richer, by a code and modernization which supplement our own traditional civilization, we hold a unique position among Far Eastern countries. Our occupation of Manchuria is not a question of taking Manchuria in a military sense, or of taking anything from Manchuria in a moral sense. It is Japan who is giving Manchuria precious principles of self-development, progress, and spirituality. This melting pot of Asia, where meet and mingle Japanese, Chinese, Manchus, Mongols, Koreans, Siberians and Russians—Red and White—one day may be able to save the whole of China.

The Lytton Commission was dispatched by the League to investigate the situation in Manchuria and report back its recommendations. The way the League handled this report led only to an experiment in nonrecognition of the Japanese army's puppet state of Manchukuo, and the loss of Japan as a member.[5]

"There is no country but China that is in a position to share with Japan the responsibility for maintaining peace in East Asia. We oppose, therefore, any attempt on the part of China to avail herself of the influence of any other country." This was Japan's official position in 1934. "The world should be divided into three parts under the influence, respectively, of American, European and Asiatic Monroe Doctrines."

Our interest in China obviously had been worth diplomatic protection only, and that had failed. The United States being unprepared to use force, there were no further protests. We had even voted to grant the Philippines their independence. Japan's sun was still rising in the Pacific but she was one of our best customers, and second only to Canada as a source of United States supplies. We were bound to each other by raw cotton and raw silk.

New York's Mayor La Guardia sent good-will dolls on a tour of Japan. When Vice-President Garner visited Tokyo to reaffirm our Good Neighbor Policy, he wondered whether he should take off his shoes in the presence of the emperor.

During the summer of 1937, Japan took decisive steps toward establishing her New Order in Asia. North China was occupied, Shanghai attacked and China's coasts blockaded. Before the year's end Japan established in Peiping what she called the Provisional Government of the Chinese Republic. The next spring another puppet government was set up in Nanking and the USS *Panay* was bombed. The United States put an embargo on the shipment of planes and plane equipment to Japan. That autumn, Japan occupied Canton and Hankow. Britain and the United States made loans to Generalissimo Chiang and he rejected Japan's third peace offer.

In 1939, China, with improved guerrilla tactics, a Russian trade agreement and some help from Britain and the United States, succeeded in preventing any further advances by the Japanese. The outbreak of the war in Europe, in September, 1939, gave Japan renewed advantage. With the fall of Holland and France, she occupied the northern part of Indo-China and, a year later, fortified by her alliance with Germany and Italy, Japan moved into South Indo-China headed for Malaya and the Philippines. The Co-Prosperity Sphere in Greater East Asia was expanding rapidly.

After the first blow on Pearl Harbor, December 7, 1941, which sank or disabled eight United States battleships and ten other ships, victory followed victory in rapid succession: Manila, January 3; Singapore, February 15; Rangoon and Java, March 8-9. Air squadrons sank the unsinkable HMS *Prince of Wales,* the world's largest battleship, and many other navy and merchant ships in the Indian Ocean. The Japanese attacked far-scattered places like Ceylon, Madagascar and Sydney. Oil wells in Sumatra and Borneo were captured undamaged. The conquest of the Philippines took longer than expected because of the strong fight that American forces put up at the entrance of Manila Harbor, but Corregidor fell on April 4.

Attu and Kiska were captured in an attack on the far-north Aleutians; the Solomon Islands, Guadalcanal and Bougainville in the Southwest Pacific were occupied. Japan's naval air arm was matchless; the army's skill in jungle warfare, incomparable; the pride of the military, overweening. Propagandists announced on the radio that they would force the United States to capitulate on the steps of the White House. The Japanese public thought the war was won.

In little more than six months, their military leaders had laid hold of a vastly wealthy empire of three million square miles and four hundred and fifty million people. The second largest empire in the modern world, including all the raw materials necessary for a great industrial power! About all of the world's natural rubber, palm oil and quinine! Rich in petroleum, copper, tin and rice! The far-flung bulwarks of the West had crumbled!

German victory was taken for granted. Japan would rush a quick victory, gathering her spoils as she went, and then turn to developing her economic supremacy in East Asia—in the Pacific—and with the fall of her long-time rivals, the United States and Russia—perhaps even throughout the world.

CHAPTER 18

DIRECT ENCOUNTER WITH THE UNITED STATES IN WAR, OCCUPATION AND SECURITY

(1942–1954)

IN May, 1942, the situation in the Pacific began to change. An engagement with United States carrier planes in the Coral Sea discouraged the Japanese from advancing toward Australia; and less than a month later (only six months after Pearl Harbor) a Japanese aircraft squadron was attacked near Midway Island. All but four of their important carriers and many of their most experienced fliers were lost. Though details were not divulged, either to the nation or the cabinet (for Japanese fighting men from feudal times had refrained from acknowledging reverses), and radio announcers left it to be inferred that American losses were greater, Midway clearly signaled a change in the relative effectiveness of their opponents. Still, with naval and air power greatly impaired, Japanese strategists did not contract their widespread battle line: they knew little of the tactics of withdrawal; retreat was impossible; fliers were given revolvers and swords but not parachutes. Before long, Japan's island bases became targets; reinforcements were sunk en route; supply by submarine was inadequate. The Americans' industrial and transportation organization was stupendous!

After 1943, munitions, food and medical supplies seldom got through. Outpost troops sometimes lived on bark, rats, roots and snakes; sometimes starved to death. Seven or eight million tons of convoyed shipping were sunk. Ore supplies from China, and oil and bauxite from the South Seas were cut off. With little aluminum available, airplane production and quality dropped.

Shortage of gasoline soon became an even more serious problem. Instead of cooperating, the army and navy competed for whatever was available. A method was devised for distilling motor fuel from the roots of pine trees, and country people were ordered to dig them up, but distribution of the necessary iron caldrons broke down; the roots dried up and were useless.

The Japanese Traveling Culture Association took sixteen-millimeter movies to rural areas to spread the national policy message. Documentary films commemorated the heroic performances of soldiers, sailors, pilots and paratroopers from Hawaii to Malaya. *Jubilation Street* publicized a drive to evacuate the cities.

Three million women from the upper classes had been organized into the Patriotic Women's Society with an imperial princess as president to assist the war effort. The Women's Society for National Defense included six and a half million women from the lower classes. All had long since given up gay colors and fancy clothes, and flag-waving, in white aprons, along the streets. They had discarded kimonos for working women's trousers, turned in their gold wedding rings and iron cooking pots, stopped collecting money for comfort kits and begun collecting pennies from children for building ships. Homes and schools were turned into factories.

In a National Self-restraint Drive people were urged to share their soldiers' hardships by not eating more than necessary—not smoking or going to entertainments. A day of idleness was called criminal. All conduct contrary to the national interest had to be eradicated.

In July, 1944, Saipan, a mandated island center of sugar cultivation and refining in the Mariannas, where thousands of Japanese had been living, became a target. Ships evacuating women and children were sunk en route to Japan and the homeland itself soon suffered United States' air attacks. Factories, homes and schools were destroyed. Where was now the great moment toward which civilians had bent all their efforts? Public bewilderment and resentment toward the military grew. Where were the fruits of all the announced victories? Why was the war so prolonged?

Industrialists and the former premiers known as Senior Statesmen and the Lord Keeper of the Privy Seal considered how they might break army domination and negotiate a compromise peace, but for fear of being themselves liquidated, and parliamentary government then overthrown, they did not speak out.

People in general began to feel that Tojo was to blame for everything. Public loss of confidence brought the Senior Statesmen to force his resignation in July, 1944. A new prime minister was appointed, and a new cabinet formed, whose expressed purpose was to explore acceptable ways of ending the war.

The fall of Iwo Jima in March, 1945, released waves of Western planes, plotting out the country by day from high altitudes and bombing the industrial areas at night. With munition manufacturing parceled out as home industries, residential areas also came to know the horrors of oil fires and saturation bombing. Fifty square miles of Tokyo lay in ruins. On one March night, in 1945, a hundred thousand corpses choked the Sumida River. What would it be like if the Americans invaded?

Industrial as well as government leaders began sending out peace feelers to the Allied Powers. Some thought that if the war continued, Japan was in danger of becoming more and more communistic with consequences, perhaps, worse than the unconditional surrender demanded by the Western Allies. After deliberation, it was decided to approach the Soviets, with whom they had carefully observed their Neutrality Pact, about mediating peace, but the Soviet ambassador in Tokyo gave no encouragement. Instead, termination of the pact was announced in Moscow.

On June 6, the war minister and chiefs of staff insisted on a fight to the finish in defense of the homeland: Japan never played at war. Suicide squads would lure the enemy ashore and destroy him. Even young boys were recruited and drilled, with bamboo spears and wooden guns. An underground palace was begun in the Japan Alps a hundred miles northwest of Tokyo to which the imperial family and the government were to be moved when the invasion began.

On July 26, the Allies declared at Potsdam specifically what they meant by unconditional surrender and with the successful test of an atomic bomb reported to them, concluded ominously, "The alternative for Japan is prompt and utter destruction."

Japanese newspapers of July 28 reported that the prime minister was reserving judgment on the Potsdam Declaration. When ten days later it was reported by the Japanese General Staff that Hiroshima, where they had established military headquarters to meet the expected invasion, had been entirely destroyed by *one* new sort of bomb, there was still a deadlock on unconditional surrender in the Supreme War Guidance Council. The Soviet declaration of war on Japan, August 8, struck another staggering blow; it would be impossible for the army to defend Manchuria and Korea. It was also impossible for Japanese leaders to agree to an enemy occupation, total demobilization and trial of war criminals, but above all to the loss of status for the emperor.

News of a *second* new sort of bomb dropped on Nagasaki reached the council at midday August 9. At three o'clock the following morning, in the imperial air-raid shelter, it was decided to send to the Allies a note of surrender.

The reply which followed made it clear that though warmaking power was to be completely destroyed and Japanese sovereignty limited to its four home islands, fundamental human rights would be respected, armed forces abroad allowed to return home, and nonmilitary industry permitted, with eventual world trade.

His Imperial Majesty himself asked the government to accept the Allied proposal. Now what was Japan to expect? This was her first experience of unconditional surrender.

On August 15, all Japanese were ordered to listen to their radios and for the first time heard the voice of their emperor. He was broadcasting to the whole nation, not that they had been defeated, but that he had acted to spare them from destruction, and the war was at an end. It was a great relief.

"Unite your total strength to be devoted to the construction for the future." He urged them, "Cultivate the ways of rectitude; foster nobility of spirit; and work with resolution so as ye may enhance the innate glory of the imperial government and keep pace with the progress of the world."

In emotional outbursts of tears and exhaustion they were united as never before in gratitude and loyalty toward their Son of Heaven. In shame for having exposed His Imperial Majesty to such humiliation, several military leaders committed suicide in their homes; a few ordinary citizens did likewise, outside the palace gates.

Preparation for Occupation was a precarious task, but accomplished with remarkably little disturbance. Completely unmolested, General Douglas MacArthur, the Supreme Commander of the Occupation, alighted at Atsugi Airfield on August 30. Each side was pleasantly surprised at the good behavior of the other.

Aboard the USS *Missouri* in Tokyo Bay on September 2, 1945, the Instrument of Surrender was signed by Foreign Minister Shigemitsu, as representative of the emperor and the government. He later wrote: "It was a wonderfully fine day. Fujisan appeared; a history of one thousand years had ended; a new epoch dawned. The future of this new Japan depends on the ability and perseverance of the Japanese race." [1]

Exhausted physically and spiritually, from fourteen years of military domination and the horrors and hungers of war, most Japanese on the day of surrender were too numb and bewildered to follow the ways of democracy with which they were confronted. The best that urban dwellers could do was carry on their daily scrounging for food, clearing away of rubble and building of makeshift shelters.

Education was virtually at a standstill. Four thousand schools had been destroyed and only about a fifth of the needed textbooks were to be had. Eighteen million students, who during the war had worked part time in defense plants or at machines installed in their schools, and spent their vacations working on farms, were now idle.

For farmers, life was somewhat better, but what with trying to provide for destitute city relatives in addition to their immediate families, they too were barely existing. True, they were being given silk kimonos, tea ceremony wares and other family treasures, in exchange for their vegetables, eggs and grains, but these relics of better days only prompted reminiscence.

Looking back, one realized how much Japan had been changed, since her first dealing with the United States; how she had been caught up and carried along by the currents of Western affairs; how she had achieved the semblance of a Westernized state in one generation, and had continued to assimilate, cooperate and integrate with the Western world. Japanese people had been giving their utmost of ability and perseverance, and yet they could not determine their future; no nation, it seemed, could freely determine its future; all were interdependent.

Readiness to accept and make the best of any situation, with at least outward serenity, was part of the well-established discipline of both the religion and the education of all Japanese, however, though miserable in circumstances and frustrated in purpose they were able to smile and follow orders politely.

When the emperor was summoned to a conference by the Supreme Commander of the Allied Powers, he impressed General MacArthur with his integrity, sincerity and good intentions. And MacArthur, in turn, well-cast for the role which was his to play, with a dramatic flare for fine phrases, impressed the Japanese with his benevolence, strong will, personal loyalty and austerity, all qualities they admired. Crowds watched his goings and comings and were grateful for the sense of direction he gave them. He helped to restore confidence. "Makkasa Tenno" (MacArthur, Son of Heaven) they sometimes called him. There was no chain reaction of hostility or violence, and necessary tasks proceeded relatively smoothly.

The first objective, according to the United States Initial Post Surrender Policy, radioed from Washington to General MacArthur before his arrival in Japan, was "to insure that Japan will not again become a menace to the United States, or to the peace and security of the world." Objective two was "to bring about the eventual establishment of a peaceful and responsible government, which will support the objectives of the United States, as expressed in the Charter of the United Nations."

An attractive program of adult education was planned and set in action. Troupes of traveling actors went to tell the farmers about democracy in variety acts and short plays. At the movies, in addition to Japanese films, such as *The Returned Soldier, Woman's Suffrage* and *Your Diet,* American documentary films, features and newsreels were shown. At the theaters, Drinkwater's *Abraham Lincoln* and Shakespearean comedies were played. There were radio roundtable programs about needed reforms. *The Man on the Street* broadcast opinions on current problems in fifteen-minute programs three times a week. *The Voice of the People* was heard for ten minutes twice daily. *The Woman's Hour* aimed to develop the social and political consciousness of women; *Farm Hour* aimed to impress the farmer with his importance; *Freedom of Thought* voiced the opinions of professional men and leaders. *The American Way of Life* told the experiences of Japanese who had visited the United States. Western music was featured. *Now It Can Be Told,* in March-of-Time for-mat, gave a "true" history of the war. Libraries of information about the United States and international affairs were established in large cities for the use of the Japanese. Special licenses were issued to *Time, Newsweek,* the *Reader's Digest* and *The New York Times* Overseas Edition, for publication in Japanese.

Japanese people soon became familiar with details of the Occupation policy in practice. Though noted for their conformity to traditional standards, they were understandably not of one mind now. City folk, especially those in Tokyo and the large port cities, had had more contact with Westerners, more education and political experience. They were ready for radical changes: many of them felt that the teachings of Karl Marx were better suited than capitalism and democracy to actual conditions in Japan. Farmers were conservative and wanted chiefly to be left to their own productive labors without strange and complicated political responsibilities.

The two million soldiers returning to Japan and three million government and industrial personnel who had been living abroad in the Co-Prosperity Sphere added their peculiar factors to the problems of food, shelter and unemployment. Thousands of Chinese merchants in Japanese cities tried to take advantage of the desperate straits of their defeated enemies, and even larger numbers of Korean laborers now released from enforced war efforts were uncooperative. Communist agitators and other political prisoners whom the Occupation had turned loose from Japanese jails, swarms of discharged members of the former National Police Force, government workers of long-established status, former political, educational and industrial leaders of high caliber, factory hands and small shopkeepers, all had their views of the United States Occupation policy and forces in action. Misunderstandings were compounded by language difficulties, official red tape, inconsistencies and incompetence on both sides, but in general it was agreed that the Americans were surprisingly well-behaved and trying to be fair; the Japanese, accepting their situation realistically and trying to cooperate.

Responsible leaders naturally showed reluctance to expose themselves to the risks and wastefulness of government by the politically inexperienced, but Occupation authorities tolerated no dalliance. In rapid succession, reforms were introduced and carried out: a bill guaranteeing political freedom and encouraging political activities was passed by the Diet on October 4, 1945; demobilization of military personnel and the dismantling of army and navy facilities were so well accomplished in three months that one of the two Occupation armies was withdrawn in January, 1946.

Drastic reforms were effected in religion also. On New Year's Day in 1946, the emperor read over the radio a rescript denying the divine ancestry of the imperial family and the Japanese people. "We have to proceed unflinchingly," he proclaimed, "toward elimination of the misguided practices of the past . . . The ties between us and our people . . . do not depend upon mere legends and myths. They are not predicated on the false conception that the emperor is divine and that the Japanese people are superior to other races and fated to rule the world . . . The emperor is not a living god . . ." [2]

Shinto was to receive no further government support. Shinto shrines and symbols were removed from schools and public buildings. No discrimination was to be shown against nonbelievers. On Sunday mornings the radio carried a Shinto program from eight to eight-thirty, a Buddhist program from ten to ten-thirty and a Christian program from eleven to eleven-thirty.

The great purge of military and nationalist leaders was begun, and trials, of those considered to be war criminals, continued for two years.

An Education Mission arrived from the United States, for a three weeks' visit, to study the Japanese school and higher education system, and render a report. Under a reorganized

Ministry of Education, courses were revised, textbooks censored to conform with the Supreme Commander's directives, and schools reopened.

Their aim was to be:

to train citizens who will be able to understand the role of the individual in local, national and world life, to develop character and sense of responsibility through living and practices in the community, and to equip students to contribute to the betterment of society.

On March 6, a draft of a new Constitution said to have the full approval of both General MacArthur and the emperor was made public. It began:

We, the Japanese people, acting through our duly elected representatives in the National Diet, determined that we shall secure for ourselves and our posterity the fruits of peaceful cooperation with all nations and the blessings of liberty throughout this land, and resolved that never again shall we be visited with the horrors of war through the action of government, do proclaim that sovereign power resides with the people, and do firmly establish this Constitution. Government is a sacred trust of the people, the authority for which is derived from the people, the powers of which are exercised by the representatives of the people, and the benefits of which are enjoyed by the people. This is a universal principle of mankind upon which this Constitution is founded . . .

We, the Japanese people, desire peace for all time and are deeply conscious of the high ideals controlling human relationship, and we have determined to preserve our security and existence, trusting in the justice and faith of the peace-loving peoples of the world. We desire to occupy an honored place in an international society, striving for the preservation of peace and the banishment of tyranny and slavery, oppression and intolerance for all time from the earth. We recognize that all peoples of the world have the right to live in peace, free from fear and want.

We believe that no nation is responsible to itself alone, but that laws of political morality are universal; and that obedience to such laws is incumbent upon all nations who would sustain their own sovereignty, and justify their sovereign relationship with other nations.

We, the Japanese people, pledge our national honor to accomplish these high ideals and purposes with all our resources . . .

The Emperor shall be the symbol of the State and of the unity of the people, deriving his position from the will of the people with whom resides sovereign power . . .

The advice and approval of the Cabinet shall be required for all acts of the Emperor in matters of state, and the Cabinet shall be responsible therefore . . . The Emperor shall appoint the Prime Minister . . . and the Chief Judge of the Supreme Court . . . as designated by the Cabinet . . .

Article 9 of the Japanese Constitution read in the light of present world relationships is startling. One of the most visionary, idealistic and daring proclamations ever published, it is the subject of continuing ardent controversy. It declares:

Aspiring sincerely to an international peace based on justice and order, the Japanese people forever renounce war as a sovereign right of the nation, and the threat or use of force as means of settling international disputes.

In order to accomplish the aim of the preceding paragraph, land, sea and air forces, as well as other war potential, will never be maintained. The right of belligerency of the state will not be recognized.

Thirty-one more articles (twenty-one more than the Bill of Rights appended to the United States Constitution) outline the rights and duties of the people, and guarantee that they shall be conferred upon "this and future generations, as eternal and inviolable rights."

All of the people shall be respected as individuals. Their right to life, liberty and the pursuit of happiness shall, to the extent that it does not interfere with the public welfare, be the supreme consideration in legislation . . .

All of the people are equal under the law and there shall be no discrimination in political, economic and social relations because of race, creed, sex, social status or family origin.

All public officials are servants of the whole community and not of any group thereof.

Universal adult suffrage is guaranteed . . .

Secrecy of the ballot shall not be violated . . .

Freedom of thought and conscience shall not be violated.

Freedom of religion is guaranteed to all. No religious organization shall receive any privileges from the State, nor exercise any political authority.

The State and its organs shall refrain from religious education or any other religious activity.

Freedom of assembly and association as well as speech, press and all other forms of expression are guaranteed.

No censorship shall be maintained, nor shall the secrecy of any means of communication be violated.

. . . Academic freedom is guaranteed.

Marriage . . . laws with regard to choice of spouse, property rights, inheritance, choice of domicile and divorce . . . shall be enacted from the standpoint of individual dignity and the essential equality of the sexes.

All people shall have the right to maintain the minimum standards of wholesome and cultured living.

All people shall have the right to receive an equal education correspondent to their ability—ordinary education, compulsory and free.

In April, 1946, with all Japanese of twenty years and over, male and female, privileged to vote and hold office, a general election was ordered to end control of the Diet by members who had been elected during the war. Thirty-nine of the four hundred and sixty-six new representatives were women.[3]

During the same month, the first shipments of food, requested from America by MacArthur, to supplement meager Japanese rations, were received. Also received was the disquieting news that the United States, the Soviets and the Far Eastern Commission in Washington were at odds concerning Japan's future.

In October, the Constitution was passed to become effective in May, 1947. Although it may not have been precisely "the freely expressed will of the Japanese people," it did seem to Japanese intellectuals to be in accordance *ideally* with world trends. Looked at realistically, however, in view of Japan's economic and cultural limitations, its ultraliberal provisions seemed impossible to implement. The role of pilot project Utopia was appealing, but it needed a very strong supporting cast, stronger perhaps than the United States would afford. Many studies of Constitutional Law were activated with a view to possible revision some years later.

Japanese women, on the other hand, who for a couple of decades had been working toward equal rights for their sex, or who had had to sacrifice their sons and husbands to the war machine, were especially enthusiastic about the new constitution. They organized impressive programs, with their leaders giving lectures throughout the country on ways in which the new rights affected women and the family system.

In response to the education-reform laws, nine years of free compulsory education were provided instead of six, many new high schools and colleges for girls were started, and universities became coeducational.

New textbooks, rewritten by Japanese historians, told the history of Japan in relation to world history, and emphasized the progress of the people, rather than the deeds of rulers and warriors. The causes and events of World War II were given frank treatment: culture and economics, importance.

Radios, newspapers, movies, film strips, posters and public speakers explained the new Land Reform Bill. Within two years, the land held by absentee landlords was to be made available for purchase by resident farmers, so that they might own the land they cultivated and bequeath it to their children. Fifty model factories were set up in rural sections to train a nucleus of technical personnel for developing rural centers for the processing of agricultural products, light manufacturing and handicraft work.

A basic labor law was passed, providing a forty-eight-hour work week and equality of employment for men and women. The newly organized unions called an embarrassing general strike, which, democratic principles notwithstanding, General MacArthur intervened to prevent.

Through the agency of the U.S. Commercial Company, a trickle of bartered exports and imports began: timber, rayon yarn, chemicals and drugs, tea, silk, furs and some machinery and equipment were exchanged for foodstuffs, salt and raw cotton.

A Japanese Christian was elected prime minister in April, 1947.

Occupation officials began to talk about a Peace Treaty and, in order to hasten her economic recovery, about paring down the reparations demanded of Japan by the erstwhile members of her Co-Prosperity Sphere. Korea had been freed of Japanese domination only to be split into Communist and Anti-Communist camps. Chiang Kai-shek was fighting for the survival of Nationalist China against Communist leaders. Communists in Japan polled ten per cent of the popular vote, electing thirty-five members to the Diet. By early 1948, it was evident that United States diplomacy in Asia was not entirely successful, and that the United States was unable to get its

Western allies to agree to hold a peace conference. Instead, on its own initiative, the United States was beginning a larger program of economic rehabilitation for Japan. This was carried on with increasing success until June, 1950; manufacturing production almost doubled; unfavorable balances of imports over exports, halved.

With desperate needs provided for, and reforms no longer urgent, the continuing presence of the Occupation forces, families included, began to rankle. As their goals in Japan were reached, officials with vision and drive moved on, their places being filled with what seemed like inferior personnel. Fresh teen-age draftees, drinking and romancing, made a nuisance of themselves.

Then war broke out in Korea with United Nations forces defending South Korea against Communist aggression from the North. Still straining to recover from the direst disaster in their history, Japanese were in no mood to be involved again in military operation. This conflict seemed of little concern to them.

Communists in Japan had been driven underground by General MacArthur's response to their violence, strikes and sabotage. There seemed to be both good and bad in both Russia and America and each was trying to use Japan against the other. The Japanese had received $1.7 billion worth of direct aid from the United States since their surrender, for which they were grateful, but they resented being used. They wanted to be free in the Free World. "Relying upon the advanced spirituality of the world to protect them against undue aggression" even Makkasa Tenno now recognized, afforded little sense of security.

United Nations' orders for war supplies and repair services, and the lavish spending of United Nations troops on furlough in Japan, provided temporary distractions but when in April, 1951, General MacArthur was relieved of his command because *he* was "no longer able to give wholehearted support to

United States' and United Nations' policies," Japanese were "unable to close their open mouths." The man in the narrow street or the two-and-a-half-acre rice paddy did not understand what was going on.

The advantage of Japan's cooperation to the Western Allies, as well as the advantage to Japan of a lenient, liberal Peace Treaty seemed to be recognized by John Foster Dulles, Secretary of State in Washington. He was flying about the world reconciling differences, making compromises, winning agreements, in preparation for a conference to be held in San Francisco; and on September 8, 1951, a treaty was signed by the United States and forty-eight allies and Japan, which "resolved that henceforth their relations shall be those of nations which, as sovereign equals, cooperate in friendly association to promote their common welfare and to maintain international peace and security."

Shigeru Yoshida, who became Minister of Foreign Affairs at the beginning of the Occupation and Prime Minister about half a year later, was the central figure in Japan's postwar diplomacy. He desired and worked for the restoration of Japan's independence with great sincerity. Many Japanese believe that when praying to the kami for help one should express sincerity by abstaining from the things most enjoyed. A story goes that Yoshida, as fond of cigars as Churchill, gave up smoking completely before the San Francisco Peace Conference and that after the treaty was signed, he was seen puffing again.

Much remained to be done, however. The countries of most immediate importance to Japan in East Asia, the Philippines, Burma, India, Indonesia, Red China and the U.S.S.R. had not signed. Reparations had to be negotiated, and strong antipathies reconciled, before normal diplomatic ties could be resumed. There was disagreement even between Great Britain and the United States about recognizing Red China.

Japan nevertheless declared its intention to apply for membership in the United Nations, to conform to its charter, strive to realize the objective of the Universal Declaration of Human Rights, and in public and private trade and commerce, to conform to internationally accepted practices. The state of war between Japan and each of the United States-Allied Powers was officially terminated by the Peace Treaty and the full sovereignty of the Japanese people over Japan and its territorial waters was recognized, but a Japan-United States Security Treaty was signed the same day.

Cut back to original size,[4] but independent! Independent? Well, yes and no. All Occupation forces were to be withdrawn as soon as possible, but there was "nothing to prevent the stationing or retention of foreign armed forces in Japanese territory under . . . agreements . . . between one or more of the allied powers and Japan."

Having been completely disarmed, Japan, the treaty stated, did "not have the effective means to exercise its inherent right of self-defense, and since irresponsible militarism has not yet been driven from the world, the United States of America in the interest of peace and security is presently willing to maintain certain of its armed forces in and about Japan, in the expectation that Japan will itself, increasingly, assume responsibility for its own defense against direct and indirect aggression, always avoiding any armament which could be an offensive threat . . ." Japan and the United States in a mutual security pact a decade after Pearl Harbor![5]

Six months later, the National Police Reserve of seventy-five thousand men which General MacArthur had ordered in June, 1950, to replace the U.S. troops taken out of Japan by the war in Korea, was developed into the National Safety Force. Aid in organization and modern army equipment for its hundred and ten thousand men was supplied by the United States. Seven U.S. frigates were leased to Japan for a new embryo navy.

In December, 1953, Vice President Nixon paid Japan an official visit, and made a policy speech pointing out that, in future, Japan would be required to contribute to its own defense and rearmament. A budget for Mutual Security Assistance was approved by the Diet the following spring. A force to defend Japan against outside aggression was not barred by Prime Minister Yoshida's interpretation of the new Constitution, but the United States seemed to want everything faster than many Japanese felt financially or politically possible.

The Prime Minister's leadership was needed and he made public a statement: "If a 'neutral' nation refuses to join a 'just' group, international justice cannot be enforced. If a nation cannot distinguish between right and wrong, it is not qualified to be an independent nation. It is cowardice to refuse to support the right. Japan believes in the justice of democratic principles and therefore has been determined to rise or fall with the democratic nations. This is basic policy in which the majority of Japanese believe." [6]

CHAPTER 19

CONTEMPORARY JAPAN
(1960–   )

FOREIGN visitors[1] taxiing up to Tokyo from Haneda International Airport, or from a superliner at Yokohama, well may think that Japan today is one of the most completely international countries of the world. Wide highways and narrow alleys seethe with trucks, buses, passenger cars and bicycles of both foreign and domestic makes, and with pedestrians wearing leather shoes, wooden geta, Western-style dress and kimonos. Buildings of reinforced concrete in good contemporary architecture crowd traditional paper-walled houses. Department stores with roof-top golf ranges and children's playgrounds are interspersed with owner-operated specialty shops and flanked by open booths. Signs and billboards combine Western and Asian scripts and pictures. Aromas of hot dogs, pizzas, curry, chop suey and sukiyaki blend around the Ginza, which is drab wood and stone by day, but aglow with colored neon at night.

Cinemas galore, many showing foreign films, are distributed throughout the city. Banks of America, China, Korea, India and Indo-China display their nameplates in the financial section, in addition to various scattered embassies, diplomatic missions, and centers of International Cultural Societies: Argentine, Ethiopian, French, Hispanic, Israeli, Nordic, Philippine, Thai and many more. Christian churches and meeting places numbering close to four hundred (including Greek and Russian

Orthodox) stand in the same neighborhoods as Shinto shrines and Buddhist temples. One sees classical Japanese gardens, formal Western gardens and perhaps a futuristic garden with metal mobiles, abstract sculpture and ceramic furniture.[2] Tokyo Tower, a giant TV antenna, rises above all.

The Tokyo metropolis sprawls over an area of almost thirteen hundred square miles (more than three times the size of New York's five boroughs). "Housing estates" are proliferating along the rail lines and city outskirts. Mass-media advertising and instalment-plan buying familiarize the tenants with electric washing machines, irons, refrigerators, and vacuum cleaners. A rapidly growing number of households have television sets.[3] Compared with Americans and Europeans, few Japanese own cars, but teen-agers join car clubs and membership entitles them to driving instructions with use of a car once a month.

In Tokyo's thick two-volume telephone directory, over four hundred listings include international as part of the name: International Airport, International Conference Hall, International House, International Theater, International Trade Fair Hall, International Christian University, St. Luke's International Hospital, International Judo Center, etc. Direct dialing operates over three million phones, long distance as well as local.

Marvelously punctual trains arrive and depart on closely timed schedules.[4] Between Tokyo and Osaka the most modern railway in the world is being built, designed to carry air-conditioned passenger cars with individual head-rest radios, at an average speed of a hundred and four miles an hour.

Osaka, like Tokyo, is actively international. It has a Sister-City affiliation[5] with San Francisco, as Tokyo has with New York, and plays host to many international conferences. Osaka also has an annual International Festival in an auditorium reputed to be acoustically one of the world's best. The 1960 festival program included: a French drama troupe, a Swiss soprano, a Spanish harpist and ballet, the Paganini String Quartet, and the Boston Symphony Orchestra, together with a grand concert of Japanese kotos, and performances of Noh dramas, Kabuki dances, Bunraku puppet plays and a modern Japanese opera about Perry's Black Ships. Not to be outdone, Tokyo planned an annual *East-West Music Encounter* also featuring famous foreign performers and musicians along with Japanese.

A few cosmopolitans with overseas connections and modern transportation and communication facilities have worked wonders in overcoming insularity and entering into relationship with other members of the world family. A very large majority of Japanese, however, are still isolated even from one another: the psychological distance between port city and country village still is very great. There is little conversation between intellectuals and fishermen, large industrialists and small operators, students and unskilled labor or government officials; there is much class soliloquy and slogan shouting.

Diplomatically, since December, 1956, Japan has been one of the United Nations cooperating "to save succeeding generations from the scourge of war" and "to improve economic and social conditions, health and education and to promote respect for human rights and fundamental freedoms."

Her industrialists have been cooperating with world trade organizations, participating in international commodity exhibits and trade fairs, lending technical assistance in underdeveloped countries of Asia and privately undertaking joint ventures [6] with entrepreneurs in other countries. They tried to concentrate on producing goods that would meet the least competition from established industries abroad; and to the textiles, toys, cultured pearls, canned fish and dinner-ware, by which they were previously known, have added electronic and optical equipment of superior quality, transistor radios, cameras and electron microscopes.

They lead the world in building ships of new design, and manufacturing for export many kinds of machinery, and rolling stock suitable for both desert and jungle conditions. Efficient techniques for the transportation and storage of agricultural products, and for construction of dams, power generators, earthquake-proof buildings, subways and underwater tunnels have also enhanced Japan's reputation abroad.[7]

The large industrialists belong to the Liberal Democratic party and, with the United States supporting their business acumen, have developed the rapidly expanding economy on which the continuing power of their party is based. They are the owners of the companies of more than a hundred million yen capitalization with thousands of employees whose wages are twice those paid to workers in industries having less than two million yen capital and less than a hundred employees. Industries whose productive power is comparatively low as well as those whose relatively uncontrolled quality standards and operations frequently give Japan a bad name abroad, naturally are not given much support by the government. About ten per cent of the population earn what is considered the minimum subsistence level, about thirty dollars a month for a family of five.

Hayato Ikeda who succeeded as prime minister after the 1960 government crisis,[8] in his speech to the Plenary Session of the newly elected National Diet in January, 1961, announced that Japan is now "starting on this brave march toward a welfare state," for the "unfortunate and unblest who belong to the so-called low-income stratum." "The State, however," according to Prime Minister Ikeda, "must not be regarded as something like Santa Claus." "The big task of the government's long-range plan" is rather to "create ample opportunities for those unlucky people to help themselves." The need to stabilize prices seems to be the one plank on which most political spokesmen stand together.

Those who feel that the government is dragging its feet and allowing great gaps between economic growth and welfare legislation in "this brave march" vote with the Socialist and newer Democratic Socialist parties.[9] These include both intellectuals and ill-informed, many of whom belong principally to register their opposition to the Liberal Democrats. Civil liberty is sometimes confused with laissez-faire; the fall of capitalism, with nirvana. Perhaps because they feel that their democracy is so new and undeveloped, though they welcomed its return after the wartime totalitarian government, Diet members of neither party seem to trust it. The party in power has ignored public opinion and tried to rush its measures through, while frustrated opposition resorted to sit-downs and "demos." Stabbings and shootings have sometimes been preferred to the slow but orderly ballot box for removing officials from office. A few Socialists seem to be aware of the challenge and herculean responsibility of preserving the parliamentary system, re-educating the nation politically, and providing practical policies for both national security and the effective use of Japan's resources for foreign trade.

The main island, as it were, of Japanese people is the rural group—farmers, fishers and foresters, who constitute over half of the total population. They live in the fishing and farming villages throughout the country, where traditional Shinto, Confucian and Buddhist doctrines still control the thinking, and TV antennae, on bamboo poles or thatched roofs, are the most conspicuous signs of foreign influence.

Seventy per cent of the more than six million farm households now, compared with a prewar thirty per cent, own their land, but the small size of individual holdings provides but little income.[10] Two and a half acres constitute the average farm, and about half of the farm families work less than one acre. Those living in the mountains often supplement their farm yield with forestry; those near the shore also engage in fishing and processing edible seaweed.

Government research centers and county agents organize agriculture-improvement associations and small cooperatives for distributing new information and equipment. Farmers are encouraged to diversify their operations by adding to their usual grain crops, a great variety of vegetables and fruits of superior quality and also a few milk goats or cows, and steers for beef.[11] With seed improvement, chemical fertilizers and insecticides, plastic covers to protect young plants, motorized cultivators, sprayers and threshers all of which help farmers beat typhoons to the harvest, the yield per acre has increased significantly in recent years. According to American standards the amount of labor required for such intensive horticulture is uneconomical, but Japan does in this way manage to produce most of her own food despite population growth and a generally improved diet, and farmers rightly feel their importance to the nation.

During the rush seasons of planting and harvest, entire families are mobilized on the farm front; between times, however, the young folk go to town for factory jobs or day labor, and through them a certain amount of urban influence filters into rural communities. In general, however, farmers remain very conservative in their thinking and doing, and concern themselves little with self-improvement or participation in public affairs. For security they rely more on their own hard work and on incantations and magic than on politicians; and, lacking the modern medical care of city clinics and hospitals, are inclined to look to new religious sects for health and longevity.

Only on Saturday nights are movies usually shown in farming villages. Country folk still prefer films about samurai swordplay to modern subjects; they find foreign pictures hard to understand and rather uninteresting. The *Asahi* (*Morning Sun*) newspaper in rural Japan has ten times the rural circulation which *The New York Times* has in America, and almost every farmer's wife gets to see the folksy and recreational, best-selling monthly, *Light of the Home.*

When elections are held, a lingering sense of loyalty inclines many farmers to vote for former landlords or the candidates and office holders whom they recommend. Large election expenditures which only the Liberal Democrats can afford also play a very influential part. Lack of informed participation in politics seems to be causing a trend toward more centralized government rather than toward self-government at the grass roots. Though farmers vote consistently for the party in power, many resist capitalist proposals for organization of the agricultural industry on a larger scale; a Labor-Farmer Union opposes capitalistic controls, and farmer demonstrations against government appropriation of hard-earned tax money for seemingly futile rearmament, and against allocation of arable land for airfields and defense installations are occasionally reported in newspapers. Nevertheless, the government seems more and more interested in modernization of farming and in correcting the imbalance between agricultural and industrial incomes by developing larger scale farm operation.

A very small, but equally deep-rooted and self-conscious group is the imperial family. Traditionally the most isolated of all, the emperor and empress now appear occasionally at a night baseball game or some other popular event. The crown prince and his lovely "commoner" wife have been traveling abroad, and thanks undoubtedly in part to his Quaker tutor, Mrs. Vining, and in spite of the official protocol which surrounded them, managed to communicate heartwarming human feelings to the American people during their visit in 1960. Imperial princesses also married outside of royalty and ventured into livestock farming and TV disc-jockeying.[12]

Scientists and creative artists by the very nature of their work belong more fully to the world than to an isolated background. Not always well supported with research facilities at home,[13] Japanese scientists participate in international conferences and projects in many fields—agriculture, metallurgy, nuclear energy, Geophysical Year researches, tidal-wave alarm systems, radiation medicine, etc. Biological and medical researchers are making valuable contributions to the world's health with microphotography of cells and cancer studies. In 1949, the Nobel Prize was awarded to a Japanese physicist, Hideki Yukawa, working at Columbia University.

The influence of Japanese house and garden architects, and interior decorators, is well recognized in the West.[14] While reminiscences of calligraphy seem apparent in many contemporary Western paintings, the preponderance of oil and canvas and Western subjects, in Japanese art shows, is clear evidence that East and West have met and mingled. Among contemporary men of letters,[15] great importance is placed on the everyday experience of the individual as such, autobiographical writing with an air of self-superiority, novels based on current events, mysteries and detective stories.

Religious organizations in Japan,[16] like the people, are constitutionally free and equal. No religion receives government support or has its doctrines taught in public schools, but each serves as a bridge or line of communication between individuals and between groups. Shinto leaders are emphasizing personal development and community service instead of nationalism; Buddhist leaders face the fact that social problems are not solved by meditation or repetition of the name of Amida Buddha; and Christians are realizing that they have no monopoly on Truth. The majority are of second and third religiously cross-fertilized generations, and might be expected to produce a strong syncretic faith for the masses; this has not happened yet: those who are ardent usually seem to be ardently sectarian; those who are liberal usually lack zeal. Joint meetings and conferences are occasionally held, however, and there is a growing awareness of what all have in common. Many contemporary Japanese on the other hand are disinterested in any religion they know of, avowedly materialistic, but nostalgic for something absolute.

Those who visit the shrines probably do so from habit, but many also seem to believe deep within themselves that "divine power is the source of all life" and feel a need to express their gratitude and devotion. Some buy charms and draw fortune papers. Some call upon priests to purify their land before building on it and to give them magic protection against disease. The grand shrine of Isé, alone, is said to distribute about seven million paper amulets a year. Attendants and priests from the various shrines affiliate and confer together on how to stimulate greater interest in Shinto ritual, how to reach more of the industrial and business population, how better to serve the community, and also how better to support themselves. Within the Liberal Democratic party, there is currently some agitation for supporting a few shrines of historical importance with government funds.

Of thirteen prewar Shinto sects, with a total of perhaps ten million adherents, many of whom formed new sects when freedom of religion was guaranteed to all, the most active and influential is Tenrikyo, the sect of Great Parent God. Founded in 1838, by a woman whose descendants are still its chief priests, it emphasizes faith healing. The ultimate reality, it teaches, is Divine Reason, a composite of ten Shinto kamis. Evil consists of the "dusts" of greed, misguided love, spite, anger, selfishness, etc. When man comes into perfect union with Divine Reason he is well and happy. Tenrikyo followers believe in reincarnation and the eventual changing of all men into virtuous agents for the kingdom of peace.

At their headquarters in Nara is a great educational center with kindergartens, elementary and high schools, advanced language schools and seminaries for training priests and missionaries for South East Asia. For their library, they are buying old and rare as well as new books from all over the world, especially books related to the history of Christian missions. For their museums they are buying up the findings of Far Eastern archeologists. From their swimming pools, gynasiums and playing fields they are producing fine physical specimens, champions of baseball and judo.

Tenrikyo members volunteer labor for public works and building homes for homeless families not necessarily connected with their church. They also carry on tuberculosis research, and sanitariums, social-service clinics, homes for orphans and occupational-training agencies.

Another vigorous Shinto sect, with its center in Osaka, and somewhat less than a million adherents in southeastern Japan, is Konkokyo. It was founded a hundred years ago by an uneducated farmer who felt himself called to communicate between mankind and the "great father of the universe, the source of all beings and of infinite mercy and love, through faith in whom men love each other, pray for peace in the world and fulfill their duties to self, family and society, in happiness and prosperity." Human suffering and calamities are attributed to ignorance of his love and violation of his laws. Konkokyo is more free than other Shinto sects from traditional ceremonies and superstitions; it relies on the creative union of man and spiritual powers, in carrying on educational and social-welfare work.

Many Shinto sects preach fortitude and loyalty to the state, ancient etiquette, personal purity and universal brotherhood, and carry their preaching and purifying even into factories and wrestling rings. Japan, like the United States, also has headline-making sects whose fanatical followers pool their property and worry the police.

A sect called House of Growth, claiming to embrace the best elements of all religions, has over a million middle- and upper-class adherents. Its original aim was to do away with superstition and formalism and to harmonize all races of mankind through belief in the one God revealed in all, but it is said to be increasingly emphasizing fatherland and national flag.

Buddhism known as the most tolerant of the world's religions is also divided into six large denominations with dozens of splinter sects. About half of the Japanese are counted as Buddhists, and though many young ones disavow affiliation they cannot avoid its everyday influence.

Japanese Buddhism through the centuries has become even more complicated and sophisticated than Christianity. In addition to its founding Buddha, there are mythical Buddhas, cosmic Buddhas and Buddhas-to-be, philosophical scriptures, interpretations of scriptures, sacred objects and rituals galore. Though there are both priests and nuns, few public services are held. At any time convenient for themselves, believers visit temples for individual prayers and worship. Preaching is more common nowadays, but still the most frequent services are funerals or memorials, and the incomes of both temples and clergy are derived mainly from offerings made for the sake of the dead.

According to the teaching of the Shingon sect, which claims about ten million followers, the whole universe is the body of the cosmic Buddha and even a grain of dust includes some of his spiritual nature. Man progresses through stages of spiritual development from a mind absorbed in thoughts of food and sex, recognition of moral laws and the illusory nature of material things, to true enlightenment and comprehension of the glories of the cosmos.

Amida Buddhism with over twenty million followers is the most active and powerful sect in Japan. According to its teachings, calling the name of Amida is sufficient for salvation; since faith is the gift of Amida, gratitude should be men's chief concern. A saved man *will* practice the ordinary moralities as a member of family and state, it teaches, to square up its deficient ethical side. The headquarters of Higashi and Nishi Honganji, the two leading sects of Amida Buddhism, are in Kyoto where both are known for their universities and their pilgrim-tourist attractions. The abbots of both are related to the imperial family. Throughout the country each has about ten thousand temples.

The Zen School of Buddhism is better known in the West because of its relevance to the current popularity of depth psychology and psychiatry. Zen teaches silent meditation and mental disciplines for detaching oneself from concern for one's self, and experiencing a unity with cosmic existence. It places little value on sacred scriptures, faith in a saviour or personal ethics. It aims at opening the seeker's mind directly to Truth and Enlightenment. Architecture, literature, painting, dramas, tea ceremony, gardens, all may serve this purpose and Zen devotees have produced much of what is known as essentially Japanese art.

A new sect which has gained remarkable numerical strength since the war is Soka Gakkai (Value Creating Academic Society). Taking their inspiration from the thirteenth-century prophet Nichiren and a twentieth-century geography teacher from Hokkaido, they appeal especially to the coal miners of that northern island and to laboring people generally. Organized for political power they send out "troops" commissioned to win converts for indoctrination. Their aim is to seek whatever has any sort of value, and to elect as many representatives as possible in national and local legislatures.

Japanese Buddhist leaders seem to be increasingly interested in cooperation with Buddhists abroad. At a recent world conference of Buddhists in Bangkok, plans were made for the international exchange of scholars, students, books and goodwill delegations and there was a joint resolution to oppose nuclear weapons. Japanese scholars together with Ceylonese are editing a Buddhist Encyclopedia in English, and there is considerable scholarly interest in exploring the ancient sites in India associated with the founding of their religion.

The approximately half million Christians in Japan are about equally divided between Catholic and Protestant churches, with Greek Orthodox claiming almost as many members as the Episcopalians. The one hundredth anniversary of the first Protestant mission to Japan was celebrated in 1960: Protestant churches have been nationalized and independent of foreign denominational controls for two decades. The continuing influence of foreign Christians is in social service, Y.M.C.A. and Y.W.C.A., hospitals and higher education. Although the total number of Japanese Christians remains small, they like to think they develop a disproportionately large number of responsible leaders. Because of the traditionally greater stature of national and private universities, where religious differences are not emphasized, the graduates of these, rather than those from Christian universities, seem to be given job preference, especially in government, politics and journalism. Both Catholics and Protestants are adjusting their programs to current world trends with mass meetings, prayer groups and lay ministries, and are making new translations of the Bible in modern simplified Japanese. The writings of Japanese theologians are also being published in the West.

Education in Japan, like religion, is helping to break down barriers, extend horizons and make people feel less insular. These advantages are somewhat offset by a downgrading of academic standards and the dilemma of a traditional morality which does not serve in the contemporary situation, while the ethics of individualism are not fully appreciated. The need for some unifying core of ideals is often noted.

Compulsory education now includes a standardized six years of elementary school plus three years of lower secondary school, corresponding to our junior high. The curriculum is designed to train for a democratic way of life. There is emphasis on speaking rather than writing, on conversation and speeches with few of the old-fashioned honorific forms of expression. History and geography are taught as social studies to help students orient themselves with the world. There is less memorizing, more evaluation, more useful rather than ornamental studies. Modern teachers encourage students to consult books, illustrations and maps, take excursions, investigate organizations, form their own opinion, explain it, test it:

How is Japan progressing in modernization?
What part do citizens play in social progress?
What attempts have been made to secure world peace?
If a foreign lady came into our classroom and sat on the teacher's desk, what would you do? 1. Push her off? 2. Explain to her that Japanese respect learning too much to sit on a desk? 3. Accept the fact that different people have different manners?

The study of English, one vocational subject and home-room activities are introduced at the junior high level which is also coeducational. More electives and another foreign language, usually French or German, is added at the secondary level. All schools are crowded, but the days of double shifts have passed.

Though there are colleges and universities throughout the country, with at least one national university in each of the forty-three provinces, the most popular ones are in Tokyo, with a total of about three hundred thousand students. Universities admit women but there are also colleges for girl students only. The proportion of male to female students in colleges and universities is about eight to one. Competition for admission to the better colleges and universities is terrific and young people frequently ruin their health and eyesight studying for examinations. Once admitted, however, they may, like European students, be irregular in class attendance, or like American ones, pursue a degree rather than knowledge.

Those who have made such a name for themselves in the papers, the Zengakuren, are an emotionally isolated and estranged generation, wanting to do something important and heroic, but overlooking opportunities of student caliber. They knew the oppressive controls, the stupidities and sufferings of war, and feel that their elders are to be blamed for failing to resist the military cliques. They admire and respect no one. The United States they know chiefly from the later, frivolous days of the Occupation, and from movies, press and television. They do not see the shift to rearm Japan as a consistent policy on behalf of world peace or Sovietism as a greater threat than the Japanese military. They are terribly confused and terribly self-righteous, but with enlightened direction their drive for self-dedication could serve their country well.

Few young people nowadays want to follow the trades of their parents, and the way to social and financial success seems to be in higher education. There are almost a million new job seekers every year. In the spring of 1961, for the first time in modern history, the Education Ministry announced that almost all this year's graduates will have jobs waiting for them, and employers will be looking for more skilled workers to run their modernized plants. Family connections persist, however, as a determining factor in employment as important as individual merit; the system is moving slowly from paternalism to democracy. For young people up to twenty-eight years old who have not finished high school, youth classes are provided by cities, towns and villages with one-third of the expense borne by the central government. About a million students are in this way studying arts and sciences and being trained in specialized work.

Prefectures send young people on educational tours through the country, twenty-five or thirty in a group, living in a farm community to study agriculture, in the mountains to study forestry or mining, or in a fishing community to study its techniques. Some university students returning to their native villages during summer vacations are assisted by their professors in an organized movement to enlighten the old folks at home about democracy. Other student groups are being sent abroad by the central government to study for two or three months and spread good will; about half of these are going to Southeast Asia and half to Western countries; about one-fifth are girls. Under the United States' Fulbright program, thousands of Japanese students have come to America to study labor management, industrial relations, public administration, legal problems, social science, educational methods, atomic medicine, etc., and hundreds of American students have studied in Japan.

City young folks, of course, have more chance of contact with foreigners than country young folks do; most have seen Americans, about one in ten has had direct dealings with them, but very few have firsthand knowledge of other Westerners.

In addition to their schooling, more than ten per cent of Japanese young people, especially in rural areas, receive education in clubs and social organizations. The Junior Red Cross with half a million members promotes citizenship and international friendship; the Seinen Dan, an organization of four million young men, ninety per cent rural, teaches improved methods of farming, fire prevention and participation in public affairs. Boy Scouts and Girl Scouts [17] and Y.M.C.A.'s and Y.W.C.A.'s provide over a hundred thousand with the usual educational and recreational opportunities of these international organizations. There is also a Japanese UNESCO Student Federation, Youth Hostels and World Youth Conference. Lack of experienced leadership, resources and public enthusiasm for such activities hampers their growth.

Mass media directors spare no efforts in reaching isolated areas of society and drawing people together; and their work is greatly facilitated by the simplification of the Japanese language recommended by the Occupation. Repeated attempts had been made to replace the peculiar written symbols, which were such a barrier to Western understanding of Japan, with the Roman alphabet, but this involved re-education of the entire nation and scrapping of their already published literature. A compromise was worked out whereby many Chinese ideographs were dropped from use and Japanese phonetic symbols took their place. Complicated ideographs were abbreviated. In place of the ten thousand ideographs or characters, which newspapers had been required to have in their type fonts, about nine hundred were selected as essential and another thousand as standard. The Japanese phonetic symbols called kana were also reduced in number and simplified in form and use, and the use of complicated expressions based on distinctions of social rank were discouraged. This made reading easier and tended to have a democratizing effect.

Japan's per capita newspaper circulation is second only to that of the United States. There is an average of more than one newspaper subscription per household, twelve hundred different periodicals and twenty thousand books a year are also published. About half of the newspaper circulation is of three big nation-wide dailies; the other half, of local papers.

The Big Three have editorial and business offices as well as color-printing facilities in Tokyo, Osaka, Nagoya, in Sapporo on the northern island, Hokkaido, and in two cities on the southern island, Kyushu. Domestic and local news is gathered by press clubs within various government agencies and by branch offices, with such facilities as planes, helicopters, walkie-talkies and cars with ultra-short-wave radio. Leased telephones and wirephoto networks cover the entire country.

In addition to having correspondents in the principal news centers of the world, the Big Three capacity for receiving, selecting, translating and transmitting news from foreign countries is tremendous. Together with the Ministry of Communications they receive almost half a million words of foreign news daily, mostly by wireless teleprinters from: the Associated Press in San Francisco, Taipei, Manila and Seoul; United Press International reports from Hong Kong and Singapore also; Reuters, from Singapore and Taipei; Tass from the U.S.S.R. Credit lines for the Nationalist China News Agency, Indian, Southeast Asian and West German news agencies also appear frequently, keeping Japanese readers informed of happenings abroad.

In addition to the regular newspapers, special sports newspapers, shipping and trade news and photo journalism are very popular. Tokyo has four English-language dailies.

To increase their prestige, many newspapers engage in cultural and charitable enterprises such as sponsoring academic research projects, industrial development programs and intercultural exchanges. Large numbers of musicians, dancers, orchestras, athletic groups and baseball teams from abroad are invited to come to Japan each year. Expeditions to the Himalayas, the Antarctic, and Patagonia have been underwritten by newspapers; donations have been collected and mobile rescue units sent to disaster areas. Local papers sponsor local art exhibitions, concerts, photographic, flower arrangement and dressmaking contests, lectures and classes.

The organizational excellence of the Japanese press is often

said to be more notable than the political responsibility it mani-
fests. There are no Fukuzawas these days at editorial desks to
give authoritative leadership to the young democracy, but
publishers do channel in a steady flow of news from the world
current.

Few countries publish more magazines than Japan, weeklies
as well as semimonthlies and monthlies catering to the interests
and tastes of all ages and classes. Women's and children's magazines, political and cultural reviews are among the most popular.
Time, Newsweek and *Life* are also readily obtainable in city
bookstores. A few intellectuals read the British *Economist* and
New Statesman, Soviet *New Time* and *International Life,* and
Communist China's *Red Flag* and *People's China;* although
foreign magazines are too expensive for the general public
they may be read at libraries and information centers.

A magazine called frankly *Mediocrity* has the largest circulation among Japanese teen-agers. It contains pictures of
actors and athletes, little gossip, nothing obscene.

Among current nonfiction best sellers in Japanese are the
primers on: *Hypnotism, Mathematics, Marriage* and *Mass Communication Media,* a photographic history of Japan's last hundred years, Miki's *World of Tomorrow,* Kuwabara's *Impres-
sions of U.S. Intellectuals.* Translations of *Lolita, Dr. Zhivago*
and *The Organization Man* are all best sellers too. Many Japanese books on subjects such as judo, flower arrangement and
paper folding are being exported.

Radio and television, as in the United States, give publishers
stiff competition. Over three quarters of all the households in
the country have radio sets. By law, radio and TV owners are
supposed to register their sets and to pay a monthly reception
fee.

The Japan Broadcasting Corporation is a noncommercial
service with over fifty TV stations, five of them educational,
giving the country very wide geographical coverage. The general service stations provide homes with music, news, melo-

drama and quiz shows, which Japanese eggheads designate as sentimental and decadent, while educational stations program for schools. Foreign shows with Japanese dialogue dubbed in are popular. Some programs, including the Perry Como show, are broadcast in color but color receiving sets are rarely seen except in waiting rooms, lobbies and museums.

Japan is one of the leading film producers in the world today; six major companies produce entertainment prolifically for small-town home consumption. About a third of the news reels shown are foreign. Japanese art films of great excellence are being exported in growing numbers.

Japanese national holidays also provide mass entertainment. Crowds swarm in the streets and parks on holidays, and sake flows freely. New Year's and Vernal Equinox are the gayest times. For New Year's, elaborate decorations symbolic of long life and prosperity appear everywhere, gifts are exchanged, and special dishes of the season served at family reunions. Vernal Equinox is "cherry viewing" time, a holiday "to love nature and think tenderly of living things." January 15 is Adults' Day, set aside to honor youth just reaching maturity. April 29 is the emperor's birthday; April 8 is Buddha's, but not a national holiday. The first week of May with three holidays is called Golden Week: May 1, which though not a legal holiday, looms largest in public demonstrations by students and laborers; May 3 is Constitution Memorial Day, "to promote the growth of the nation"; and May 5, formerly Boys' Day is now Children's Day to wish all children happiness and prosperity. September 23 is a day for adoring and worshipping ancestors. November 3 is Culture Day "to love freedom and peace and to advance culture." November 23, Labor Thanksgiving, to respect labor and felicitate production. The first week in October is set aside as Newspaper Week with meetings, lectures and exhibits highlighting the importance of the press in a democratic government; to highlight the importance of the rule of law, Law Day was celebrated for the first time in 1960.

Many Japanese feel that the Occupation reform most successful in operation is the new court system. Though many able jurists,[18] recognized for personal integrity and independence, have suffered frequent provocation by political leaders, labor unions and Communist agitators, the rule of law has increased in strength. As elsewhere in the world, however, and despite economic improvement, crimes have increased to three times the prewar rate; most are aimed at material profit, gambling, theft, fraud and assault. Among the causes given are the stimulation of teen-age appetites for pleasure by films, TV and magazines, weakened parental controls following the democratic constitution, and the inability of the old religions to offer new inspiration. There are special Laws, Courts, Classification Officers and Correction Institutions for Juveniles, and a Big Brothers and Sisters organization supported by the Ministry of Justice to help wayward youth. Trial by jury, a totally incongruous system from the Japanese point of view, has never been introduced.

The government has "adjusted its posture" since the body blow delivered to the National Diet in the spring of 1960, and Prime Minister Ikeda at the reopening of its thirty-eighth Regular Session announced his firm resolve to establish "proper democratic practice" and to settle "by discussion with tolerance and patience any dispute that may arise in the political, economic or social fields.

"I think the world is now approaching a momentous turning point," he went on. "It is time we paid greater attention to how we may unite East and West, rather than dividing them.

"The fundamental aim of Japan's foreign policy is first to grasp clearly these new circumstances; and then by holding fast to the collective security system, to secure the peace and prosperity of our country and consolidate an international environment such as will contribute to the creation of world peace. I strongly hope the sincerity and good intentions of Japan will come to be trusted by all nations."

ADAPTED FROM M.I.T. MAP OF

JAPANESE EMPIRE

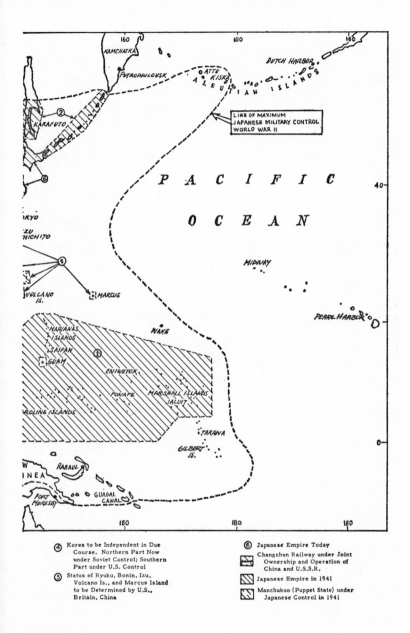

160　　　　　180　　　　　160

KAMCHATKA

DUTCH HARBOR

PETROPAVLOVSK

ATTU

KISKA

A L E U T I A N   I S L A N D S

② KARAFUTO

LINE OF MAXIMUM
JAPANESE MILITARY CONTROL
WORLD WAR II

⑥

P A C I F I C

40—

O C E A N

KYO

ZU
HICHITO

⑤

MIDWAY

VOLCANO
IS.

MARCUS

PEARL HARBOR

MARIANAS
ISLANDS

WAKE

SAIPAN

GUAM

③

ENIWETOK

PONAPE

MARSHALL ISLANDS
JALUIT

ROLINE ISLANDS

TARAWA

GILBERT
IS.

0—

W

RABAUL

INEA

PORT
MORESBY

GUADAL
CANAL

160　　　　　180　　　　　160

④ Korea to be Independent in Due
Course. Northern Part Now
under Soviet Control; Southern
Part under U.S. Control

⑤ Status of Ryuku, Bonin, Izu,
Volcano Is., and Marcus Island
to be Determined by U.S.,
Britain, China

⑥ Japanese Empire Today

Changchun Railway under Joint
Ownership and Operation of
China and U.S.S.R.

Japanese Empire in 1941

Manchukuo (Puppet State) under
Japanese Control in 1941

325

PERIOD	GOVERNMENT	FOREIGN RELATIONS	RELIGION AND THOUGHT
NEOLITHIC			
B.C. 1200		Migrations from the continent	Animism
SIDEROLITHIC			
B.C. 200	Clan system	Introduction of Pre-Han and Han culture from China via Korea	Fertility rituals and divination
IRON AGE			
A.D. 300	Clan system	Increasing migration from Korea Yamato troops invited to assist warring Korean kingdoms establish settlement on Korean peninsula	Deities of the land— Shrines at Izumo, Ise, Usa Conflict between native Shinto and immigrant Buddhism
PROTOHISTORIC			
A.D. 600	Imperial clan versus Soga clan. Prince Regent Shotoku's attempt to centralize gov't. Kamatari, Tenji-Tenno and First Great Change; census and land survey made. Nippon adopted as official name. Law-making activity based on Chinese.	Korean nobles and Buddhist priests welcomed as teachers Students sent to Chinese court Adoption of Chinese calendar, system of measurement, medicine	17 Article Constitution Buddhism officially adopted Onyodo (pseudo-science of Yin-Yang)
NARA			
A.D. 710	First permanent capital, modeled after Chinese city Yamato court under Chinese and Buddhist tutelage Buddhist designs on throne frustrated War God: Sustain imperial clan Accession of Emperor Kwammu (782) Removal of capital from Nara	Envoys exchanged with T'ang Court Arrival of priests from China and India with temple and palace accessories	University established for study of Chinese literature, history, philosophy Shomu's abdication of throne and devotion to Buddhism Medicine, a monopoly of Buddhist priests
EARLY HEIAN			
794	Establishment of Heian-Kyo (Kyoto) Subjugation of rebellious Ainu Gradual passing of imperial power into hands of Fujiwara regents Ceremonial regulations and commentaries on codes of law	Cessation of relations with China on advice of Sugawara Michizane (895)	Court free from temple control Mountain centers of Buddhism: Tendai sect on Hieizan Shingon sect on Koyasan Michizane (died in exile) deified as God of Letters Persistence of Shinto
LATE HEIAN			
967	Fujiwaras as regents, civil dictators and maternal relatives of emperors Rule of retired sovereigns Domination of feudal lords in struggles between emperors, retired emperors and Fujiwaras	Taira Kiyomori's efforts to carry on trade with China	Esthetic Amida-worship, glorification of palace life Rapprochement of Shinto and Buddhism
KAMAKURA			
1185	Military dictatorship initiated by Minamoto Yoritomo, carried on by Hojo regents	Sung political refugees welcomed Kublai Khan's envoys Mongol Invasions (1274–81)	Popular revival of Buddhism: Jodo, Zen and Nichiren sects Revival of Shinto deities

PERIOD	ARTS AND CRAFTS	LITERATURE	SOCIAL & ECONOMIC CONDITIONS	IN WEST
NEOLITHIC B.C. 1200	Stone implements Comb and cord design potteries		No private property Scattered settlers; hunting, fishing	Bronze age Trojan War Plato
SIDEROLITHIC B.C. 200	Yayoi pottery (red) Paintings on tomb walls Bronze swords and bells		Rice culture introduced from Korea Slaves used for farming —division of labor	Roman supremacy in Mediterranean
IRON AGE A.D. 300	Iron weapons and farming implements. Imported Buddhist art and artists, small statues of gilded iron. Haniwa (grave) pottery figures. Bronze mirrors. Weaving.	Introduction of Chinese script Records kept by Korean scribes	Leaders with iron axes and farm implements felling forests and extending cultivated areas Growth of social distinctions	Gaul, Spain, Britain, Roman provinces Christianity recognized
PROTOHISTORIC A.D. 600	Temple building— Horyu-ji Buddhist sculpture in wood and bronze Embroidery Korean music and dancing	History by Shotoku and Soga Commentaries on sutras Development in use of Chinese script	Chinese court life introduced Private administration of lands theoretically abolished Land distribution and tax systems instituted Peerage compiled	Constantinople envoys to China Celts and Teutons in Britain
NARA A.D. 710	Palace roof tiles Minting of copper Silk weaving and dying Casting of huge bronze statues Wood-block printing Dry lacquer sculpture	Kojiki and Nihongi (official histories) Kaifuso and Manyoshu (anthologies of poems) Adaptation of Chinese script Sutra-copying	Social service work of Buddhists: dispensaries, dormitories, schools, bridge, road and harbor construction, irrigation and land reclamation Innovations concentrated in capital, outlying districts little affected Smallpox epidemic	Arabian invasion of Gaul Lowest ebb of culture
EARLY HEIAN 794	T'ang style sculpture; bulky, stern, or voluptuous statues of deities Buddhist painting; formularized representation of theology in mandaras	First dictionary Vogue for Chinese poetry *Kokinshu* and other official anthologies Religious essays Official histories First monogatari	Lack of communication between capital and provinces, and between upper and lower classes Growth of tax-free manors belonging to court officials and temples Farmers' desertion of taxable lands, increasing vagrancy	Charlemagne Christianity a unifying force to cement conquests Vikings
LATE HEIAN 967	Calligraphy. Yamato-e, native style paintings. Painted wood sculpture; Jocho School. Buddhist painting; lavish use of gold, elegance, gentleness and grace. Golden Age of palace architecture.	Court ladies' diaries, notes, novels, in colloquial Japanese. Sei Shonagon's *Makura no Soshi.* Murasaki Shikibu's *Genji, Monogatari.* Development of Japanese script.	Passing of real power into hands of provincial landlords Growth of bands of armed defenders of local landlords Dependence of court on provincial troops for collection of taxes	Capture of Rome by Otto, king of all the Germans Norman Conquest
KAMAKURA 1185	Portrait sculpture in wood: Unkei Metal work and swordmaking Narrative scroll paintings	Official anthologies, histories Quasi-historical narratives Biographies of famous priests	Efficient and economic justice for all classes Courtiers supporting themselves	Crusades Magna Charta Dante Cathedrals

PERIOD GOVERNMENT	FOREIGN RELATIONS	RELIGION AND THOUGHT
DUAL DYNASTIES		
1331 Collapse of Kamakura government. Ascendancy of Ashikaga Takauji. Simultaneous emperors at Kyoto and Yoshino (1336–92).	Flourishing piracy along China coast	Zen priests as political and trade advisers *History of the True Succession*
ASHIKAGA		
1392 Ashikaga shoguns ruling in Kyoto Imperial succession dispute settled by Yoshimitsu Feudalism and anarchy throughout the provinces	Diplomatic intercourse and official trade with China	Bushido, the Samurai's code based on Confucian loyalty, Zen stoicism, Shinto reverence for ancestors, social and economic conditions of the times O-cha-no-yu (tea estheticism)
WESTERN CONTACTS		
1550 About 300 autonomous feudatories Most powerful feudal chiefs contending for control of Kyoto General Nobunaga's attempt at unification by force Organization of feudal lords under leadership of Hideyoshi at Osaka Supremacy of Iyeyasu after Sekigahara (1600)	Arrival of Portuguese traders and missionaries Religious envoys to Rome (1582) Japanese carried off as slaves by Portuguese traders Trade routes and spheres of influence through south Pacific islands and Asiatic littoral Arrival of Spaniards from Philippines and shipping with them to New Spain (Southern California) Expeditions to Korea (1592–8)	Introduction of Christianity by St. Francis Xavier. Growth of Jesuit influence in southwestern Japan. Destruction of Mt. Hiei temples by Nobunaga (1571). Rivalry between Franciscans and Jesuits and Buddhists. Zen influence in diplomacy. Loss of faith in spiritual and intellectual superiority of China.
TOKUGAWA		
1603 Centralized feudalism under Tokugawas New political center at Yedo Rigid regulations and strict supervision of all classes Officially prescribed education Policy of Isolation, internal and external (1640–1854) Decline of Tokugawa authority Leadership assumed by southwestern seacoast clans	Temporary trade agreement with Dutch, English and Spanish. Will Adams in Shogun's employ. Closed door: prohibition against Japanese going abroad and expulsion of all foreigners. Foreign trade restricted to Dutch and Chinese at Nagasaki. Knowledge of Western imperialistic expansion obtained from Dutch Arrival of Perry (1853) Intercourse with West resumed Extraterritoriality and control of tariffs granted (1858) First embassy to U. S. (1860)	Suppression of Christianity (1628) Official adoption of Neo-Confucianism Neo-Shinto and growing nationalism Carnal materialism and travesty Interest in medicine and science learned from the Dutch Decline of Buddhist influence
MEIJI		
1868 Restoration of imperial dignity Satcho clans, the power behind throne. Tokyo (Yedo) made imperial capital. All land theoretically returned to emperor, regranted to occupants in return for taxes. Universal conscription for imperial army. Granting of Constitution and first election (1890).	Numbers of students and envoys sent to U. S. and Europe Western authorities retained as advisers by new government Trade treaty revision (1894) Sino-Japanese War (1894–5) Boxer Rebellion (1900) Anglo-Japanese Alliance Russo-Japanese War (1904–5)	Enthusiasm for intensive study of Western civilization at home and abroad Uniform education system Official revival of Shinto
MODERN		
1912 Universal manhood suffrage (1925). Capitalist-bureaucrat leadership. Rise and fall of totalitarianism.	World War I: Germany driven from Pacific. Expansion in China by negotiation. Racial equality denied at Paris Peace Conference (1919). Growing apprehension of Russia and Communism. Nine Power Treaty (1922). U. S. Exclusion Act (1924). Expansion in world markets. Armed attempt to control Chinese policies and activities. Greater Asia Co-Prosperity Sphere. Totalitarian Alliance vs. U. S., Britain, France and Russia.	Buddhist adaptation of Christianity. Liberalism and internationalism followed by reactionary nationalism in late 1920's. Emphasis on physical fitness. Militarism. Doctrine of Japanese superiority.

PERIOD DUAL DYNASTIES	ARTS AND CRAFTS	LITERATURE	SOCIAL & ECONOMIC CONDITIONS	IN WEST
1331		*Tsuredzuregusa,* miscellany by a hermit excourtier	Hojos and people bank- rupted by defense against Mongols Feudal disturbances	Hanseatic League Gunpowder

ASHIKAGA

| 1392 | Importation of tea utensils
and other Chinese works of
art. Landscape gardening
and tea-house architecture
characterized by shibumi,
restrained estheticism.
Gold and Silver Pavilions,
Noh masks, netsuké, pot-
tery, lacquer. Black ink
paintings; Sesshu. | Noh dramas and
Kyogen
Zen writings | Shogun enriched by
overseas trade
Populace impoverished
by epidemics and
famines
Onin Civil War (1467–77):
Kyoto in ruins, shoguns
powerless, court penni-
less, anarchy in provinces
Rise of trade guide | Renaissance
Gutenberg's
printing
Columbus
Reformation |

WESTERN CONTACTS

| 1550 | Castle building on heroic
scale
Heroic wall and screen
painting; Eitoku and
Sanraku
Intricate carving of wood
panels and gates
Development of purely
decorative and secular art
First moveable type
printing | Introduction of
Jesuit litera-
ture and
Aesop's Fables | Freedom and opportun-
ity for individual
initiative, enterprise,
ability
Development of mercan-
tile interests | Spaniards in
North America
Elizabeth
Shakespeare |

TOKUGAWA

| 1603 | Artists from Hideyoshi's
employ scattered to
feudal castles throughout
country under patronage
of feudal lords
Nikko, epitome of period's
art
Genroku Renaissance:
Ukiyo-e, wood block
prints, silk textiles,
lacquer and other applied
arts
Erotic music for samisen
and voice
Pantomime dancing
Highly developed theatre | Realistic novels;
Saikaku, etc.
Drama;
Chikamatsu
Haiku; Basho,
etc.
Heuristic studies
Philosophical,
historical and
economic
writings | Agrarian foundation of
Shogunate
Enforcement of peace
and order
Persecution of Christians
Internal and external
trade monopolized by
Shogunate
Enormous increase of
urban populace
Rise of bourgeoisie
Farmers' revolts against
high taxes
Static population and
dwindling natural
resources | Galileo
Settlement of
New World
Rembrandt
Bach
U.S.A.
Napoleon
Steam engines
Industrial
Revolution
Slavery
abolished
Imperialistic
expansion
Anesthetics
Victoria |

MEIJI

| 1868 | Two simultaneous schools
in all forms of art:
Traditional school
School of Western
influence
Commercialization of
applied arts | Translation of
Western works
Fiction and
dramas based
on Western
models | National system of com-
pulsory education
instituted (1872)
Economic straits of
samurai due to end of
special privileges
Development of indus-
tries | Telegraph
Darwin
Electric Light
Telephone |

MODERN

| 1912 | Music: develop-
ment of sym-
phony and other
Western forms.
Publication of
Fine Art Cata-
logues and repro-
ductions. | World War I prosperity. Increasing de-
mocracy, strikes and communistic activi-
ties. Imported raw materials essential to
industries. Tokyo-Yokohama earthquake
(1923). Worldwide depression and bank
panics. Centralized organization of people
and industries. Distress of farm popula-
tion. Overpopulation. Widespread destruc-
tion in cities. | | Improved transporta-
tion and communica-
tion facilities. World
War I. League of Na-
tions. Communism.
Fascism. World War II.
United Nations. |

PERIOD	GOVERNMENT	FOREIGN RELATIONS	RELIGION AND THOUGHT
MODERN			
1945	U. S. Occupation. New Constitution. Votes for women. Accommodation of U. S. democracy and Japanese tradition.	Loss of empire. Reparations. Peace Treaty and U. S.-Japan Mutual Security and Trade Treaty. Membership in United Nations. Expanding world trade. Cooperation with world organizations.	Disillusionment. State religion abolished. Renunciation of war. Rise of materialism. Neutralism.

PERIOD	ARTS AND CRAFTS	LITERATURE	SOCIAL & ECONOMIC CONDITIONS	IN WEST
MODERN				
1945	Popularized in West. Use of Western design.	Simplification of writing. U. S.-Japan exchanges, translations, and expanded libraries.	Constitutional freedom. Educational reforms. Redistribution of land. Status for women and Labor. Reconstruction. Population control. Industrial prosperity.	Welfare states. Nuclear power. Cold war. Increasing cultural exchange. Space exploration.

NOTES

1. A recent study of Japanese archeology in English is the excellent and profusely illustrated *Japan Before Buddhism* by Jonathan E. Kidder, New York, Praeger, 1959, to which I have referred in revising this chapter.
2. An American zoologist, archeologist, anthropologist, Edward S. Morse, excavated one of the largest and most famous of the Japanese shell mounds at Omori (between Tokyo and Yokohama) in 1879, while he was a professor at Tokyo Imperial University. His collection of Japanese pottery is now owned by the Boston Museum of Fine Arts.

   Another collection of neolithic Japanese pottery and ceramic statuary dating from 1500 B.C.–A.D. 500 was sent to the United States by the Japanese government and exhibited in several cities as part of the Centennial Celebration in 1960 of the first Japanese diplomatic mission to the U.S.
3. See: *The Coming of Man from Asia in the Light of Recent Discoveries,* by Ales Hrdlicka, and *The Antiquity of Man in America,* by N. C. Nelson, both of which are published in the 1935 Annual Report of the Board of Regents, Smithsonian Institution.

   Until 1926 it was thought that Asiatic migrants had been in North America only three to four thousand years, but manufactured objects and fossils discovered in New Mexico in that year indicated that they had been there for almost ten thousand years. The discovery in 1959, near the capital of Old Mexico, of a fragment of fossilized mastodon bone inscribed with animal pictures, however, appears to push their arrival date back another twenty thousand years, according to the report of Dr. Juan Armenta, Director of the Department of Anthropology, University of Puebla, Mexico, *The New York Times,* July 22, 1960.
4. For the art of this early period see *Handbook of Japanese Art,* by Noritake Tsuda, Sanseido, Tokyo, 1935, *A Glimpse of Japanese Ideals,* by Jiro Harada, Kokusai Bunka Shinkokai, Tokyo, 1937, and *2000 Years of Japanese Art,* by Yukio Yashiro, New York, Abrams, 1958.
5. Though the Wei dynasty followed the Latter Han, its official history was compiled first, about A.D. 297, and the description of Wa in the *History of the Latter Han,* which was not compiled until 445, seems to have been based on the earlier work. The translation quoted is by Tsunoda and Goodrich; *Sources of the Japanese Tradition,* compiled by Ryusaku Tsunoda, William de Bary and Donald Keene, New York, Columbia University Press, 1958, pp. 6–9.
6. Translated from the original Chinese and Japanese, of the *Nihongi, Chronicles of Japan from the Earliest Times to A.D. 697,* by W. G. Aston, New York, Dutton, 1924, p. 221.
7. Translation from *History of Japanese Religion,* by Masaharu Anesaki, London, Kegan Paul, Trench and Trubner, 1930, pp. 32–33.
8. Rice, too, was brought from China, not indigenous to Japan.

9. The Kojiki was translated by Basil Hall Chamberlain, Kobe, Thompson, 1932.
10. A flourishing shrine to Susanowo has existed at Izumo through the centuries since. It is known as a place of compromise, where fortunate marriages are performed.
11. Communities of Ainu still exist on Hokkaido, the northernmost island of Japan. Though they put on bear-hunt dances as a tourist attraction, these Ainu have attended Japanese schools and intermarried with Japanese, no longer learning the Ainu language or keeping up Ainu traditions. The Rev. John Batchelor spent many years among the Ainu and wrote *Ainu and Their Folk Lore*, London, Religious Tract Society, 1901, and *Ainu Life and Lore*, Tokyo, Kyobunkan, 1927.

CHAPTER 2. YAMATO LEADERS AND CHINESE TUTORS

1. See: *Lo-Lang: A Report on the Excavations of Lo-Lang, Wang-Han's Tomb in Lo-Lang Province an Ancient Chinese Colony in Korea*, by Harada and Tazawa, Tokyo: Toko-Shoin, 1935.
2. *Nihongi* (see above Chap. I, note 6), vol. II, p. 72.
3. This peerage, *Shoji-roku*, is no longer extant, but much that it is supposed to have contained is embodied in a later one, *Shinsen Shoji-roku* (Revised Family Register) comp. in 815.
4. *Nihongi* (see above Chap. I, note 6), vol. II, p. 66.
5. For fuller translations see *Nihongi*, pp. 129–133, or Brinkley: *A History of the Japanese People*, New York, Encyclopædia Britannica, 1915, pp. 140–2.
6. For illustrations see H. Minamoto, *An Illustrated History of Japanese Art*, tr. by H. G. Henderson, Kyoto: Hoshino, 1935. Also *The Craft of the Japanese Sculptor*, by Langdon Warner, New York, McFarlane, 1936, also Yashiro (Chap. I, note 4).
7. The complete cycle of twelve is shown on the face of the Japanese clock, illustration p. 154.
   The day was divided as follows:

Symbol	Japanese Hour Number	Our Corresponding Hours
Rat	9th	11 P.M. to 1 A.M.
Ox	8th	1–3 A.M.
Tiger	7th	3–5 A.M.
Rabbit	6th	5–7 A.M.
Dragon	5th	7–9 A.M.
Serpent	4th	9–11 A.M.
Horse	9th	11 A.M to 1 P.M.
Sheep	8th	1–3 P.M.
Monkey	7th	3–5 P.M.
Cock	6th	5–7 P.M.
Dog	5th	7–9 P.M.
Boar	4th	9–11 P.M.

According to B. H. Chamberlain, *Things Japanese*, London, Murray, 1905, in the section on "Time," pp. 474–9, "Three preliminary strokes were always struck in order to warn people that the hour was about to be sounded. Hence, if the numbers one, two and three had been used to denote any of the actual hours confusion might have arisen . . . The hours were never all of exactly the same length except at the equinoxes. In summer those of the night were shorter, in winter those of the day. This was because sunrise and sunset were always called six o'clock throughout the year." According to Ernest W. Clement, *Japanese Calendars*, Trans., Asiatic Society of Japan, vol. XXX, 1902, part I, p. 3, Japanese time computations were based on multiples of 9 ($1 \times 9 = 9$, $2 \times 9 = 18$, $3 \times 9 = 27$, etc.), and the last figure of the product was used as the name of the hour.

8. The Gregorian Calendar was officially adopted in Japan in the fifth year of Meiji (1873). Years, however, are still more frequently designated with respect to the beginning of a new imperial reign, rather than to the Christian Era. On postal cancellation stamps, for example, instead of 1961, one finds 36 Showa, the current period which began with Emperor Hirohito's accession in 1926.

9. *Nihongi* (see above Chap. 1, note 6), vol. II, p. 139.

10. Ibid., pp. 206–8.

CHAPTER 3.   PEOPLE OF NARA, THE FIRST CAPITAL

1. *Manyoshu*, Lay No. 92, tr. by F. V. Dickens (see below note 6).

2. An illustrated *English Catalogue of Treasures in the Imperial Repository, Shoso-in*, by Jiro Harada, was published by the Imperial Household Museum in Tokyo in 1932. Nara and Kyoto survived World War II and occupation forces were ordered to keep these treasures intact.

3. This festival, called Tanabata, is still celebrated in Japan on July seventh. See *Children's Days in Japan*, Tokyo, Japanese Government Railways Tourist Library, vol. 12, 1936. "Day of the rat," the twelve animal cycle (Chap. 2 above, note 7) was applied to months and days also.

4. See Yosaburo Takekoshi, *The Economic Aspects of the History of the Civilization of Japan*, New York, Macmillan, 1930, 3 vols., vol. I, Chap. VI.

5. For an excellent account of the introduction and development of writing in Japan see *An Historical Grammar of Japanese*, by G. B. Sansom, Oxford, Clarendon Press, 1928, pp. 1–68. Further discussion is also given in Chapter 6 of this book.

6. For translations see Donald Keene's *Anthology of Japanese Literature* from the earliest era to the mid-nineteenth century, UNESCO, New York, Grove Press, 1955; F. V. Dickens' *Primitive and Mediæval Japanese Texts*, Oxford, Clarendon Press, 1906, and *Masterpieces of Japanese Poetry, Ancient and Modern*, tr. and annot. by Asataro Miyamori, Tokyo, Maruzen, 1936, 2 vols.

7. The former interpretation is given by J. Ingram Bryan, *Literature of Japan*, New York, Holt, 1930, p. 42; the latter by Professor Tsunoda.

8. Highly imaginary adventures of Kibi no Mabi in China are depicted in a scroll painting which in 1932 was added to the West's best collection of Japanese Art, in the Boston Museum of Fine Arts. Like the famous Ban Dainagon scroll it is attributed to Fujiwara Mitsunaga who painted during the early days of Kamakura (early thirteenth century). For illustrations see Kenji Toda, *Japanese Scroll Painting*, Chicago, University of Chicago Press, 1935.

9. For the development of katakana see Chapter 6.

CHAPTER 4.   BUDDHIST PRIESTS AND THEIR NARA TEMPLES

1. See *Handbook of the Old Shrines and Temples and Their Treasures in Japan*, Bureau of Religions, Department of Education, Tokyo, Sanshusha, 1920.

2. For a translation and exposition of the Lotus Sutra, which is said to be to the Buddhist what the Gospel of St. John is to the Christian, see *The Lotus of the Wonderful Law,* or *The Lotus Gospel,* by W. E. Soothill, Oxford, Clarendon Press, 1930.

3. These details from a document in the Shoso-in are to be found in Ishida Mosaku's *Shakyo yori Mitaru Nara Cho Bukyo no Kenkyu* (Study of Nara Period Buddhism based on Sutra manuscripts)—with a summary in English-Tokyo, Toyo Bunko, 1930.

4. See *Textile Fabrics of 6th, 7th and 8th Centuries A.D. in the Imperial Household Collection,* Tokyo, Imperial Household Museum, 1929.

5. See K. Okakura, *Ideals of the East,* London, Murray, 1920, p. 118.

6. The Daibutsu (Great Buddha) was 53½ feet high and weighed over 500 tons. It was the world's largest metal statue, according to Sir Percival David, who gives a beautiful description of the Eye-Opening Ceremony in his article on the Shoso-in, Trans. and Proc., Japan Society of London, vol. XXVIII. As a result of fire and earthquake the statue has had to be repaired several times. The present head was cast in 1692.

7. The "three treasures" always associated with Buddhist temples are the sacred image, the sutras, and the priesthood.

8. This message was reported as the oracle of the deity Hachiman revealed at his shrine at Usa in Kyushu. See also p. 98.

9. *English Catalogue of Treasures in the Imperial Repository, Shoso-in* (see above Chap. 3, note 2), p. 155.

10. See *Medicine in Ancient Japan,* by Keizo Dohi, *The Young East* (mag.) vol. II, no. 5, Oct. 1926.

CHAPTER 5. THE IMPERIAL COURT, KYOTO

1. Though of doubtful significance, it may be interesting to note that the active volcanoes of Japan were situated in these districts last to be controlled—Mt. Asama and Mt. Fuji in the northeast, and Mt. Aso in Kyushu. (Mt. Fuji has been inactive since 1707.)

2. According to the Yin Yang philosophy of the Chinese *Canon of Change.*

3. The phœnix was an imperial emblem in China.

4. For details see R.A.B. Ponsonby-Fane, *The Capital and Palaces of Heian,* Trans. and Proc., Japan Society, London, vol. XXII, 1924–5.

5. See Matsuyo Takizawa, *The Penetration of Money Economy in Japan,* New York, Columbia University Press, 1927. Chapter II.

6. Posthumously Saicho was honored with the name Dengyo Daishi (Great Teacher or Propagator of the True Religion) and Kukai, Kobo Daishi (Great Teacher or Propagator of the Law) Saicho on his return from China founded the Tendai sect; Kukai, the Shingon. For details see Sir Charles Eliot, *Japanese Buddhism,* New York, Longmans, 1935; also, *History of Japanese Religion,* Masaharu Anesaki, London, Kegan Paul, 1930.

7. See Sir George Sansom *Japan, A Short Cultural History,* New York, Century, 1931, p. 223.

8. The following translation is somewhat condensed from Sansom's *Early Japanese Law and Administration* reprinted from Trans., Asiatic Society of Japan, 1932.

9. Sugawara Michizane (845–903), banished from court to the Dazaifu in Kyushu

by Fujiwara rivals, but after his death deified as Tenjin-sama, patron saint of literature.

10. See W. G. Aston, Shinto, New York, Longmans, 1905, pp. 97–132.

11. For history of the mirror, the bead and the sword see C. D. Holtom, *Japanese Enthronement Ceremonies with an Account of the Imperial Regalia,* Tokyo, Kyo Bun Kwan, 1928.

CHAPTER 6. THE POWER AND GLORY OF THE FUJIWARAS

1. Though Fujiwaras lost much power to the military clans in the twelfth century, seven hundred years later they still represented the court and the imperial heritage and had sufficient prestige to play an important part in the Restoration of 1868. Sanjo Sanetomi, a Fujiwara, then became premier; Prince Konoye who became premier in June, 1937, was also a Fujiwara.

2. These quotations and the following descriptions of Michinaga's palace and temple are from *Eiga Monogatari* (Tale of Splendor), attributed to Akazome Emon, a court lady of the early eleventh century. See *Two Tales of Historic Japan* (a comparative study of *Genji Monogatari* and *Heike Monogatari*), by Ryusaku Tsunoda, *Columbia University Quarterly,* June, 1935.

3. The original painting, Amida Raigo, is now in the Reihokwan Museum on Mt. Koya. It was attributed to the priest-painter Eshin Sozu (942–1017), but according to recent scholarship dates from somewhat later. For a reproduction see Minamoto (above Chap. 2, note 6). For superb illustrations of Buddhist sculpture and painting see *2000 Years of Japanese Art* (above Chap. 1, note 4).

4. *The Pillow Book of Sei Shonagon* (see below note 7), p. 135.

5. From an unpublished paper on *Nenju Gyoji,* the Court Calendar, by Shunzo Sakamaki.

6. *The Tale of Genji,* a novel by Lady Murasaki, tr. by Arthur Waley, Boston, Houghton, 1935, 2 vols. The following is a slightly condensed quotation from vol. I, *Wreath of Cloud,* Chaps. VI and VII, pp. 479–80 and 497–98 respectively.

7. *The Pillow Book of Sei Shonagon,* tr. by Arthur Waley, Boston, Houghton, 1929, p. 37 and p. 101.

8. There are only five vowel sounds in Japanese—father, gasoline, coo (u in many words is elided), end, hope. The usual arrangement of hiragana differs from that of katakana; it is based on a short Buddhist psalm which contains all the syllables. Katakana, the symbols next to the roman letters, are used for rendering foreign names and words into Japanese; hiragana, to denote grammatical forms and pronunciation of Japanese words. Blank spaces in the table indicate symbols deleted in recent simplification of the written language. See pages 89, 319.

9. *Taketori no Okina no Monogatori,* written in the tenth century (author unknown,) tr. by F. Victor Dickins, London, Trübner, 1888. A modern version of this story for children is called *Kaguya Hime* (The Moon Maiden).

10. In addition to Sei Shonagon's *Makura no Soshi* (Pillow Book), and Murasaki Shikibu's *Genji Monogatari,* see *Diaries of Court Ladies of Old Japan,* tr. by Annie Shepley Omori and Kochi Doi, Tokyo, Kenkyusha, 1935. Some think that *Tosa Nikki* (Tosa Diary), tr. by Wm. Porter, London, Frowde, 1912, and *Ochikubo Monogatari* (Tale of Lady Ochikubo), tr. by Wilfrid White-house, London, Kegan Paul, 1934, were also written by ladies.

11. See Toda (above Chap. 3, note 8).
12. (See above note 2).

CHAPTER 7. COURTIER GIVES PLACE TO PROVINCIAL SOLDIER

1. Used as introduction to *Tale of Heike,* a long narrative of the struggles between the Taira and Minamoto, parts of which are quoted on pp. 104–112 (see below note 4).
2. See *A Biographical Approach to Shinto,* by Ryusaku Tsunoda, in *About Japan,* New York, Japan Society, Nov., 1933.
3. Brinkley (see above Chap 2, note 5), p. 199.
4. *The Tale of Heike,* tr. by A. L. Sadler, Trans., Asiatic Society of Japan, vol. XLVI, part II, 1918, p. 13. A modern version by Eiji Yoshikawa, tr. by Fuki Uramatsu, New York, Knopf, 1956.
5. From *Hojoki,* written by Kamo Chomei in 1212. Tr. by W. G. Aston in his *History of Japanese Literature,* New York, Appleton, 1899, pp. 145–56.
6. One of three scrolls of the *Tale of Heiki* said to be by Sumiyoshi Keion is in the Boston Museum of Fine Arts. Its depiction of battle scenes, and especially of the burning of a palace, is superb. For illustration see (above Chap. 3, note 8, Toda), p. 88, and also photogravure p. 91.
7. The thirteenth century witnessed a great revival of Buddhism in a popular form designed to appeal to common people. Four sects, especially, began to flourish under the leadership of four very remarkable evangelists.

Sect (*Shu*)	*Leader*	*His Dates*
Jodo	Honen	1133–1212
Zen	Eisai	1141–1215
Shin	Shinran	1173–1262
Nichiren	Nichiren	1222–1282

8. Selected and condensed from Trans., Asiatic Society of Japan, vol. XLVI, part II, pp. 1–278, and vol. XLIX, part I, 1921, pp. 1–354 (see above note 4).

CHAPTER 8. CAMP ADMINISTRATION AT KAMAKURA

1. See *Some Striking Personalities in Japanese History,* by Tan Hamaguchi, in the Trans. and Proc., Japan Society of London, vol. VI, part II, p. 256.
2. From *Tsuredzuregusa* (Sec. 184), by Yoshida no Kaneyoshi, tr. by Sir George Sansom in the Trans., Asiatic Society of Japan, vol. 39, 1911.
3. Emperor Go-Toba (1179–1239) ruled 1184–98.
4. See *Kyoto, Its History and Vicissitudes Since Its Foundation in 792 to 1868,* by R. A. B. Ponsonby-Fane, Hong Kong, Rumford, 1931.
5. From translation of Nichiren's *Rissho Ankoku Ron* (The Establishment of Righteousness and the Security of the Country) by Arthur Lloyd, in his *Creed of Half Japan,* London, Murray, 1911, pp. 307–9.
6. See *Nichiren the Buddhist Prophet,* by Masaharu Anesaki, Cambridge, Harvard University Press, 1916.
7. Zepangu, in Europe, came to be spelled and pronounced Japan. See *The Book of Ser Marco Polo, the Venetian, Concerning the Kingdoms and Marvels of the East,* newly tr. and ed. with notes by Colonel Henry Yule, London, Murray, 3rd ed., 1921, vol. II, Book 3, Chap. 2, p. 253 et seq.

8. Letter given in full in James Murdoch's *A History of Japan*, London, Kegan Paul, 1926, 3 vols., vol. i, p. 499. (What is now Vol. II was published first by the *Japan Chronicle*, Kobe, 1903).

9. Quoted by Murdoch, vol. i, p. 499.

10. For details of sword-making see J. J. Rein *The Industries of Japan*, New York, Armstrong, 1889.

11. See *Bushido, the Soul of Japan*, by Inazo Nitobe, Tokyo, Kenkyusha, 1935, p. 120.

12. An incident from *Taikoki* (History of Hideyoshi) by Ose Hoan (1564–1640), this story really belongs to the well-developed bushido of the sixteenth century, but, though slightly anachronistic, is given here for its context. The treasures included two swords, a ceramic tea caddy, a blue glazed water jar, a tea bowl, a ceramic incense box named "plover," a painting of a hawk by a Chinese emperor. The incense box later came into the possession of Hideyoshi and is said to have mysteriously given warning whenever his life was in danger. The attitude of the samurai is further elucidated in the beautiful volume *A Glimpse of Japanese Ideals*, by Dr. Jiro Harada, Tokyo, Kokusai Bunka Shinkokai, 1937, Chapter IX.

13. For Jodo, see Eliot and Anesaki (above Chap. 5, note 6), or *Honen The Buddhist Saint, His Life and Teaching*, by Coates and Ishizuka, Kyoto, Chion-in, 1925. Zen is described more fully in the next chapter.

14. This and the following story is told by Dr. Nitobe in his *Bushido* (note 11 above), p. 31.

CHAPTER 9.   DUAL DYNASTIES, DILETTANTI AND DISORDER

1. Translation of part of Kitabatke Chikafusa's *Jinnoshotoki*, given by W. G. Aston in his *History of Japanese Literature*, pp. 164–9. Aston calls this *Jinko shotoki*. Y. Kuno, in his *Japanese Expansion on the Asiatic Continent*, vol. i, Berkeley, University of California Press, 1937, p. 352, calls it *Shinko Shoto-Ki*. This shows how ambiguous and confusing transliteration and translation of Japanese may be.

2. *Tsuredzuregusa* (Sec. 120) (see above Chap. 8, note 2).

3. The derivation of maru as applied to ships is still somewhat of a question. According to one interpretation maru meant darling or precious and was applied to ships because they brought such highly prized treasures from China. The following tribute ship records and the diary notes are given by Takekoshi (see above Chap. 3, note 4) vol. I. pp. 16–25. Perhaps wisely, he makes no attempt to evaluate kwanmon in modern currency, for standards of exchange were continually changing in accord with local circumstances; for kwanmon, ryo and hiki see glossary.

4. *Kwadensho*, by Seami, 1363–1444, tr. in part in Arthur Waley's introduction to his *Nō Plays of Japan*, New York, Knopf, 1922. See also *Japanese No Plays*, Japan Travel Bureau, Tourist Library, vol. 16 (1956). For translations of Noh plays by Seami and his notes on the art of Noh, and also of Kyogen, see *Anthology of Japanese Literature* (Chap. 3, note 6).

5. Most Japanese are still extremely sentimental about Cha no Yu, or Tea Ceremony. See K. Okakura, *The Book of Tea*, Edinburgh, Foulis, 1919; *Tea Cult of Japan*, Japan Travel Tureau, Tourist Library ,vol. 4; also A. L. Sadler, *Cha no Yu, the Japanese Tea Ceremony*, London, Kegan Paul, 1933. Some Westerners perhaps can understand the quiet pleasure of holding a warm cup

in both hands, savoring the refreshing liquid, and meditating on themselves as clay vessels, like the cup, containing a fluid something, warm, and refreshing.
6. Emperor Go-Hanazono, 1419–71, reigned 1429–64.
7. A popular phrase from Ichijo Kaneyoshi's *Shodan Chiyo* (Woodcutter's Remarks), written about 1480.

CHAPTER 10. CATHOLICS AND CASTLES

1. Murdoch (see above Chap. 8, note 8), vol. II, p. 42.
2. On this site (supposedly) in Yamaguchi a monument to St. Francis Xavier was recently erected.
3. Quoted by Murdoch, vol. II, p. 64, from the Letters of St. Francis Xavier. See also H. H. Gowen, *Five Foreigners in Japan,* New York, Revell, 1936.
4. Murdoch, vol. II, p. 155.
5. Ibid., p. 170.
6. See *Japan As It Was and Is,* by Richard Hildreth, Boston, 1855, p. 88.
7. See *Toyotomi Hideyoshi,* by Walter Dening, Tokyo, Kyo Bun Kwan, 1904.
8. A detailed account of Hideyoshi's invasion of Korea is given by W. G. Aston in the Trans., Asiatic Society of Japan, vol. VI, part II, pp. 227–245, vol. IX, pp. 87–93 and 213–22, vol. XI, pp. 117–25.
9. Murdoch, vol. II, p. 288.
10. This explanation is based on *Jokaku no Kenkyu* (Study of Castle Strongholds), by Nobu Orui, Tokyo, Rekishi Koza Series, 1915. For illustrations see *Castles in Japan,* Japanese Government Railways Tourist Library, vol. IX.
11. Quoted from *Taikoki,* by Fane (see above Chap. 8, notes 4 and 12), p. 261.
12. Murdoch, vol. II, p. 386.

CHAPTER 11. AN OLD SOLDIER ORGANIZES FOR PEACE

1. Rice was the principal food and until after the seventeenth century the most important medium of exchange but its value changed almost every day. In the summer of 1732 when insect pests attacked the rice crop the price jumped from 40–50 to 130–150 momme of silver during one night. Money was thought to be the most degrading element in society, self-respecting people did not discuss it. When finally a daring intellectual wrote a treatise on the price of rice in relation to general price levels it was kept in hiding for generations. See Takizawa, *Penetration of Money Economy in Japan* (above Chap. 5, note 5).
2. See *Yedo Castle,* by Thomas R. H. McClatchie, Trans., Asiatic Society of Japan, vol. VI, 1877.
3. See *The Maker of Modern Japan,* the life of Tokugawa Iyeyasu, by A. L. Sadler, London, Allen and Unwin, 1937, p. 167. Toward the end of his life Iyeyasu referred to a "line which I learned in my boyhood, and always retained in my mind, 'Requite malice with kindness,' from Lao Tzu, it has been useful to me on many occasions." *Sources of the Japanese Tradition* (see above Chap. 1, note 5), page 340.
4. See *Five Foreigners in Japan* (above Chap. 10, note 3) and Wilson Crewdson, *The Dawn of Western Influence in Japan,* Trans., and Proc., Japan Society of London, vol. VI, part II.
5. Brinkley (Chap. 2, note 5), p. 568.
6. Ibid., p. 577.

7. Ibid., p. 574.
8. See *Judo,* Japan Travel-Bureau, Tourist Library, vol. 22, Tokyo, 1956.
9. See *Japan, the Official Guide,* Japan Travel Bureau, Tokyo, 1958, pp. 410–20.
10. Brinkley (Chap. 2, note 5), p. 555.

CHAPTER 12.   THE GOLDEN AGE FOR BUSINESSMEN

1. Takekoshi (Chap. 3, note 4), vol. II, p. 243, p. 252 for Yodoya inventory p. 190.
2. See (Chap. 11, note 1).
3. *Art, Life and Nature in Japan,* by Masaharu Anesaki, Boston, Marshall Jones, 1932, p. 150.
4. *History of Nations,* Henry Cabot Lodge, Editor, New York, Collier, 1916, vol. VII, p. 153.
5. Genroku literally means "good fortune."
6. In his novel, *Koshoku Ichidai Otoko* (Middle-aged Gentleman of Passion).
7. See *Japanese Music and Musical Instruments,* W. P. Malm, Tokyo, 1959, Tuttle. And also *Kabuki Drama,* Japan Travel Bureau, Tourist Library, vol. 7.
8. *The Autobiography of Fukuzawa Yukichi,* translated by Eiichi Kiyooka, Tokyo, Hokuseido, 1934, p. 4.
9. See *Masterpieces of Chikamatsu,* translated by Asataro Miyamori, New York, Dutton, 1926.
10. "Ukiyo" originally was Buddhist terminology for this "transient world" as opposed to the eternal realm. The sacrilegious use of it was typical of the Genroku Age in which all things sacred were travestied For illustrations see *2,000 Years of Japanese Art* (above Chap. 1, note 4).
11. See *The Art of Japan,* by Louis V. Ledoux, New York, Japan Society, Inc., 1927, and *Handbook of Japanese Art,* by Noritake Tsuda, Tokyo, Sanseido, 1935, and *Japanese Art,* Encyclopædia Britannica, Inc., 1933.
12. *The Bamboo Broom, An Introduction to Japanese Haiku,* by Harold G. Henderson, Boston, Houghton, 1934, p. 25.
13. *History of Japanese Literature,* by W. G. Aston, New York, Appleton, 1899, p. 292.
14. *The Bamboo Broom* (see note 12 above), p. 35.
15. Each year during the climbing season, about six weeks in July and August, thousands of pilgrims, old and young, make their way to the top, chanting *"Sange, sange rokon shojo"* (recognizing and admitting our faults, doing penance to purify our six senses) [the mind is included as a sense].

CHAPTER 13.   WHEN PERRY CAME WITH U. S. GUNBOATS

1. Quotation from Murdoch, vol. III, p. 499. See also *Jan Compagnie in Japan, 1600–1817,* by C. R. Boxer, The Hague, Nijhoff, 1936.
2. Engelbert Kaempfer (1651–1716), a German medical doctor resident at Deshima 1690–92, in the employ of the Dutch East India Company, wrote the first complete history of Japan by a Westerner, an English translation of which, in two volumes, was published in 1792.
Carl Peter Thunberg (1743–1828), Swedish scientist and scholar resident at Deshima 1775–77.
Isaac Titsingh, statesman and gentleman, who impressed the Japanese by refusing to be searched by their officials, saying it was beneath his dignity; a book-

hunter, interested in social customs, made two trips to Yedo during his stay in Japan 1779–84, and kept up correspondence with scholarly Japanese friends for years after he left the country.

Philip Franz von Siebold (1796–1886) resident at Nagasaki, 1823–30, forced to leave the country for having received from a Japanese official a map of Japan in exchange for a *Life of Napoleon*. He revisited it again in 1859, after its doors were opened. During his first period of residence his home was thronged with eager Japanese students who were required by him to write dissertations in Dutch on all sorts of Japanese subjects on which he wanted information. Based on these dissertations, Siebold published in Leyden in 1832 an encyclopædic work, *Nippon, Archiv zur Beschreibung von Japan un der dessen Neben und Schutzlandern*, with two volumes of illustrations (new edition by Japan Institute in Berlin in 1930).

3. Especially popular were the scientific treatises written in Chinese by the Jesuit Fathers and printed by them in China with no evidence of their Christian origin.

4. There is still preserved a print of the one Dutch wife and child who managed to visit Deshima. It is reproduced in Boxer (note 1 above), p. 92.

5. For these and a wealth of other details from native sources see *Tokugawa Japan* (Materials on Japanese Social and Economic History), ed. by Neil Skene Smith, Tokyo, Asiatic Society of Japan, 1937.

6. See *Tadataka Ino (The Japanese Land Surveyor)*, by R. Otani, tr. by K. Sugimura, Tokyo, Iwanami, 1932.

7. See *Hiroshige and Japanese Landscapes,* Japan Travel Bureau, Tourist Library, vol. 2.

8. Such a flag was first used as a symbol of the nation on the bow of the United States Navy's steamship, *Powhatan,* which carried the first official Japanese embassy to the United States in 1860. The standard proportions of the national flag were determined by official proclamation ten years later. The red disc is suggestive of both the rising sun and the mirror which Amaterasu charged her descendants to reverence. The populace first used rising sun flags on the occasion of the opening of the railway from Tokyo to Yokohama in 1872.

9. For illustrations see *Japanese Architecture*, Japanese Government Railways Tourist Library, vol. 7, and *Folk Crafts in Japan*, by S. Yanagi, Tokyo, Society for International Cultural Relations, 1936.

10. See *House Beautiful,* vol. 102, No. 8, August 1960, an entire issue on Japan for illustrations and discussion of shibui.

11. *Onna Daigaku,* by Kaibara Ekken (1630–1714), a distinguished Confucianist. A partial translation is given by B. H. Chamberlain in his *Things Japanese,* London, Murray, 1905, pp. 502–8. "The five worst maladies that afflict the female mind [it says] are: indocility, discontent, slander, jealousy and silliness. Without any doubt these maladies infest seven or eight out of every ten women, and it is from these that arises the inferiority of women to men. A woman should cure them by self-inspection and self-reproach. The worst of them all and the parent of the other four is silliness."

12. See Shinto Revival, *Sources of the Japanese Tradition,* (Chap. 1, note 5) pp. 506–51.

13. See *Narrative of the Expedition of an American Squadron to the China Seas and Japan, Performed in the Years 1852, 1853 and 1854 under the Command of Commodore M. C. Perry, United States Navy,* comp. from the original notes and journals of Commodore Perry and his officers, published by order of the

Congress of the United States, Washington, 1856. Also, Edward Morley Barrows' *The Great Commodore,* New York, Bobbs Merrill, 1935.

14. See *The Complete Journal of Townsend Harris,* New York, Doubleday, 1930, p. 484.

CHAPTER 14. OLD JAPAN TANGLES WITH MODERN WORLD

1. Many of the details, concerning the foreign settlement, to be found in this chapter the author has drawn from M. Paske-Smith's *Western Barbarians in Japan and Formosa in Tokugawa Days,* Kobe, Thompson, 1930.

2. Opening of the Comstock Lode in California in 1859 made large quantities of cheap silver available for exchange at great profits for Japanese gold.

3. *Autobiography of Fukuzawa* (Chap. 12, note 8).

4. See *Sources of the Japanese Tradition* (Chap. 1 above, note 5) pp. 592–637, "The Debate Over Seclusion and Restoration," for Fukuzawa and Aizawa quotes.

5. W. W. McLaren, Japanese Government Documents, TASJ vol. XLII, part I, 1914, pp. 1–2.

6. For description see Holtom (Chap. 5, note 11 above).

7. These seventeen, Tokugawa adherents, were coerced by "Government" forces.

8. See *Japanese Thought in the Meiji Era,* edited by Kosaka Masaaki, Centenary Culture Council Series, Tokyo, Pan-Pacific Press, 1958. Meat was not generally considered proper food before the Christian missionaries came. Owners of cows or oxen regarded them virtually as members of the family. To kill one was a crime punishable by a scolding, a fine or even banishment. The sale of beef in Tokyo began in 1869.

CHAPTER 15. ON THE WAY TO WORLD POWER

1. Two studied at Vassar, the youngest, many years later, graduated from Bryn Mawr and returned to Tokyo to establish the Institute of English Learning for girls, now called in her honor Tsuda College. These and other details about Japanese students in the U.S. and American advisers in Japan are to be found in *The Intercourse between the United States and Japan,* Inazo Nitobe, Baltimore, Johns Hopkins Press, 1891.

2. The president of the society was an ardent champion of women's rights. The leading newspaper of the day, the *Tokyo Nichi Nichi* with a circulation of about eight thousand in February, 1875, reported his wedding as follows: "Mori Arinori's Fancy Wedding—Fukuzawa witnesses wedding contract . . . bridegroom was in formal attire, and bride wore Western dress, her face covered by white veil. Bride and groom walked arm in arm. In front as witness was the well-known Mr. Fukuzawa. After the ceremony there was a Western-style banquet." (See Chap. 14 note 8). Kosaka gives abundant details.

3. The majority of teachers in Japan today are men.

4. See *Grant in Peace, From Appomattox to Mount McGregor,* a Personal Memoir, by Adam Badeau, Hartford, Scranton, 1887.
   It is interesting to note that Grant went on to say, "A day of retribution is sure to come, these people are becoming strong, and China is sure to do so also. When they do, a different policy will have to prevail from that imposed now."

5. See *Sources of the Japanese Tradition,* (Chap. 1, note 5) pp. 654–7.

6. See *Prince Ito,* by Kengi Hamada, Tokyo, Sanseido, 1926, and *Three Meiji Lead-*

ers—*Ito, Togo, Nogi,* by James A. B. Scherer, Tokyo, Hokuseido, 1936. Also see *Sources of the Japanese Tradition,* (Chap. 1, note 5) p. 673.
7. This quotation and also the following one is from the *Encyclopædia Britannica,* 14th ed., vol. XII, p. 950.
8. Known as "The Twenty-one Demands" of Baron Kato.
9. Again in 1960, at the dramatic Fifteenth Session of the United Nations' General Assembly, the Foreign Minister of Japan called attention to the principle of racial equality. "To translate this principle into practice . . . is an indispensable condition for enabling all nations to join hands, each as an equal member of the world community."
10. See *Sources of The Japanese Tradition.* (Chap. 1 note 5) pp. 703–717.

CHAPTER 16. UNEASY JAPAN

1. According to agreements reached between China and Japan in May, 1925, Japan proposed to establish:
    1. A cultural research institute and library at Peking.
    2. A natural science research institute at Shanghai.
    3. Fellowships and scholarships for Chinese students abroad.
    Work was begun on these projects in 1926. The institute at Shanghai initiated studies of medicinal herbs, fish of the Yangtze, bacilli, local and epidemic diseases, and carried on a geological survey. Needless to say, this whole project was "temporarily discontinued" in 1931.
2. In two provinces alone the number of newborn infants killed annually during the late Tokugawa period exceeded sixty thousand.
3. Short-term temporary loans of large sums were made to the Bank of England and to Russia; some investments were made in other European countries. Large sums were also lent to China for development projects.
4. See *Japan, government-politics,* by Robert Karl Reischauer, New York, Nelson, 1939.
5. A cursory glance through The *New York Times Index* for this period reminds one of nation-wide strikes of railroad and marine workers which prevented the movement of raw materials and resulted in the closing of many mills and factories, the arrest of two hundred Reds in Chicago, prohibition, bootlegging and the high cost of law enforcement, profiteering, Teapot Dome oil scandal, notification of Eugene Debs in Atlanta penitentiary of his nomination for the presidency of the United States, white slave traffic, bank bandits and holdups, and an increasing number of divorces.
6. Ginza—so called from the Tokugawa Silver Mint—now the street of Tokyo's most fashionable shops and restaurants.
    Perhaps the most remarkable of these literary men was Dr. Shoyo Tsubouchi, who translated Shakespeare's complete works into Japanese, and was the pioneer of a New Theater movement in Japan. For English translations of the works of many contemporary Japanese authors see *Anthology of Japanese Literature,* vol. II, compiled and edited by Donald Keene, New York, Grove Press, 1955.
7. See *The Japanese Film, Art and Industry,* Joseph Anderson and Donald Richie, Rutland, Vermont, and Tokyo, Tuttle, 1959.
8. Annual quotas were drawn by lot from all physically fit males twenty years old. In 1937, 60 per cent of the age group were rejected as unfit but the remaining 40 per cent were remarkably sturdy. About 85 per cent of the conscripts had only the compulsory six years of elementary education: about one-third were farm

youth; one-third, factory workers, and the rest office workers, teachers, fishers, miners, etc. See *Japan's Military Masters* by Hillis Lory, N.Y., Viking, 1943.

9. Thereupon, the emperor is reported to have displayed a rare burst of anger. "They had said they could clear up their problem in China within one month and yet more than four years had passed." See *Japan and Her Destiny*, London, Hutchison, 1958, pp. 245–522, from which this and following anecdotes about Prince Konoye and Ozaki and the poem-quoting of the emperor were taken.

10. Son of a Meiji General, Tojo was a capable field commander and able administrator, largely responsible for Japan's great air strength and success in mechanized warfare. Prince Konoye, it may be recalled, committed suicide just before the War Crimes Trials began.

CHAPTER 17. STRUGGLE FOR SUPREMACY IN EAST ASIA

1. For a fuller account see:
   Borton, Hugh, *Japan's Modern Century*, N.Y., Ronald Press, 1955.
   Reischauer, Edwin O., *The United States and Japan*, Cambridge, Mass., Harvard University Press, 1957.
   Sansom, Sir George, *The Western World and Japan*, N.Y., Knopf, 1950.
   Yanaga, Chitoshi, *Japan Since Perry*, N.Y., McGraw Hill, 1950.

2. Dulles, Foster Rhea, *Forty Years of American-Japanese Relations*, New York, Appleton, 1937, p. 63.

3. As far back as 1875 Japan, applying lessons learned from the West, had drawn Korea from her traditional isolation into the world of commerce, and had championed Korean independence from China. As a result of the Russo-Japanese War, Korea had become a protectorate of Japan, but a very troublesome and expensive one it proved to be. In the summer of 1910 the following announcement was made: "An earnest and careful examination of the Korean problem has convinced the Japanese government that the regime of a protectorate can not be made to adapt itself to the actual condition of affairs in Korea, and that the responsibilities devolving upon Japan for due administration of the country can not be justly fulfilled without the complete annexation of Korea to the Empire." Then Japanese troops were moved in, and the Korean dynasty was superseded by a Japanese governor general and his officials.

4. Before World War I, immigration to the United States had grown to such proportions that restrictive measures were considered necessary. All Anglo-Saxon countries had long since barred Asiatics from citizenship. In 1917, in the United States the entry of illiterates was prohibited. In 1921, another temporary measure for limitation was taken. With revisions, this was passed as the Immigration Act of 1924. Together with provisions for reducing European immigration by a quota system was the provision, brought on by agitators in California, prohibiting the entry of aliens ineligible to become naturalized citizens except as stipulated in existing treaties. In accordance with the Gentlemen's Agreement which both Canada and the United States had made with Japan, the desires of our immigration authorities had been complied with. The excess of entries over departures of Japanese between 1907 and 1923 was less than nine thousand, building up a total of about 110,000 in the United States. The great majority of them, however, about 72,000, were concentrated in California, and constituted about 2 per cent of the total state population. The Gentlemen's Agreement was not considered a Treaty.

5. According to Mr. Frederick Moore who served as American counselor to the

Japanese Government from 1927–1941, and in his official capacity accompanied the Japanese delegation to Geneva in 1932, Mr. Matsuoka fancied himself as a sort of Japanese Mussolini and was one of the real war criminals. He was embittered toward Americans by his experiences as a struggling student and, for a short time thereafter, as a struggling young lawyer in the State of Washington. The dramatic "crucifixion" speech and walkout of the Japanese delegation from the League of Nations meeting was Matsuoka's own show, and not in accordance with orders from Tokyo. He cabled his plans to the Foreign Office, which simply acquiesced. For other interesting insights to Japanese diplomacy, see *With Japan's Leaders,* by Frederick Moore, New York, Scribner's, 1942.

CHAPTER 18. DIRECT ENCOUNTER WITH THE UNITED STATES

1. According to a Japanese proverb, "High minded men refuse to remember past reverses." Shigemitsu, an able bureaucrat who did his duty courageously was, understandably, an unpopular statesman and is but dimly remembered today. He had attended the Versailles Peace Conference after World War I as a junior secretary and later served as ambassador to China, the Soviet Union and England. For two years after the surrender he served as minister of foreign affairs, but then was arrested and kept in Sugamo Prison during two and a half years of war crimes trials. When he was released in 1950, and on his way to home and freedom, he had the car in which he was riding stop opposite the Palace Gate (the English author of the preface to his *Japan and Her Destiny* writes) while he got out, limping on his wooden leg, to bow in obeisance toward the emperor. (Chap. 16, note 9).

2. The Japanese word *kami* which Westerners have translated *god* does not connote the usual European idea of God but rather, superior and highly respectable. Our Judaic-Christian ancestors also were created "in the image of God," and we have been called temples of the Holy Spirit.

3. Mrs. Masa Nakayama, a graduate of Ohio Wesleyan University, and six times elected to the Lower House of the Diet, was appointed in 1960 as Minister of Welfare, Japan's first woman Cabinet Member. She was replaced a few months later by the new Prime Minister Ikeda but continues as a member of the Welfare Committee of the Diet.

4. Japan is smaller than California with a population about ten times as great, the fifth largest in the world: 75 per cent living on Honshu, 15 per cent on Kyushu and 5 per cent each on Hokkaido and Shikoku. Of these four main islands, Honshu is the largest with the major industrial centers. Hokkaido, the northernmost island, has Japan's most extensive forests and grazing lands in addition to mines and fisheries. The southernmost island, Kyushu, is noted for its coal mines and heavy industries, and Shikoku, the smallest, has some salt beds and copper mines as well as agriculture and forestry.

5. Back in 1860, a member of the first Japanese mission to the United States had written: "Today, six years after that great national Crisis [Perry Expedition] we are here in the midst of the friendly American nation, welcome guests in the home of the very Commodore whose great fleet might have stirred our peaceful land into battle! The time has come when no nation may remain isolated and refuse to take part in the affairs of the rest of the world." Muragaki Awaji-no-Kami, *Diary of the First Japanese Embassy to the United States of America,* Tokyo, 1920.

6. This speech seemed to echo public statements of John Foster Dulles. Yoshida was censured as a "tool of America" by opponents of rearmament and military alliance with the United States and forced out of office in December, 1954. Although the Liberal Democratic Party, of which in 1961 he is still the leader, remains the party in power, its policies are conservative and inclined toward centralized controls.

CHAPTER 19.   CONTEMPORARY JAPAN

1. Mostly Americans, followed in decreasing numbers by British, Nationalist Chinese, Filipinos, Indians, French and Canadians bringing an estimated tourist revenue of over a hundred million dollars.
2. At the Sogetsu School of Flower Arrangement, attended by many American garden club ladies.
3. About five million in 1960.
4. Engineers are rebuked for bringing their trains in either early or late. Less than half a minute variation in either direction is the tolerance.
5. Over twenty such affiliations, designed to develop goodwill have been promoted: Boston-Kyoto, Hiroshima-Honolulu, etc.
6. With India in developing fisheries, exploring for iron ore and giving on-the-job training in making clocks and watches, cameras and radios. They are also establishing pulp mills near Sitka, Alaska, for the rayon manufacturers of Japan, and prospecting for mines and oil fields in our undeveloped forty-ninth state.
7. A new ten-year hundred billion yen project for reclaiming islands in the Tokyo Bay area and providing specialized dock facilities for receiving and dispatching forty-seven million tons of cargo, as well as truck highways and short-haul railroads, and warehouses, storages and residential districts for a foreign trade center involves very imaginative and advanced engineering plans.
8. Without making clear to the public the pros and cons of the new Japan-U.S. Security Treaty, Prime Minister Kishi was determined to force the signing of it; and the opposition to block its passage. Students with their natural hatred of war and armaments and of Kishi's autocratic methods, inflamed perhaps by communist agitators, staged demonstrations (demos, for short) which brought about the cancellation of Eisenhower's visit, the resignation of the Prime Minister, and the dissolution of the Diet, followed by a general election.
9. A socialist movement in Japan was started principally by Christians about the turn of the century. Repressed and outlawed, revived, fractured and reunited, it plays the role of critic better than effective reformer and seems to be more concerned with how to win votes than with what needs to be done. Total disarmament and independence from the United States, with a neutrality like India's, economic and cultural exchange with red China on the basis of political non-interference, and nationalization of electric power, coal, iron steel and chemicals seems to be their platform.
10. According to a U.N. Food and Agriculture census for the five years ending Jan. 1, 1960, the average farm family consisting of about six members earns the equivalent in yen of from $55—$275 for a year's work.
11. Farmers do not usually have herds on pasture but a couple of animals which they keep in a shed. Lack of exercise together with frequent massaging and an occasional drink of beer is credited with making very high quality beef.
12. See *Windows for the Crown Prince* and *Return to Japan* by Elizabeth Gray Vining, N.Y. J. B. Lippincott, 1952 and 1960.

13. The Esaki diode was developed in the U.S. because Esaki the inventor, a Sony radio research engineer, was unable to find adequate research facilities and financial backing in Japan.

14. It is expressed in the Japanese word shibui, to which *House Beautiful* devoted two special issues in August and September, 1960. Literally, astringent, like the taste of persimmons whose juice is used to produce a tough and durable yet pleasant paper, shibui was introduced by the Zen Masters of Tea Ceremony who taught the Japanese that art for art's sake is unnecessary, but that beauty bound up with everyday human life is vital. Shibui is still an everyday word, used of baseball players, wrestlers or politicians who are able to do the important thing at the important time, as well as of teacups, gardens or paintings which convey the beauty of good taste without showiness, and some of the truth of life-as-a-whole rather than the fame of the artist.

15. Yukio Mishima is probably the best known in America of these contemporary writers. Several of his novels have been translated and published here.

16. See *Religions in Japan*, Wm. K. Bunce, Tokyo, Tuttle, 1959.

17. Many conservative families do not approve of scouting, for their daughters.

18. Chief Justice Tanaka of the Japanese Supreme Court upon reaching compulsory retirement age was appointed by the United Nations to the International Court of Justice in the Hague. Dr. Tanaka is a devout Catholic, an ardent advocate for world peace and fluent in several European languages, with a gift rare among Japanese for speaking out a clear "Yes" or "No."

GLOSSARY AND DICTIONARY OF
JAPANESE PROPER NAMES

Ainu — Aborigines of Japan.

Akechi Mitsuharu (d. 1582) — A soldier in the service of Nobunaga.

Amaterasu — Sun Goddess, ancestress of the imperial family.

Amida Buddha — Buddha of the Western Paradise; a deity of mercy.

Ashikaga — A district about 100 miles north of Tokyo; the ancestral estate of the Ashikaga shoguns.

Ashikaga Takauji (1305–1358) — First Ashikaga shogun (1338–1358).

Asuka — A region south of Kyoto, site of ancient capital.

Bakufu — Camp administration; government with headquarters at Kamakura, 1185–1333.

bashi — Bridge.

Basho (1644–1695) — Japan's greatest poet; leader of haiku movement.

be — A sort of craft guild (early Japan).

Biwa, Lake — Largest lake in Japan, close to Kyoto.

bodhisattva — Buddhist saint.

Bungo — Province in northeastern Kyushu.

bushido — The warriors' code.

Byo-do-in — Part of villa built at Uji in 1053.

cha no yu — (see o-cha-no-yu).

Chikafusa (Kitabatake Chikafusa), (1293–1354) — Leader of the Southern Dynasty and author of political treatise.

Chikamatsu (Monzaemon Chikamatsu), (1653–1724) — The most celebrated Japanese dramatist.

Chion-in — Headquarters of the Jodo sect in Kyoto; built in 1211.

cho — (surface) 2.45 acres, linear 119 yards.

Choshu — District in southwestern Japan, which belonged successively to Ouchi and Mori clans.

Chu Hsi (A.D. 1130–1200) — A Chinese philosopher on whose teachings official education in Japan was based during the Tokugawa period.

Daibutsu — Great statue of Buddha.

Daigo — Emperor, 897–930.

daimyo — Lit. "Great Name," a feudal lord.

Daruma — Indian Buddhist priest (of the sixth century) and saint.

Dazaifu — Government headquarters in Kyushu (Nara and Heian periods).

Deshima — Island off Nagasaki; center of Dutch trade.

Dokyo (d. 772) — Buddhist priest consort of Empress Koken; aspired to become emperor.

e — A painting, drawing, picture.

Eisai (1141–1215) — Famous Zen priest, architect.

Eitoku (Kano Eitoku) (1548–1590) — Official painter in service of Nobunaga.

Esaki, Leo (1926–)

eta — The most despised class of Japanese society, traditionally engaged in occupations having to do with the handling of dead bodies.

Fubito (Fujiwara Fubito) (659–720) — Son of Kamatari; minister during four reigns, father-in-law of Emperor Shomu.

Fugen — Bodhisattva of all-pervading wisdom, usually shown mounted on an elephant.

Fujisan, Mt. Fuji — Japan's sacred and highest mountain (12,467 ft.).

Fujiwara — District in central Japan given to Kamatari, from which Fujiwara family name is derived.

Fukuzawa, Yukichi (1835–1901) — Educational leader, founder of Keio University, Tokyo.

Gempei — Era of the Genji and Heike.

Genji (or Minamoto) — Military clan, derived from imperial princes during ninth and tenth centuries.

Genji, Prince — Fictitious hero of Japan's most famous novel by Lady Murasaki (c. 1000).

Genroku — Name of period of great commercial prosperity (1688–1703).

Genryaku — Name of period 1184–1185.

Ginkaku-ji — Silver pavilion built in Kyoto in 1473 by Ashikaga shogun, Yoshimasa.

Ginza — Silver mint, name of fashionable street in Tokyo.

giri — Duty.

Go-Daigo — Emperor (1319–1338).

Gyogi (670–749) — Buddhist priest.

Hachiman — Shinto god of war; tutelary deity of Minamotos.

haiku — Seventeen syllable poem.

Hakodate — Principal seaport of Hokkaido.

Han (206 B.C.–A.D. 220) — Ruling dynasty in China.

Hayashi — Family of Tokugawa Education Ministers, wrote *Honcho Tsugan* c. 1650.

Heian — Peace and ease; name of period 794–858.

Heian-kyo — Capital of peace and ease; i.e. Kyoto, founded 795.

Heike (or Taira) — Clan descended from great-grandson of Emperor Kwammu.

Hideyori (1593–1615) — Son of Toyotomi Hideyoshi.

Hideyoshi (Toyotomi Hideyoshi), (1536–1598) — "The Taiko," military ruler of late 16th century.

Hieizan, Mt. Hiei — Mountain northeast of Kyoto, famous temple center.

hiki — A unit for measuring cloth — about 25 yards.

Hirado — Island off northwest coast of Kyushu; Portuguese and English trading center.

hiragana — Phonetic symbols in running script.

Hirohito, Emperor (1901–) — His reign, Showa, began Dec. 25, 1926.

Hiroshige (1797–1858) — Color print artist.

Hizen — Province in Kyushu.

Hojo — Branch of the Taira clan which ruled Japan 1199–1333.

Hojo-ji — Temple built c. 1000 by Fujiwara Michinaga in conjunction with his palace.

Hojo Tokimasa (1138–1215) — Father of Masa, wife of Yoritomo.

Hokkaido — Large northern island of Japan.

Horyu-ji—Buddhist temple founded by Prince Shotoku, early seventh century.

Ikeda, Hayato (1899–) — Prime Minister 1960– .

Isé — Province in central Japan where Sun Goddess is enshrined.

Ito (Hirobumi, Prince), (1841–1906) — Leader in Restoration movement and author of Constitution.

Itsukushima — Island of Inland Sea, better known as Miyajima.

Iyeyasu (1542–1616) — First Tokugawa Shogun, appointed 1603; had son appointed shogun in 1605.

Izumo — Province in northwestern Japan where Susanoo was enshrined.

ji — clan.

Jimmu — Traditionally first emperor of Japan, 660–585 B.C.

Jingu, Empress — Traditionally first empress of Japan, A.D. 170–269 and conqueror of Korea.

Jocho (d. 1657) — Buddhist priest sculptor.

Jodo — Name of Buddhist sect founded by Honen, thirteenth century. To Jodoists, repetition of the name, Amida, was sufficient for salvation.

kabuki — Popular type drama.

Kai — One of the eastern provinces of Japan.

Kaifuso — Anthology of Chinese poetry of Nara period.

Kamakura — Headquarters of first shogunate, 1192–1333.

Kamatari (614–669) — Founder of the Fujiwara clan.

kami — Superiors or gods of the land.

kana — Phonetic symbols.

karuta — Playing cards.

kastera — Spongecake.

katakana — Phonetic symbols in block script.

Kato, Takaaki (1860–1926) — Prime Minister and Count, 1924.

ke — Family, clan.

Kebiishi — Law-enforcing agency of the Heian period.

Kenzan (1663–1743) — Kyoto artist, designer in applied arts.

Kibi no Mabi (693–775) — Minister and scholar.

Kii — Peninsular province in central Japan.

Kinkaku-ji — Golden pavilion built in Kyoto by Ashikaga Yoshimitsu, 1397.

Kiyomori (Taira Kiyomori), (1118–1181) — Ruler 1159–1181.

Kojiki — Earliest history of Japan, 712.

Koken — Empress of Japan 749–759; reascended throne six years later as Empress Shotoku.

koku — Dry measure used for rice, about five bushels.

Komyo, Empress (701–760) — Wife of Emperor Shomu.

Konoye, Fumimaro (1891–1945) — Prime Minister, 1937–1941.

Korin (Ogata Korin), (1661–1716) — Artist.

koto — The classical stringed instrument.

Koyasan, Mt. Koya — Temple center of Shingon sect, founded by Kukai 816.

Kukai (745–835) — Founder of Mt. Koya, center of Shingon sect; posthumously known as Kobo Daishi.

Kwammu — Emperor of Japan (782–805).

kwan mon — Unit of weight — 1000 mon, 1 mon (or monme) = .12 oz. (troy); pertaining to currency, usually copper.

Kwanto — Half of Japan east of Lake Biwa.

kyogen — Lit. "foolish words"; short, humorous folk plays; used for comic relief on programs of Noh.

Kyoto — Capital founded by Emperor Kwammu, 795.

Kyushu — Southern island of Japan.

Lolang — Chinese colony in northern Korea in late Han period.

Manyoshu — "Collection of 10,000 Leaves"; anthology of Japanese poems, Nara period.

Masa (Hojo Masa), (1157–1225) — Wife of Yoritomo.

Matsuoka, Yosuke (1880–1946) — Diplomat.

Meiji — Reign of Enlightenment (1868–1912).

Michinaga (966–1027) — Fujiwara who brought family to zenith of its power.

Minamoto — See Genji.

Mishima, Yukio — (1925–) novelist.

Mito — City about fifty miles east of Tokyo.

Mitsukuni (1628–1700) — Head of Mito branch of Tokugawa family; initiated great historical work.

miyako — Capital.

Momokawa (Fujiwara Momokawa), (722–779) — Minister during two reigns; arranged succession of Emperor Kwammu.

monogatari — Narrative, tale.

Mori, Arinori (1847–1889) — Educator, statesman.

Moronobu (Hishikawa Moronobu), (1688–1703) — Painter.

Motoori (Motoori Norinaga), (1730–1801) — Famous man of letters.

Murasaki, Lady — Author of Tale of Genji, c. 1000.

Musashi — Province in eastern Japan, especially Musashi Plain, the broadest in Japan.

Muso (1275–1351) — Zen priest and poet.

Nagasaki — Chief port of Kyushu, center of Dutch learning.

Naka, Prince — Associated with Kamatari and First Great Change; became Emperor Tenji (662–671).

Nara — First permanent capital of Japan, established 710.

Netsuké — Carved pendant.

Nichiren (1222–1282) — Nationalistic evangelist, founder of Buddhist sect.

Nihongi — Ancient chronicles of Japan, 720.

Nikko — Mountain shrine to Tokugawa Iyeyasu.

Ninigi — Grandson of Sun Goddess.

ninjo — Sentiment.

Nippon (or Nihon) — Ni (or hi) = sun, pon (or hon) = root, source. Nippon has recently been made the official pronunciation.

Nobunaga (Oda Nobunaga), (1534–1582) — Hero-general.

noh — Classical drama.

Nyorai — Saviour; name applied to certain Buddhist deities.

o-cha-no-yu — Lit. tea's hot water; tea ceremony.

Ogata — Kyoto scholar and schoolmaster, middle nineteenth century.

Onin Civil War — 1467–77 around Kyoto.

onyo-do — The way of Yin and Yang; a Chinese pseudo-scientific philosophy of natural phenomena used for divination.

Osaka — Castle town and seaport, central Japan.

Ouchi — Clan with capital in Yamaguchi, southwestern Japan, middle sixteenth century.

Owari — Province of eastern Japan.

pan — Bread.

roju — Members of Tokugawa shogun's council.

ryo — Old name for yen; standard of currency, varying in value in different periods.

Ryo no Gige — Commentary on law code, published 833.

Ryukyu Islands — Between Japan and Formosa.

Sado — Island in Japan Sea, frequent place of exile; contains gold and silver mines.

Saicho (767–822) — Founder of Hiei-zan temple center; posthumously Dengyo Daishi.

Saigo Takamori (1827–1877) — Army leader and hero of Satsuma clan.

Saikaku (d. 1693) — Realistic novelist.

Sakai — Seaport of central Japan, now part of Osaka.

sake — Rice wine; alcoholic content about 17%.

samisen — Three-stringed musical instrument usually associated with popular type music.

samurai — A feudal warrior and retainer.

san, zan, sen, yama — Various pronunciations of the symbol for *mountain*.

Sanraku (Kano Sanraku), (1559–1635) — Official painter in service of Hideyoshi.

Satcho — Combination of Satsuma and Choshu clans (abb.).

Satsuma — District of S.W. Kyushu belonging to Shimazu family.

Seami (1363–1444) — Noh writer and actor.

Sei, Lady — Author of *Pillow Book*, notes on Fujiwara court, c. 1000.

Sei-i- Tai Shogun — Great Barbarian-subduing General.

Seika (Fujiwara Seika) (1561–1619) — Founder of school of Chu Hsi philosophy in Japan.

Sekigahara — Village near Lake Biwa, site of Iyeyasu's conclusive victory in October, 1600.

Sesshu (1420–1506) — Famous Zen painter.

shibumi — (also shibui) Lit. astringent taste; refined estheticism.

Shigemitsu, Mamoru (1887–1957) — Foreign Minister 1954–56.

Shikoku — One of the four main islands of Japan.

Shimoda — Port where first United States consulate was established in Japan, southeast of Izu Peninsula.

shinchu — An alloy very closely resembling gold in appearance.

Shingon — Buddhist sect founded in Japan in 806 by Kukai, with center at Mt. Koya.

Shinto — Way of the Gods; national religion of Japan.

shogun — General.

Shomu, Emperor, 724–748 — Devout Buddhist.

Shoso-in — Storehouse belonging to Todai temple with treasures preserved from 756.

Shotoku, Prince — Regent (572–621). "Father of Japanese Culture."

shu — Sect or denomination.

Shuko (1422–1502) — Importer and connoisseur for Ashikaga Yoshimasa; first master of tea ceremony.

Soga — Clan which usurped imperial power in 7th century.

Sui — Ruling dynasty in China (A.D. 589–618).

Suiko, Empress (593–628) — For whom Prince Shotoku was regent.

Susanowo — Impetuous Male, brother of Sun Goddess.

sutra — Buddhist scripture.

Taiho — Code of laws promulgated in 701.

Taiko — Lit. Great Lord (title of Hideyoshi), from which is derived our colloquial tycoon, industrial magnate.

Taikwa — Great Change; name for period 645–649.

Taira — See Heike.

tairo — Chief officials of the Tokugawa shogunate.

Tamura Maro (or Saka-no-Uye) (758–811) — First Sei-i Tai Shogun, Great Barbarian-subduing General.

T'ang — Ruling dynasty in China (618–907).

tanka — Thirty-one-syllable poem.

Temmu — Emperor 673–686.

tempura — Fish (usually shrimp) or vegetable covered with batter and fried in deep vegetable oil.

Tenji, Emperor (662–671) — See Naka.

Tenjin-Sama — God of letters.

Tenno — Son of Heaven, Emperor.

Tenryu-ji — Zen temple west of Kyoto, built by Muso, 1342.

Todai-ji — Buddhist temple erected at Nara in 728.

Tosa — Province in southwest Japan.

tripitaka — Buddhist Bible.

T'sin—Chinese dynasty (255–202 B.C.).

Tsubouchi, Shoyo (1859–1935) — man of letters.

Tsunoda, Ryusaku (1876–   ) — scholar, educator.

Tsurumi, Yusuke (1885–   ) — roving diplomat.

Uji — Scenic site of Byo-do-in and of teagrowing.

ukiyo — Buddhist terminology, "fleeting or transient world"; in Genroku travesty, "floating world," the gay pleasure quarters.

Unkei (d. 1223) — Great sculptor.

Uraga — Fishing village near Kamakura where Perry landed.

Usa — Place in Kyushu where shrine to Hachiman has been in existence since early eighth century — probably longer.

Vairocana — Buddhist deity identified with Sun Goddess; the deity represented by the Nara Daibutsu.

Wa — Ancient Chinese name for Japan.

Yamaguchi — City in southwest Japan.

Yamato — District in central Japan; original settlement of imperial clan.

Yamato-e — Native Japanese style of painting.

yang — In Chinese philosophy the active, light elements of the universe.

Yayoi — A type of Stone Age pottery.

Yedo — Castle town and capital of Tokugawas; since 1868, Tokyo.

yen — Standard of currency, corresponding in buying power in Japan to dollar in U. S. At par worth $.50.

yin — In Chinese philosophy the passive, dark elements of the universe.

Yoritomo (Minamoto) (1147–99) — First Military Dictator of Japan.

Yoshida, Shigeru (1878–   ) — statesman.

Yoshimasa (1435–1490) — Eighth Ashikaga Shogun.

Yoshimitsu (1358–1408) — Third Ashikaga Shogun.

Yoshinaka (Minamoto) (1154–1184) — A hero in the *Tale of Heike*.

Yoshino — Mountainous district in central Japan, famous for cherry blossoms, capital of southern court.

Yoshitsune (Minamoto) (1159–1189) — Younger brother of Yoritomo.

Yukawa, Shigeru (1907–   ) — meson research physicist, Columbia Univ. 1949.

za — Trade guild (mediæval Japan).

Zen — Buddhist sect; emphasis on meditation and practical accomplishment.

Zojo-ji — Temple in Tokyo built by Tokugawas.

INDEX

abacus, 185
Abraham Lincoln, 292
actors, 142–143, 167, 194–195, 198, 206, 209, 292
Adams, Will, 179
Aesop's Fables, 164
agriculture, 32, 36, 206, 318; fertility cult, 8–9, 10; new methods of, 15; economic aspects, 23, 93, 99, 101, 138; mainstay of nation, 161, 171, 249; Tokugawa, 206–207; reforms in, 246, 260, 308–309, 310. *See also* rice
Ainu, 11, 21, 25, 47, 60, 66, 99, 101, 125, 202, 334n.11
air power, Japanese, 285–287; United States, 286
airplane production, 287
Aizawa, 233–234
Akechi Mitsuharu, 128–129
Alaska, 205, 276
Aleutian Islands, 285
aluminum, 286
Ama Shogun. *See* Masa
Amaterasu (Sun Goddess), 10–11, 20, 38, 39, 40, 73, 74, 76, 84, 134, 215, 238, 267
America. *See* United States
American Revolution, 5
American Way of Life, 292
Amida, 98, 109, 112, 119, 159, 311, 314; in art, 82–83, 149, 337n.3
ancestor worship, 10, 74, 78, 80, 84, 129
ancestry, 1–2, 38, 73, 78, 80, 96, 213, 267, 294, 333n.3
Anglo-Japanese Alliance, 253; abrogation of, 279–280
animal worship, 9
Antarctic, 320
Arabs, 135
archeology, 1, 2, 3, 4, 6, 246, 312, 333n.1, 3

archery, 33, 56, 57, 62, 84, 104–105, 110–111, 182
architecture, primitive, 14, 29, 152; at Nara, 30; palace, 30, 62–63; Ming, 139; temple, 47–48, 186; Zen, 149, 314; of modern Japan, 304, 311. *See also* castles, homes, Nikko
art, Nara, 29, 48; Fujiwara, 73–74, 91; Zen, 149, 168, 314; Genroku, 193–199; Western, 205, 245, 270. *See also* architecture, painting, sculpture
artists, 16, 29, 49, 51, 83, 101, 168–169, 186. *See also* art, list of plates
Asaki (Morning Sun), 309
Associated Press, 320
astrology, 19, 71
Ashikaga, 134, 135, 139, 145, 146, 149, 150, 168, 264. *See also* Takauji, Yoshimasa, Yoshimitsu
astronomy, 38, 154, 204, 208, 215
Asuka, 28
atomic bombs, 188, 289
Atsugi Airfield, 290
Attu, capture of, 285
autographs, selling of, 132, 148
automobiles, 266, 305

Bakufu, 114, 115, 124, 125
Bank of Japan, 249
Basho, 193, 200–202
bathing rites, 5, 8, 209
bauxite, 273, 286
Belgium, 280
Bernard, 155
Bible, translations of, 316
birth control, 208
Biwa, Lake, 27, 61, 67, 128, 165
boats, 87–88, 121, 189, 210; pleasure, 198, 199, 202. *See also* ships
books, 38, 45, 49, 59, 68, 71, 91, 138, 148, 205, 219; theological, 215; Dutch,

Middle Aged Gentleman of Passion, 193
Midway Island, 286
migration, 2, 3, 4, 11
military, 72, 97, 103–104, 113, 114, 122,
124, 134, 136, 145, 152; conscription,
34, 66, 239, 255, 258; of Yoshinaka,
107; life of, 116–117; employment of,
160; science, 245; training, 247. *See
also* Bushido, Hachiman, samurai, war
Minamoto, 81, 96–97, 99, 100. *See also*
Yoritomo, Yoshinaka, Yoshitsune
Ming Dynasty, 139, 140, 141
Mining, development of, 171, 179, 247;
government control of, 219; lands,
239–240; depletion of mines, 261
Minister of the Right, 174
mirrors, 4, 57, 100; of Amaterasu, 10–
11; found in Lolang, 13; bronze, 14;
sacred, 77, 106, 108, 129; glass, 190
missionaries, 46, 47, 151, 155–156, 164,
167, 215; martyrdom of, 164–165;
banished, 186
Mito, 178, 216, 233
Mitsubishis, 258
Mitsuharu. *See* Akechi Mitsuharu
Mitsuis, 258
Miyajima, 100
Miyako, 62
Momohawa, 60
monasteries, 136; Zen, 149; demolished
by Nobunaga, 158
money, use of shells as, 7; Chinese, 13,
15; in Japan, 26, 35, 66, 72; coinage,
138, 152; borrowing of, 192; issuance
of paper, 249. *See also* rice
Mongolia, 254
Mongols, 120–124, 132, 133, 136, 138,
139, 150, 161, 233, 264
Moronobu, 198–199
Motoori, 214–215
Mt. Fuji. *See* Fujisan
Mt. Hiei. *See* Hieizan
Mt. Koya. *See* Koyasan
movies, 270–272, 304, 309, 317; docu-
mentary, 287; American, 292; foreign,
309
moving picture film production, 322
Mukden Incident, 282
Murasaki Shikibu, 91
Murdoch, James, 159
Musashi, 116, 134

music, 15, 19, 33, 49, 54, 71, 72, 77, 84,
85, 100, 103, 142, 148, 156, 193, 198,
292, 306; Genroku, 194; appeal of
Western, 270
musical instruments, 30, 49, 57, 71, 77,
83, 85, 103, 110, 153, 164, 194
Muso, 137
Mutual Security Assistance, 303

Nagasaki; crucifixions at, 165; port
closed, 187, 189; Dutch in, 204; prints,
205; opening of port, 222; atomic
bombing of, 289
Naka, Prince, 23–28, 239. *See also*
Tenji
Nakayama, Mrs. Masa, 346n.3
Nanking, 284
Napoleonic Wars, 205
Nara, 37, 39, 41, 42, 43, 44, 50, 51, 52,
54, 88, 90, 92, 125, 132, 135; build-
ing of, 28, 29–30, 44, 47, 98; treas-
ures of, 30–31; court at, 32–33, 35,
36, 45, 69, 70; abandoned as capital,
55, 61, 67
National General Mobilization Bill, 273
National Learning Movement, 213, 216.
See also Neo-Shinto
National Police Reserve, 293, 302
National Safety Force, 302
National Self-Restraint Drive, 287
national unity, 151, 235, 238, 250
Nationalist China News Agency, 320
natural resources, 3, 161, 261, 265, 273
naval power, 234; of daimyos, 238; race
for, 279, 280; reduction of, 280, 282
needlework, 32
Negroes, first in Japan, 157; with Perry,
217, 219
Neo-Shinto, 213, 216, 238
Neutrality Pact, with Russia, 273; ter-
mination of, 288
New Proposals, 233–234
New Year, 25, 32, 39, 84
New York Times, 309
New York *Tribune,* 280
news correspondents, 320
newspapers, 247, 267, 278, 317, 319–
320
Nichiren, 120, 315
Nihongi, 4, 28, 37–39, 90, 134, 142
Nikko, 185–186

Nine Power Treaty, 280
Ninigi, 11, 38, 73
Ninjo, 195
Nippon, 27, 28, 41, 46, 121, 122, 123;
    bashi, 175, 178, 209
Nishi Honganji, 314
Nixon, Richard, 302–303
Nobel Prize, 310
Nobunaga, 128–129, 151, 156–159, 161,
    165, 168, 171, 172; quoted, 157; assas-
    sination of, 158, 159–160
Noh, 142–143, 148, 150, 167, 193, 306
North China, 274, 276
Northern Court, 133
nunneries, 47, 53, 149

official express messengers, 210, 240
Ogata school, 228–230
oil, 2, 146, 210, 254, 273–274, 285,
    286
Okinawa, 2
Okubo, 248; assassination, 249
Old Bamboo Hewer's Story, 90
Omi, 61, 70
Open Door Policy, 277, 280
Osaka, 44, 160, 163, 173, 174, 176, 188,
    191; castle, 165, 166, 177; siege of,
    180–181, 182, 188; importance of, 188,
    189; commerce in, 192, 230; wealth
    of, 237; an international city, 305
Ouchi, 153
Owari, 158, 178
Ozaki, 275

Pacific Islands, Japanese demands for, 279
painting, 16, 82–83, 91, 103, 139, 144,
    145, 150, 168–169, 198–199; oil, 205;
    Zen, 314. *See also* Art, architecture
palaces, at Kyoto, 62, 107, 115, 119, 121,
    158, 166–167; of Michinaga, 81; of
    Kiyomori, 100; of Yoshimitsu, 141,
    145; burning of, 146; comparison of,
    148; Heian, 199; underground in
    World War II, 289
paper making, 51
Paris Peace Conference, 255
Patriotic Women's Society, 287
Peace Treaty (1951), 300–301, 302
Pearl Harbor, 275, 285, 286, 302
peerage, 16, 334n.3
Peking, 122, 141, 252, 284

Perry, Commodore M. C., 206, 217–220,
    226, 227, 306
Pescadores, 252, 279
Peter the Great, 205, 231
Philip II of Spain, 157
Philippine Islands, 2, 173, 179, 273, 275,
    276, 278; granted independence, 284;
    Japan strikes at, 285
Pillow Book, 193, 337n.10
Pimiko, 5–6
piracy, 117, 121, 132, 138, 139, 189
plagues, 8, 53, 79, 119, 120, 138, 145
playing cards, 164
poems, 12, 42–43, 44, 93, 109, 172, 174,
    197, 201, 202, 214, 227, 241, 274
poetry, Chinese, 28; Japanese, 37, 40–41,
    93; writing of, 39–44, 141; Chinese in-
    fluence on, 44; tanka form, 41; contests,
    84; compilations of, 90; at court of
    Kiyomori, 100; taught in schools, 184;
    of Basho, 200–202; haiku, 200–202
political parties, Liberal Democratic
    Party, 307, 308, 312; Socialist, 307;
    Democratic Socialist, 308
politics, internal, after World War I,
    257–260; after World War II, 307–308,
    309–310
polo, 84, 86
Pope Gregory XIII, 157, 158
Pope Sixtus V, 158
Port Arthur, 279
Portsmouth (New Hampshire) Confer-
    ence, 277
Portugal, 155, 157, 179
Portuguese, 151–153, 155, 160, 161, 162,
    163, 164, 166, 186, 187, 189, 218
Portuguese language, 156
postal system, 240
Potsdam Declaration, 289
Powhatan (ship), 342n.8
priests, Buddhist, as educators, 46, 48,
    49–50, 51–52, 78, 135, 148, 150, 238,
    264; culture and education of, 49, 50;
    political ambition, 52, 54, 55, 59;
    knowledge of medicine, 57, 83; Shinto,
    68, 76, 115; emperor as, 74, 80; mer-
    chant, 132; Zen, 136, 137, 138, 139,
    140, 141, 150, 161; Shingon, 137;
    education of Confucian and Buddhist
    compared, 215–216; Catholic, 153–159.
    See also Dokyo, Eisai, Gyogi, Kukai,